MW00471321

Tales of
Canyonlands
Cowboys

Tales of

Canyonlands

Cowboys

Richard F. Negri

Editor

Foreword by

David Lavender

Utah State University Press
Logan, Utah
1997

Copyright © 1997 Utah State University Press
All rights reserved

Utah State University Press
Logan, Utah 84322-7800

Typography by WolfPack

Cover photograph: Ned Chaffin in Ernie Country, 1938; courtesy of Ned Chaffin.

All photos in the text are by the author unless credited to another source.

ISBN: 978-0-87421-800-8 (paper)
ISBN: 978-0-87421-801-5 (e-book)

Library of Congress Cataloging-in-Publication Data

Tales of Canyonlands cowboys / Richard F. Negri, editor; foreword
    by David Lavender
        p. cm.
    ISBN 978-0-87421-800-8 (paper)
        1. Cowboys—Utah—Canyonlands National Park—Interviews.
2. Canyonlands National Park (Utah)—Description and travel—
Anecdotes. 3. Ranch life—Utah—Canyonlands National Park—
Anecdotes. I. Negri, Richard F., 1926-   .
F832.C37T35   1997
979.2'—dc21   97–4900
                                                               CIP

Contents

Illustrations

Maps

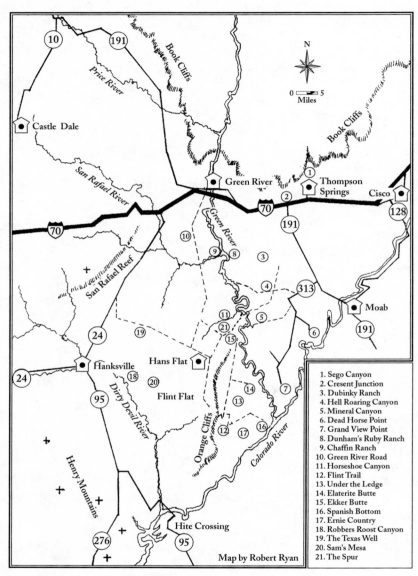

The Western Canyonlands Region.

Foreword

Hanging On

David Lavender

If you ever have a youngster
And he wants to foller stock,
The best thing you can do for him
Is to brain him with a rock.
Or if rocks ain't very handy
You kin shove him down the well;
Do not let him be a cowboy,
For he's better off in hell.

—Gail Gardener, Arizona cowboy poet[1]

As a practiced old-timer, I read with interest the tales Richard Negri extracted from seven men and three women by means of a tape-recorder—oral history, the process is sometimes called. Since a good deal of the significance of the tales depends on their stern setting, I'll risk condensing some of what Negri has already said about the backdrop. The reason will become apparent as we thread our way through the rock jungles on both sides of Canyonlands National Park.

---

1. Quoted in Patricia Nelson Limerick, *The Legacy of Conquest: The Unbroken Past of the American West* (New York: W. W. Norton, 1987), 148.

If you enter Negri's territory, as I'll call it, in an automobile, you'll soon find yourself immersed in a broad expanse of brush and fragile desert grass. At first the countryside appears either flat or slightly undulant. Actually, it is seamed here and there by rimrocked canyons, blistered by red buttes, embroidered by piñon pines and runty junipers. It stretches eastward from the whale-shouldered San Rafael Swell and the Waterpocket Fold to a sudden long drop into hidden benchlands guarded by tumults of stone. The lower area is known locally as Under the Ledge. The Ledge's drainage, such as it is, funnels quickly into the placid twinings of the gray-canyoned Green River.

The first tale I want to mention deals with an errant cow that fell irretrievably from one of the Ledge's hair-raising trails into a cluster of crags and boulders. Since she could not be moved, she faced a slow death from choking. As used throughout the Canyonlands area, "choking" means dying of thirst. To prevent that, one of the cowboys Negri tells about clambered down beside the animal and sawed through her jugular vein with his pocket knife. Clearly he thought quick deaths preferable to slow ones, a mercy forbidden to humans.

Another story tells of a cowboy slowly riding toward his own death by choking. The 110 degree heat was reflecting mercilessly from the bare ground and naked stone cliffs when he chanced across a thin patch of damp sand. Dismounting, he managed to scratch a shallow trough in the soil. One faint hope: he lay motionless in the depression. Slowly his body absorbed enough moisture from the earth to let him continue his ride to a surer source of water. Choking cow, choking cowboy: there are ironic equities in the desert.

The riders, though, could bring balance to their lives by indulging in their favorite sports. Their playing fields were the semicircular bottomlands carved out of the lower cliffs by the meandering Green River. At certain seasons, deer congregated in the back parts of those canyoned bottoms. Aware of this, two or three riders would pick a rough way down into a place chosen in advance. Shooting was permissible, but the real sport was roping a high-antlered buck in full flight before it crashed through the brush into the river. More throat cutting followed, preparatory to butchering. Incredibly, we are assured, a good horse can outrun a deer every time, provided, of course, the horse doesn't stub a toe jumping a boulder and so turn himself head over heels.

The wives, meanwhile, stayed at home with the children, packing in stove wood and water while their husbands were away. Routines were similar. Each woman canned beef in old-fashioned pressure cookers, prepared crocks of sauerkraut, tied bandages onto scraped shins, and laundered the menfolk's pungent long johns, socks, shirts, and Levis by scrubbing them back and forth, back and forth, over the metal corduroys of her washboard. How she hailed that first gasoline-powered Maytag washing machine! She also moved supplies, when necessary, in the ranch's stuttering, slat-sided Model-T flatbed truck, wondering how long it would be before one of the thin, bald tires blew. If an extra hand was needed at branding time or for driving a few head of cattle from one overused swale to another, she provided it.

Richard Negri diligently recorded all this, even after one of the people he was interviewing remarked, "Oral history means we can tell you whatever we want." To flesh out the reminiscences, he gathered suitable photographs. Most chapters include their own maps. In short, Negri has done what he set out to do.

Still, I continue to puzzle over one factor. The country Negri concerns himself with had been settled during the 1880s. A generation passed before the characters he lays before us were born. Most of them spent the major part of their lives in or near the region where the recorder found them. (An exception: the Seely brothers left Negri's territory when they were still young. One brother found a wife and both prospered elsewhere, raising sheep in the kindlier climes of northwestern Colorado. Let's remember, though, that the brothers were descendants of a famed pioneer, Orange Seely, weight 320 pounds, who led the first colonists into what became Emery County, some miles north of Negri's chosen area. Orangeville is named for him. Reputedly his wife blasphemed on stepping down from their wagon, "Damn a man who would bring a woman into such God-forsaken country." So the spirit is there, even if time and geography are stretched a little.)

To resume: except for one drifter, the people who told their tales to the inquiring reporter knew, or should have known, the onerous demands that would be imposed on them by the land they settled in. Inevitably, then, questions arise. Why did they stay *here*? What made them believe they could achieve fulfillment *here*?

While I was mulling over these questions, an extraordinarily visual epiphany appeared to me. It took the form of a heavy-shouldered, slightly stooped, slab-cheeked rancher whose blue eyes could pierce a forgetful hand or bothersome government official with the force of a cactus thorn. To me, thirty-seven years his junior, he was always Mr. Scorup. To his contemporaries, he was Al. His full name was John Albert Scorup.

Like the people of Negri's territory, he'd had very little school when, aged nineteen, he threw his saddle on one horse, his skinny pack on another, and with one five-dollar bill in his pocket turned his back on his home town, Salina, in central Utah. The year was 1891. He rode east to Hanksville and then slanted southeast to the straggling little placer mining camp of Hite, beside the Colorado River. After fording the river, he entered the huge dryness of White Canyon. There, as arranged beforehand, John Albert Scorup began overseeing a small bunch of cattle on a sharecrop basis.

In time his brother Jim joined him. Still working on a sharecrop basis, they moved four hundred or so animals to the Wooden Shoe district north of White Canyon. Like some of the ranchers Under the Ledge, they developed procedures for utilizing the maximum amount of the little feed that was available. They stayed close to their animals, moving them from swale to swale as the presence or absence of water dictated. Sometimes moisture was locked in almost unapproachable, deep rock tanks. At other times the cattle had to lick snow off the branches of the sagebrush or off little drifts blown into wiggly patterns on the soil. Like the Under the Ledge ranchers, the brothers could sometimes reach water or grass only by building hair-raising trails among the boulders or across the slickrock.

They lived as the prehistoric Indians had, under overhanging sections of cliffs they called caves. In those shelters the brothers and the helpers they sometimes hired built pantries and crude tables, packed in Dutch ovens, skillets, and coffee pots. They stored oats for their horses and bacon and beans for themselves in the fine, dry sand of the cave floors. The sand slid back faster than raiding rodents could dig in their frantic efforts to get at the food. Whenever the brothers needed supplies or a recharging of their inner batteries, one of them took the long ride across Elk Ridge and between the Bear's Ears to the little Mormon colony of Bluff beside the San Juan River. Bluff was where Al found his first wife and the mother of his half dozen daughters. No sons.

Pretty soon the cattle they herded belonged entirely to them. They discouraged human competition by inching their cattle through the rocks to the best grass before anyone else got there. They protected other parts of their range by shooting, according to their own estimate, seven hundred wild horses. They ran down, lassoed, and delivered bony, unmanageable wild cattle to less enterprising owners for five dollars a head.

They had expanded their range noticeably when the first world war broke out. They made money practically by the ton. Part of it they used buying a fine hay ranch and feed lot near Salina. There, under Jim's management, they could raise purebred bulls of their own. They could use a lot of bulls, for Al was in the process of taking the biggest financial leap of either of their lives.

Circumstances helped. They had a better summer range in the Blue (Abajo) Mountains than any of the Under the Ledge people had. But their greatest advantage was this—although Al Scorup had received little formal education, he had developed—heaven knows how—a keen understanding of how the American capitalistic machine works. He could, and did, bring neighboring ranchers together into a shareholding company with himself at its head. They were able to accumulate and manage capital in a way the Hanksville people never learned.

In 1919, he completed the formation of the giant Scorup-Somerville Cattle Company. All told, the firm held about thirty-five thousand acres of private holdings, most of it controlling all access to the water holes, springs, and little creeks of the area. Their public-domain range stretched out across more than a million acres, from the junction of the San Juan and Colorado Rivers (a spot drowned now under Lake Powell) north into what became Canyonlands National Park. No one challenged them because there was practically no water anyone outside the company could get at. But, as will be clear shortly, size wasn't what counted.

The company had scarcely taken shape when Jim's wife died at the Salina Ranch. The spirit went out of Jim's body. He soon followed. Shortly thereafter an unprecedented blizzard swept across southeastern Utah. Hit especially hard was the area around the new ranch headquarters at Indian Creek. Hundreds and hundreds of cattle died. All the company salvaged were the hides stripped from the carcasses by skinners Al hired. He survived that. He survived the Great Depression of the 1930s, a period when I was fortunate enough to get to know him. He was elected to the Cowboy Hall of Fame. But very little of that was what counted at the end.

As Al aged and the old breaks in his bones began to twinge more than ever, he agreed, at the urging of the shareholders, to sell the ranch to a consortium from Kansas. I do not know the price, but the figure I've heard bandied about most frequently was $750,000 for the ranch and its grazing permits.

The deal was to be completed at the home of Al's lawyer in Moab, Utah. Al insisted that the hefty down payment be brought to him in cash. The buyers arrived with an armored car. One account says that when Scorup saw the cavalcade coming, he disappeared out the back door. Another tale insists he refused to close the deal because it was Sunday and he never worked on Sunday, which would be news to several generations of cattle.

Later, under order from the Supreme Court of the United States, he paid a $25,000 penalty for nonperformance. And still later, after he had been paralyzed by a stroke, he did sell to the Redd Ranches of La Sal, Utah. (Charles Redd, a long time friend of Scorup's, was head of that extensive company. Charlie's oldest son, Hardy, married one of Orange Seely's great granddaughters, a happening that helps put us back on the track to Negri's territory.) In 1959, John Albert Scorup died, aged eighty-seven.

The inevitable question comes: why on earth did he back out on that sale?

I think it was because the ranch, that massive pile of mostly barren sandrock, was his commitment to life. The work, the place, the soil, and Al Scorup were one unit. Splitting that unit as if it were no more than a piece of stove wood proved to be, for Al, a physical and spiritual impossibility. The desert had caught him and would not let him go.

That unity of man and woman and the earth may be why the people who live west of the canyons, roving from Under the Ledge to Hanksville, also hung on. They were committed beyond the understanding of outsiders. Maybe comprehension comes to you only after you have fought all the demons there are to fight. You love your enemy, the desert, as yourself.

All I can say in answer to the poet Gail Gardener is, Don't, don't brain that youngster with a rock. Hell has its recompenses.

Acknowledgments

I want to thank Ned Chaffin for allowing me to join the cowboy caucus reunion. It was a privilege to be there and become acquainted with some people whose families were among the very first settlers in the desert and canyon country of southeastern Utah. My thanks to those interviewed who permitted me to intrude into their privacy. Perhaps by publishing these interviews I can repay them for putting up with my presence. Thank you as well to those who submitted comments about the original draft, perhaps especially John Alley, executive editor of the Utah State University Press. John contributed many cogent suggestions for preparation of the manuscript.

I am indebted to Marlys Ryan for her suggestion to include regional maps within each chapter, and to her husband, Bob, who unselfishly designed the maps and whose uncanny four-wheel driving skill allowed us to invade the remotest of areas and return safely. Walt Dabney, Superintendent of the National Park Service office in Moab, graciously allowed me to utilize the map of Canyonlands National Park. Dick Seely of Green River and Betty and Sam Emmanuel read an early draft and made several important suggestions. Frank Tidwell of Centerville, Utah, and Barbara Ekker, the regional historian and Jill-of-all-trades in Hanksville, Utah, have been very helpful sources of juicy bits of lore throughout the two years involved in gathering facts for this writing. My literary agent, David Spilver, has been a Gibraltar of support and has provided much sound advice. His devotion has had an instrumental role in organizing the text.

Without my wife, Taff, whose contributions and encouragement have made this more readable, and whose mastery over a computer will forever hold me in awe, this collection of stories would have quickly become a burden. My many thanks to her, for she has made this writing an enjoyable task.

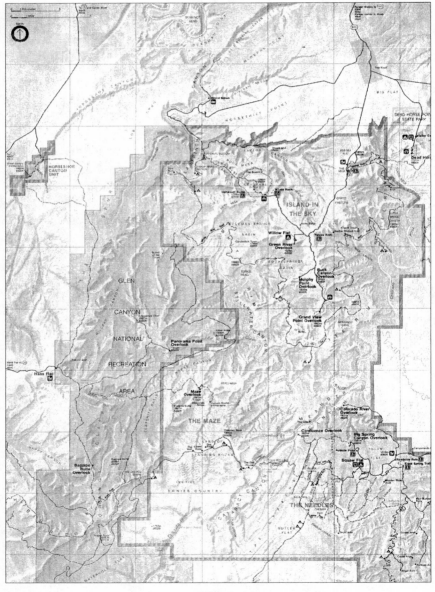

Used by permission of the National Park Service.

Introduction

Raising cattle or sheep is not an easy life. Even on the fairway-like pastures found in parts of Texas or Wyoming where the land is normally blessed with ample rainfall, riding a horse ten or twelve hours a day or being afoot in the dust behind a flock of sheep takes a special breed of person. To raise stock in eastern Wayne, Emery, or Garfield counties in southeastern Utah demanded an extra degree of determination on the part of those hardy women and men who operated isolated ranches and scratched out a living on the San Rafael Desert and in the rugged canyon country west of the Green and Colorado Rivers that is now part of Canyonlands National Park.

Established in 1964, the park was enlarged by a 1971 boundary change that added the detached Horseshoe Canyon to the park and enabled its world-acclaimed panels of pre-Columbian pictographs to come under the protective umbrella afforded by national park status. Ranchers whose stock grazed on the grasslands added to the national park were given a period of ten years to phase out their grazing activities. In that general area the annual moisture from rain and snow rarely exceeds nine or ten inches a year. Raising animals that depend upon native grasses in such a semi-arid climate is a sure formula for a rough way to make a living. Ned Chaffin, one of those ranchers and one of the principals in this book, put it succinctly when he described it as "a tough go for short dough."

The ranch hands not only had to trail their herds up and down precipitous paths to reach grazing lands or water holes, they had to learn to shoot fallen rocks off the trail and knock down ledges with dynamite

1

to a height their stock could scramble over without breaking a leg. The art of canning was a must, required to allow home-prepared meat to be taken to a cow camp and safely used over a period of months. Biscuits made in a kettle along with plenty of cowboy coffee were menu regulars. As Bill Racy learned at the time he first cooked rice over a campfire and ended up with enough rice for every soul in Wayne County, it took some knowledge of what you were doing to be a successful camp cook. As important as any of the above, the cowboys learned to become survivors in a land often manifesting itself as a harsh and dangerous companion.

From the town of Green River on the north to the site of the Hite Crossing of the Colorado River on the south and from Hanksville on the west to the Green and Colorado Rivers on the east, this unevenly shaped two hundred square miles contains one of nature's most magnificent assemblages of contrasting geography. Undulating pastures, bordered on the west by the awe-inspiring San Rafael Reef, flow eastward. The reef, a monocline of sedimentary rock, is but one of an uncounted number of the geologic features found on the Colorado Plateau. Though the pastures are fractured by arroyos and rock outcroppings such as those that Arth Chaffin named Goblin Valley, the grasslands of Robbers Roost, Hans Flat, Ernie Country, and The Spur all support a rich variety of plant life and, depending upon the particular terrain and rain belts, clusters of pinyon/juniper forests. The grasses—Indian rice, needle and thread, western wheat, and other species—naturally withstand arid conditions and are tolerant of alkaline soils. These grasses are loaded with nutrients. Cheat grass, an invasive grass that dies out in summer, is another matter. As Ned Chaffin notes, it became a problem as grazing increased:

> The stock didn't like cheat grass, and I think the reason was in many cases, not all, animals know what is good for them to feed on and they avoided cheat grass because it had little nutritional value. It became more and more pervasive as the good old grasses like buffalo grass got thinned out because of a combination of stock grazing it and those dry years. We talk of the dry years as though it is something of recent years, but heck, that country was always dry. If it wasn't for the BLM and some of the steps it took to limit the size of the herds, those areas would be without any grass or shrubs today.

Finally the flowing pastures reach the brink of the Orange Cliffs, and at this point a visitor enters another world. The geography changes dramatically. This row of cliffs, with perpendicular faces plunging from four hundred to nearly a thousand feet, is an important boundary line the early-day ranchers used to differentiate the country they called Under the Ledge, most of which is now encompassed by Canyonlands National Park and its adjacent Glen Canyon National Recreation Area.

Whether above or under the ledge makes no difference to the desert wildflowers. They seed themselves equally well on the higher ground west of the ledge or down at the level of Waterhole Flat or Elaterite Basin. The flowers, with an abundance of colors and fragrances, remain prolific and proud, whether they be Indian paint brush, aster (or its look-alike, fleabane daisy), primrose, Sego lily, scarlet gilia, lupine, or the ever lovely Prince's plume. Together they create a colorful palette. Other plants too common for the comfort of cattlemen are larkspur (*Delphinium*) and locoweed (*Astragalus*); both can be deadly to the cattle. Sagebrush, blackbrush, serviceberry, rabbitbrush, Mormon tea, and Gambel oak are dominant bushes and shelter small creatures.

The jump down from the rim to Under the Ledge, where cattle and sheep browsed in Waterhole Flat, Ernie Country, or Andy Miller Flats, delivers one into truly an up-and-down country. Those grassy areas are home to Elaterite Butte and Ekker Butte. Both rise abruptly from the fields and soar hundreds of feet into the heavens, as do Bagpipe Butte and Buttes of the Cross, each and every one a prominent landmark. One eye-catching, fingerlike projection reaching for the sky was named the Standing Rock by Major John Wesley Powell. In close proximity are other red rock monoliths: the Plug, Chimney Rock, the Wall. This is the Land of Standing Rocks. Each makes its contribution to one of the most beautiful places on earth.

It always was and remains a sightseer's paradise, a paradise admired and protected by the early ranchers who developed and improved the outflow of the life-sustaining springs. When standing on the rim of the Maze and looking below at the carved-up, white-colored Cedar Mesa Sandstone's snaky canyons, one would think no person could ever trek across them. But people have done so. Long before cowboys drove their cattle through those bottomlands, pre-Columbian Archaic, Fremont, and Anasazi peoples occupied the area. Their legacy can be discovered on the canyon walls; their pictographs, glyphs, granaries, and other artifacts attest to their lives.

There are not many foot trails or vehicle roads to transport humans from the grazing lands atop the mesa down through the Orange Cliffs to the territory Under the Ledge. The earliest trails after the Indians'

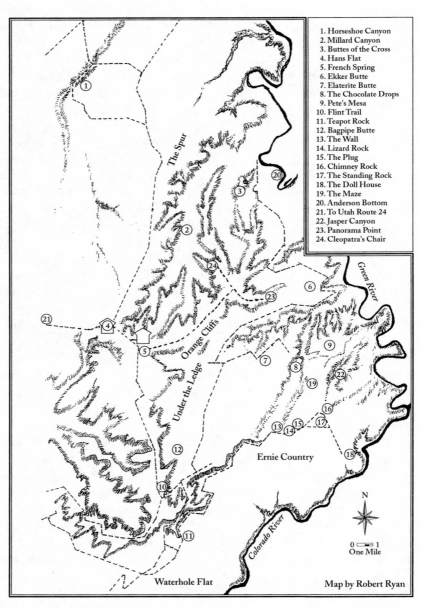

1. Horseshoe Canyon
2. Millard Canyon
3. Buttes of the Cross
4. Hans Flat
5. French Spring
6. Ekker Butte
7. Elaterite Butte
8. The Chocolate Drops
9. Pete's Mesa
10. Flint Trail
11. Teapot Rock
12. Bagpipe Butte
13. The Wall
14. Lizard Rock
15. The Plug
16. Chimney Rock
17. The Standing Rock
18. The Doll House
19. The Maze
20. Anderson Bottom
21. To Utah Route 24
22. Jasper Canyon
23. Panorama Point
24. Cleopatra's Chair

The Spur

Green River

Orange Cliffs

Under the Ledge

Ernie Country

Colorado River

N

0 ▭ 1
One Mile

Waterhole Flat

Map by Robert Ryan

Under the Ledge.

may have been those of outlaws in the 1870s or 1880s, but they were followed soon by cowmen and sheep herders who pushed or led their stock down paths through Horseshoe Canyon or the Flint Trail or to the Horsethief Trail, where water and the luxuriant grazing areas mentioned earlier were found.

This is the country where those stockmen and their families made their living. A characteristic of all, whether raising cattle or sheep, was an uncommon level of dedication to their chosen life. Success was not automatic. The nearest towns were thirty, forty, fifty, or more miles away. When ranchers drove their cattle Under the Ledge from the Chaffin or any other ranch, it was no afternoon jaunt. They planned and stocked up with water and grub and stayed out in the pastures in cow camps or sheep camps for two or three weeks at a time. Smart stockmen stayed with their herds and moved them from one feeding area to another, from one watering hole to another. Accidents could be a disaster. A broken leg became a logistics nightmare. There was no handy twenty-four-hour clinic in this country. There is none even today. In more recent times the Bureau of Land Management or mining or oil companies hacked out emergency landing strips, and today these can mitigate the complexity of hauling someone out. And now there is a national park ranger station located at Hans Flat with trail-smart rangers, rugged vehicles, and mobile radios. But at the turn of the century and for the next fifty years or so it took a special quality to survive.

One of those survivors, Ned Chaffin, organized a cowboy caucus that took place on Memorial Day 1994. He followed it with others in 1995 and 1996. The caucus was a gathering of old saddlemates, men and women who had ridden together all over the San Rafael Desert and the Maze District of Canyonlands National Park. A few of these friends had not seen each other in fifty-six years. The families of several of them also participated in the caucuses.

The following interviews, which I completed at various times during and since that first caucus, offer a profile of a few of those early cowboys and cowgirls, sheepmen and sheepwomen. I made no attempt to vary or alter the colloquialisms, western flavor, or strong opinions common to the ranch folk interviewed. There weren't many families in those two hundred square miles. Universally they loved the land, and most treated it with respect. Some continue to ranch on parts of the subject territory and will continue to do so as long as they can sit in a saddle. To all of them it was home, and with a few friends, a few neighbors maybe a day's horseback ride away, they had some fun too.

To assist readers, especially those not familiar with the area, I have included both general and more localized maps. Specific maps identify the approximate locations of many of the places discussed in corresponding interviews. Students of the Maze District of the national park will note an occasional discrepancy between the names of places shown on modern commercial maps and places named on my maps. An example of this is the grazing area labeled "Ernie's Country" on commercial and park service maps. The historically correct name is "Ernie Country." I've spoken to perhaps fifty persons who live in Wayne or Emery County and not one of them refers to it by other than Ernie Country. Other places, like Valley City, have simply faded away and no longer exist.

Ned Chaffin speaks of Dave Rust's guide services. Rust was the official guide for the Claflin-Emerson archeological expeditions to the Under the Ledge country and to certain places in the San Rafael Swell and also when the archeologists ventured into the Book Cliffs. Those expeditions were under the auspices of Harvard University's renowned Peabody Museum of Archeology and Ethnology, and various expedition members made important contributions to the recording of Fremont and Anasazi artifacts, including extensive photographic files and drawings of the petroglyphs and pictographs of those ancient cultures.

Rust was well chosen and eminently qualified to be the chief guide. He was one of the first to establish river running tours in Glen Canyon and horseback tours in Utah's canyon country. While discussing some of those archeological surveys, Ned acknowledged that Rust hired locals, including Ned, Leland Tidwell, and Les McDougal, at different times to show him around Under the Ledge. Ned would be hired by Rust as a guide for a particular area such as the canyons leading into or out of Waterhole Flat, and when the lead archeologists wanted to explore a canyon or trail that Leland was more familiar with, they would dismiss Ned and take on Leland. In turn, that guide would be replaced by Ned or by another guide who was familiar with a newly chosen locale. As described in Ned's interview, that hiring/firing practice led to some hard feelings, but Dave Rust wasn't about to hire a guide who had never been into a canyon targeted for exploration. As Ned says, "That's the way it was," and he always respected Rust for his cautious ways.

This canyon country is complex, a challenge for even skilled cartographers. The map preceding Wiladeane Hills's interview shows the approximate locations of Lou's Spring and Clell's Spring. Both are located in narrow, twisted canyons that are practically parallel to each other and can be found south and southeast of the Land of Standing

Rocks. True of many of the named places in this oral history, neither is shown on modern maps. There is a Robbers Roost Canyon, a Robbers Roost Flat, a Robbers Roost Spring, a Robbers Roost Cave, and there used to be a Robbers Roost Ranch. The ranch was founded and developed by Joe and Millie Biddlecome in 1909.

Before finding Crow Seep, where he developed the Robbers Roost Ranch, Biddlecome had ranched on the north slopes of the La Sal Mountains near the junction of the Dolores and Colorado Rivers. Some say he was encouraged to leave there by his neighbors, whose cattle herds frequently appeared to be shy a few head while his herd was experiencing overnight growth in numbers. Ned refers to this practice as "a midnight requisition."

The Biddlecomes had two daughters, Pearl Biddlecome Baker and Hazel Biddlecome Ekker. In 1939 Art Ekker, a rancher who married Hazel, bought the Robbers Roost Ranch and renamed it the Ekker Ranch. One of their sons, A. C. Ekker, manages the historic ranch today for the surviving children as a working cattle ranch and also runs a tour business, Outlaw Trails, Inc., from the remote ranch site. Whenever I'm anywhere close to it, I can't resist stopping at the ranch. The original buildings and cedar corral remain. The spring, Crow Seep, still flows and continues as the sole source of water for the ranch.

Although other "cowboys" included here had experiences raising or herding sheep, Lowry, Gwen, and Hugh Seely come from a prosperous ranching family whose principal success came from sheep raising. Before them, their parents and grandparents ran both cattle and sheep either Under the Ledge, on the San Rafael Swell, on the pastures in the Book Cliffs, or in a combination of all of the above. Lowry and Hugh's grandparents were original settlers in the area of central and southeast Utah around Orangeville, Castle Dale, Huntington, and Green River, and they prospered by ranching, as did Lowry and Hugh's father, David Randolph Seely.

Eventually the family gravitated east out of the Utah desert to the richer lands of western Colorado. Earlier though, they ran herds on the grassy valley pastures of Nine Mile Canyon, in the Sinbad area of the San Rafael Swell, in the Hill Creek country that is up in the Book Cliffs, at the head of Florence Creek where Jim McPherson's ranch was anchored, and over at Walker Draw where David Randolph Seely filed a homestead.

(Walker Draw was named after Joe Walker, a member of Butch Cassidy's gang. A posse cornered Joe Walker and two other outlaws in the draw and shot and killed all three of them in a furious exchange of gunfire. Lowry told me people went to Walker Draw with metal detectors and picked up shell casings for years after the incident, and that one could see bullet chips on the sandstone walls of the draw.)

Although Lowry and Hugh had an advantage over most of the hardscrabble cowboys interviewed here of growing up under the wing of their successful rancher father, that advantage in no way diminished the requirement for muscle strength and determination while they were helping their dad or, later, when they independently developed their own herds and ranches.

After 1921, Lowry and Hugh's dad moved north out of the Under the Ledge country and onto the Swell and the Book Cliffs. In those days between 1921 and 1934, before the Taylor Grazing Act became the rule of the land, they ran herds of fifteen hundred cattle and six thousand sheep. While on drives the cowhands and herders stayed with the herds for two or more months at a time. Hugh tells of their dad going Under the Ledge with a herd of sheep in November and not returning to civilization until April. Pack animals were worth their weight in gold; pack horses or mules were essential when moving camp or when reprovisioning was needed and someone had to take a pack outfit to town. When Lowry was a boy of twelve, his dad sent him from their cow camp on upper Florence Creek with a train of six mules to the town of Thompson to load up supplies that were needed at the camp. For a boy of twelve to ride fifty miles to Thompson, load 300 pounds of supplies on each of six pack mules and ride back to the camp surely required a massive portion of grit.

Ranching was the driving economic force of the region. Between 1934 and 1950 the town of Craig, Colorado, shipped more wool from its rail yards than any other inland shipping point in the United States. Furthermore, Hayden, just east of Craig, shipped more live lambs than did any other inland shipping point in this country. The pastures of central and southeastern Utah and northwestern Colorado supported the vast herds of sheep and cattle important to the economies of both states.

In 1942 the sheep industry peaked at 56 million sheep and lambs in the U.S. Today that figure barely reaches 8.5 million. Hugh attributes this dramatic change to several factors, including difficulties encountered with predator controls, the price of labor and related problems with the scarcity of qualified cowboys and herders today, the price of wool and lamb, and the overall costs associated with ranching operations. Everything from taxes to gasoline to food costs more, and though those costs may rise in a consistent trend, livestock returns can rocket up or down, often responding to the vagaries of international market vibrations. No wool carpet is manufactured in the United States today. It is all imported from England, Australia, and other wool-producing countries.

Throughout these interviews reference is made to still-existing small towns: Green River, Hanksville, Ferron, Thompson, Orangeville, Castle Dale, Orderville, La Sal. Most have populations of less than one thousand, some less than five hundred souls, but they exemplify Utah's pastoral heritage. In several the federal government is among the largest employers, through its offices for the Forest Service, the BLM, and National Park Service. No large manufacturer can be found—there is a power plant or a coal mine here or there, but the harvesting of hard minerals is nearly nonexistent. Tourism is contributing more and more to the economies of these small rural towns. New motels are rapidly replacing those of 1950s vintage, and a few shiny new restaurants are cropping up.

In these towns, it is not uncommon to find that individuals who work full time for one of the government agencies, or in a retail store, or who own a gas station or garage, also run a few head of cattle on the side—not many, maybe twenty-five to forty head. Why not? There sure isn't much opportunity for part-time work, and those jobs in tourism are definitely not high paying. Besides, no cow ever raised a labor dispute.

The area is rich in history and even richer in its scenic splendor. The fabled Outlaw Trail that ran from Montana to Mexico traversed these pastures and canyons. Since the advent of Canyonlands National Park the beauty of this canyon country has become widely known across our United States and in foreign countries. Much of its real beauty, though, is found within the people who lived there. Thanks to Wiladeane and Ned, to Lorin and Bill, to the Seelys (Gwen and husband Lowry and Lowry's brother Hugh), to Guy and Nina, and finally to that full-time detester of the Bureau of Land Management, Chad Moore, we have here a few of their stories.

At the picket corral at Waterhole Flat, 1995. From left to right: Frank Tidwell, Lorin Milton, Ned Chaffin, and Wiladeane Chaffin Hills. The youngster is Jod Booker, the son of Bill Booker, a BLM ranger in Hanksville, Utah.

1

Wiladeane Chaffin Wubben Hills

Wiladeane Chaffin Wubben Hills is Ned Chaffin's niece and grew up on the Chaffin Ranch. Her story gives us a rare opportunity to learn what it was like for a child growing up in an environment dominated by cow and horse talk. During her first five and a half years on this isolated ranch, before her sister Claire came along, she had to make do with a favorite dog and horse for playmates. There were other children at neighboring ranches, but those neighboring ranches were ten to thirty miles distant.

Wiladeane coped very well, and in addition to learning early in life the ways of a ranch woman—canning, cooking, sewing, and hauling water—she became a first-rate cowhand and performed most of the duties of any cowboy when it was time to drive the cattle from one grazing area to another.

She is retired now and recently moved to Grand Junction in order to be nearer to her children, and so that her bright eyes will be closer to Utah's wonderlands. In spirit, Wiladeane has never been far removed from them.

July 17, 1995 and May 31, 1996
Grand Junction, Colorado

This is my story of the Chaffin family and its role in the early history of the land that is now a part of the west side of Canyonlands National Park (the Maze District and the detached Horseshoe Canyon Unit), the north and east part of Glen Canyon National Recreation Area south to where Hite used to be on the Colorado River, and our ranch on the San Rafael River one mile west of where it joined the Green River.

Wiladeane Chaffin Wubben Hills, 1938, at the Chaffin Ranch at age ten. Ned, her uncle, is in the foreground with the horse. Bill Racy is in the background. Photo courtesy of Wiladeane Chaffin Wubben Hills.

Back in the early days my family on both my dad's and mother's side were Mormon pioneers and had settled in the middle of Utah around Loa and Torrey. The Chaffin family was one branch. At the funeral in 1968 of my grandmother, Alice Brian Chaffin, all her pallbearers were relatives or had been Mormon bishops. My mother's maiden name was Hunt and on her side of the family were the Hunts and the Curtises. For many, many years every summer we have had Hunt family reunions near Torrey, Utah.

My grandparents were Louis (Lou) Moses Chaffin and Alice Brian Chaffin. My parents were Faun and Violet Hunt Chaffin. Dad was the eldest of eleven children and the smallest of the boys.

Granddad Lou was a big man with a magnetic way of getting things done. The Colorado River had a hold on him from an early age when he placer mined many places with his dad. My father told me how Lou, in his teens, went down the Colorado River through the Cataract Canyon with Bert Loper in their homemade boat in the late 1880s, and how his dad walked out from Spanish Bottom to Hanksville, and that Lou had explored all that area long before they took cattle into the Under the Ledge country.

Dad recalled taking their first cattle from Torrey, Utah, to Hanksville, to Hatch Canyon, through Sunset Pass into Waterhole Flat and Ernie Country, and later over the North Trail to Big Water. This was in 1918 and he was eighteen years old.

I was born in 1928 at Green River, Utah, in a house that my dad and mother and my grandparents lived in. My folks had gotten married in July of 1927 at the time of the Mormon Pioneer Days celebration that honors the date of the Mormon arrival in Utah in 1847. They lived in Green River, and my mother told me she found out the day after they were married that Dad was in a partnership arrangement with his family, L. M. Chaffin & Sons. This was much to her surprise. At the time of their marriage the Chaffins were already running cattle Under the Ledge. When I was two or three I went to live at Chaffin Ranch. Several of Dad's brothers, my uncles, were always at the ranch, working it together. I have a photograph of me on a horse, and my little legs were just hanging down on top of the horse. I could ride a horse soon after I could walk, and Dad always told me I was the best cowhand ever.

From the very beginning, when you live on a ranch, when I was four or five years old I started helping my mother around the kitchen with cooking and canning and all of the things that have to be done around a home. Everybody pitched in; you did what was necessary. My family taught me and they were good teachers. In other words, I wasn't out playing like most kids do. I was working on the ranch doing whatever needed to be done and learned at an early age to help in the house, and sometimes to totally take care of the house. That is, whenever Dad wasn't enticing me to go outside.

As soon as I could do anything at all, he had me out helping with the cattle and horses and doing errands for him out on the range. As soon as I could lift a saddle he started me saddling horses. Often when little I just rode bareback. Mother had a hard time keeping me in the house. Dad would just take me off and she would be left without me. My big love was the outdoors, so any chance I got, I was outdoors. I loved to be out with the cattle and horses and riding. I got thrown on several occasions when I was a child, but I was never hurt. In all of my life I never got a broken bone. When young and the horse would throw you, you'd just get up and get on again and ride him right away. We kids used to ride some of the calves when people were there. Just for fun.

I remember how lonely it was with no other children around. There were all these guys, the uncles and the ranch hands. The house was large; it had a front room with a big fireplace, a kitchen with a wood burning stove with a big reservoir that you heated water in, bedrooms, and a big cellar. The stove had lots of space for cooking with big kettles and we had a large griddle for hot cakes. The hot water reservoir supplied us with hot water for washing dishes or clothes. Because we cooked all of our meals on a wood burning stove we always had hot water. It held at least ten gallons, maybe it was twenty.

We had running water from a cistern west of the house on a little hill. The water flowed by gravity from the cistern through water pipes they had put in before the house was set on its foundation. That was how we got running water in the sink. We had a wagon with fifty-gallon barrels, and whenever we ran out of water we'd go down to the Green River and fill the barrels with buckets. The wagon was horse drawn, and was still out there in 1990 when I visited the ranch.

We also had an ice house, and we owned one of the first automobiles in the area. I don't know when the Lou Chaffins got their first automobile, but I have a picture of him holding me with my mother and Aunt Gwen looking on. Aunt Gwen had, I think, a 1930 or 1931 Nash with a rumble seat. We had some pickups too, but I can't remember how we got out to the ranch the first time, whether by car or by wagon.

Four of the Chaffin brothers were at the ranch. By the time I got there, Gay, the youngest, had died at age twelve of blood poisoning. He didn't live at the ranch. My earliest memories were about that house and being there with my mother and dad. My grandparents and uncles lived there, and there was an extra bedroom that people stayed in on the west side of the house. Grandmother and Granddad stayed in the middle section. We had a big bunk house for the guys. It seemed my grandparents, the Chaffin boys, and I were all out there at once sometimes. We frequently had big dinners and there was a big table where everybody would sit around and talk about horses and cattle. Mother and Grandmother made delicious pies and big dinners for everyone. No one was ever turned away hungry.

There was a small house where we farmed to the west, upriver about a half mile from the main ranch house. Sometimes when everybody was at the ranch, I and my part of the family would go and stay in the small house. We had more privacy there, but it was scary when there were big floods and the river came up close to the house.

I remember Granddad drilling the well, and how everyone was so excited when all that water started coming. But they found it was so mineralized they couldn't drink it. Later, we built a cooling system at the well so we could keep our milk and things cool.

After the Chaffin brothers and my grandparents had left the ranch around 1936, Dad didn't use the ice blocks from the cinder icehouse. Maybe it depended upon the weather being colder sometimes because there were huge chunks of ice in there. They must have been ten or so inches square and were cut and brought from the Green River in winter. I used to go down there and scrape cinders off to get to the ice. We had an ice box, one of those you put a block of ice in the top. We mainly kept everything cool in the later years with water from the well. The well became a cold water geyser. It still spouts up in the air ten or fifteen feet. At the geyser we planted the tamarisk that Uncle Ned gave my mother many years ago. It was one of the first ones in the country. Now they are taking over everything.

I did a lot of haying, helping to drive the team and, when strong enough, I ran the mower. One time I cut a rabbit in two and remember how bad I felt. I also helped by tromping down the hay when the men would pitch it onto or off the hay wagon. I did a lot of shoveling to help Dad with the irrigating and kept debris out of the ditches when we ran water from the dam rather than from the pump. It was hard work because we had big old ditches and we had to constantly build little dirt dams to move the water around to different crop rows. There was a big pump on the ditch to get water from the San Rafael River into the irrigation ditches. Claire was little and I was only eight and served as Dad's handy helper whenever he had to work on the pump or around the ranch.

We had lots of fences and I rode them a lot to check for breaks where cattle could get through. Our farm was about 670 acres, not all farmed, but most of it was fenced. We had a fence west of the house that went north to the big hills and sand dunes near a big rock. That fence kept the cattle out of the living area and away from the crops. All of our farm machinery was horse drawn. We never had a tractor. I milked and fed cows a lot, but I never liked milking.

What I liked best was being around the cattle and going Under the Ledge. The farm work was hard and a lot of it was too heavy for me. Like hay raking, that was too much for little me. We had a big ensilage pit and grew corn in a field. In the late summer or fall we would cut up the corn and put it in the ensilage pit. Then I would get on my horse and ride back and forth over the ensilage to tromp it down. During the winter the cut-up corn would stay warm in the pit and made good cattle feed.

I don't think Mother ever moved the cattle when the brothers were around. The way she and Grandmother were brought up in the Mormon religion, a woman's place was in the home. They took care of their husbands and the children and made a happy home. Everything a woman did, pretty much, was the cooking and the cleaning and the social part at the church and all of those kinds of things.

The pioneer women often had to do other things. I recall in my younger days when the brothers and grandparents were here, Mother was mainly doing the cooking and helping to run things. But she did have a say in the financial end of running the ranch.

The ranch was twenty-three miles from town and when we needed something like groceries we went to town in a truck on the old dirt Green River road. Sometimes we went to town only once a month and once in a while we'd get stuck in the sand or clay hills or the truck would break down.

We raised almost everything that we served at those meals because mother canned a lot: corn and string beans, meat, potatoes, carrots, and beets. She made her own cheese, and we always had a big old crock of sauerkraut. There was always canned meat and vegetables that we took Under the Ledge. We had a pressure cooker for canning, meats mainly.

I remember Mother's uncle, Frank Hatt. Each September he would bring us ten or so bushels of peaches from the Fruita, Utah, orchard that is now part of Capital Reef National Park. His wife was

Ruby Curtis, a sister of Grandmother, Alta Curtis Hunt, and my grandfather was Charles Hunt. She canned beef, and we'd go down to the Green River with catfish traps. They are outlawed now. We put a rabbit or chicken in this little trap, and the fish would swim in the trap. We would go back in a few days to get the traps out, and there would be maybe thirty fish in it. Mother would can those with a pressure cooker and they tasted like salmon, but they were catfish. If we got carp, we fed them to the turkeys. We raised a lot of turkeys for selling and canning. When we went fishing or to get water, we went swimming. That was a big thing, a fun thing.

I remember when Claire was little she would ride with Mother on old Smokey, the mule, down to Waterhole Flat. Claire would ride on a blanket in the saddle in front of Mother until she could ride by herself, and later got her own horse called Rowdy. Mother always wanted to ride Smokey because he was very gentle and easy-gaited, and he was sure-footed and could be used as a pack mule if needed.

When we went Under the Ledge we had to check gates. Like at Spanish Bottom, I used to have to go down to the bottom to check on the cattle. At the trail head, up on top where we found those trilobites and crinoids on a rock ledge, we had a brush gate made out of cedar and juniper trunks and branches. You would take the cattle down and close the gate and leave the cattle there until spring. I don't know if the gate is still there; I haven't been there since I was fourteen or so.

We had a main cowboy camp Under the Ledge at Waterhole Flat. We usually stayed out there for two or three weeks at a time. I was eight years old the first time I went Under the Ledge. We had to move the cattle around when it rained to where the water had collected in the potholes and the ponds. If it didn't rain, we would have to move them to places where they could get water. The later years were very dry and Dad said one year it didn't rain enough to wet his shirt. When not at the camp at Waterhole we took kettles, potatoes, rice, and beans to cook, but we didn't have sleeping bags. We just rolled up our quilts. At Waterhole we had a permanent tent with cedar logs up about three feet on the sides and canvas above that. The tent was under a big cedar tree that is still there, but the tent and logs are gone. We slept on cots outside and there was a camp stove Mother used to bake bread. She'd bring one cake of yeast that would last only long enough to bake yeast bread once and the rest of the time we'd have baking powder biscuits that we cooked in a Dutch oven.

We would go down for two to three weeks at a time. This was during the summer because I was in school during the winter, but I missed a

Spanish Bottom on the Colorado River.

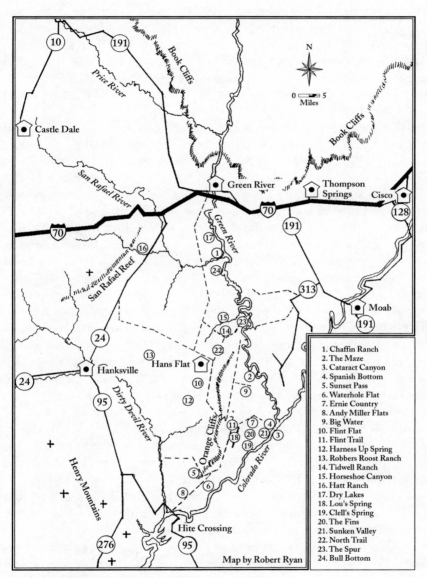

Wiladeane Chaffin Hills's Canyonlands.

lot of school. Mother taught me a lot at home. The cattle herds we moved around were usually small in number. We had to separate the older calves from the mothers because they would be having calves again. We put the older calves in different places such as Calf Canyon, which is east of Waterhole Flat. You didn't run them in one place at the same time. We ran cattle in Big Water, Ernie Country, Andy Miller Flats, and sometimes in Cove Canyon and down in Hatch Canyon, but Waterhole Flat was our main area. All of those areas are located in what we called Under the Ledge.

Many times down there I would have to help with the branding and moving the cattle around. Once Dad had gotten me started moving some cows from Waterhole Flat to Big Water. That meant I had to take them over very rough places and get the cows up onto the Black Ridge to trail them over and down into Big Water. What we called Big Water is now known as Elaterite Basin. The cows were very ornery, and I had a hard, hot time getting them onto the trail. I was thankful for the cairns marking the trail. Often when I was a cowgirl, a cowhand, there was just me, all alone, taking care of the cattle just as Uncle Ned did. I took the place of another man and did what the men would do with the cattle. Mother helped with the cattle and she had her own cattle and her own brand too. She got them as part of the partnership arrangement Dad had with the L. M. Chaffin & Sons partners. The fellows factored in the work the women did and they got cattle and a brand as payment. She worked right alongside of all of us to do what had to be done. I never went Under the Ledge alone, but I handled the cattle on the range by myself a lot. The men sure went down there and into the canyons alone on many occasions.

The terrain was very rough and the trails were scary. There were no roads, not even wagon roads. There were rocks and ledges you'd have to go down or get over and a lot of areas would be washed out after big rains. You'd have to watch for the rock cairns. It was a very beautiful area, rugged and clean, with high grasses and flowers. There wasn't any cheat grass in those days; it came later when weather started getting dryer and the ground got worn down from the sheep. Not from us, for as I recall, we usually had lots of grasses except in dry years.

Dad always stressed safety, but even so I had a lot of close experiences. We always were very careful to put our fires out and never had a grass fire on the range. I don't remember any sort of a stampede. I think, in bigger herds on a trail drive, if a mountain lion attacks or someone starts shooting, or bad thunder storms come along, there might be a stampede. In a small herd you had them under control, although when herding them, once in a while one would dart back quickly and two or three others would dart back with him. You would have to whirl your horse around quickly and head them off.

I did help with the branding, but didn't actually put the brand on because I wasn't strong enough and it was dangerous. I was the one who roped the cattle and brought them to the guys to brand or get them in the chutes or whatever they were going to do to the cattle. I was pretty good with a rope. Not as good as Uncle Ned, but pretty good considering how little I was. I always had a lariat on my saddle. We never had guns along that I can recall, except when we hunted deer.

To get down to Under the Ledge we would drive the car to the head of the Flint Trail. Hired hands or Daddy drove the horses there. I always rode in a car going out there. At Flint Flat, up on top, we never liked to stay in the cabins that Edwin T. Wolverton and the Chaffins built because of the mice in the cabins. We just slept under the trees. There is a spring about a mile to the northwest of the cabins and we'd take the horses to water there. It was called Harness-Up Spring. There was water dripping and troughs for the horses. You would take the horse over at night, and take water jugs there. The jugs would be filled by morning. The spring faced the Henry Mountains to the west. We left the horses there at the spring or over at the Gordons and got them when we were ready for the next trip Under the Ledge.

We would drive back to our ranch, and we often stopped at the Robbers Roost Ranch if we hadn't stopped on the way out. The Ekkers were there, Art and Hazel and the children, Eddyjo and Tissy. Those are the ones I knew. It was always a fun thing to go there. I never went to the Tidwell's ranch east of Horseshoe Canyon, but finally went into Horseshoe Canyon in 1995 to where the Great Gallery pictographs and petroglyphs are. We went down into the canyon on the old road that Granddad Lou and his brother Arth had built through a contract with Phillips Petroleum in 1928 and 1929. A Phillips crew was in there to drill for oil at the Tidwell ranch. Even today there is a lot of cable and timbers laying around at the site of that old well. They never brought in anything worth producing. This was about the same time they built (for Phillips again) the old bridge across the San Rafael River about a mile upriver from our ranch. That bridge was an engineering feat, and it's still standing although not useable. It was exciting for me to go through the canyon on the trails my dad, granddad, uncles, in-laws, and Bill Racy had traveled many years before bringing the cattle into Green River and going past our San Rafael Ranch on the way to market.

Around our ranch we had milk cows. Sometimes you just raised them to milk and sell because milk cows were always in demand. We had Jersey cows almost always. The Herefords were okay to handle except some of the bulls were mean. When they were mean they would paw the ground and you have to get out your rope while you were on a horse and act as if you meant business and turn them away. Once Dad had sent me out to bring this bull in from just across the San Rafael River. When I came up on him he suddenly charged my horse. There were two large horn marks left on the horse after the collision. Because I was a good rider I managed to stay on the horse and chased the bull back to the ranch.

The Tidwells, both Leland's family and Delbert's, and their kids came by our San Rafael Ranch often, Chad Moore and Billy Moore, and the Ekkers, sometimes. We always had big meals, huge meals. It was good to have the kids come over, but it seemed like they couldn't stay long enough. As a kid I really looked forward to visits with other kids. Frank Tidwell and me were two who grew up alone for a long time unlike Eddyjo and Tissy Ekker who were over at the Robbers Roost where there was always a lot of things going on. Frank was isolated on the Tidwell Ranch, over on the other side of Horseshoe Canyon. I was, too, at our San Rafael Ranch, so we really had fun when he came to visit. There were times when I would hear a car coming because we were only about a mile from the road to Green River, and I would listen hard and always hoped someone would turn down the road to our place and come to visit with us.

Frank reminded me recently about a time when their truck had broken down on a little bridge that we were building across a ditch near where our pump was and they couldn't get through and all of them came down to spend the night. It was dark and it was Halloween, but he probably hadn't realized that. As he started to come towards the house, there was this big witch all dressed in black and making lots of noise. All of a sudden he recognized my voice and my nose and was really relieved and glad it was me and not a witch. He was about eight then and I was ten.

I know whenever he came to the house, as well as the other kids, his cousins, we would always go off doing something fun, like swimming or riding. Frank liked to ride my horse, Tony, so we would get on together and cross the San Rafael River a bunch of times. We would talk and have fun together and all of us would swim. Those were fun times.

It was good to go to town once in a while because we had been so alone on the ranch. I lived in Green River when I went to school through my freshman year, and had lots of friends there. Through the Mormon church and the school there were many social activities—a lot of dancing. I think I had my first prom dress when I was in eighth grade. I liked Green River, but I preferred the ranch and going to Under the Ledge. One thing I missed out on because of living on a ranch that far from town was the social part. The kids in town had more social and childhood interaction while growing up.

There were a lot of kids in Green River who came from farms and ranches and, like me, lived in town to go to school, so it was not unusual for me living on a ranch. The other kids treated me respectfully, but in later years while in high school after we moved to Grand Junction, it was kind of neat for my classmates there to talk to someone like me who lived out on a ranch and had their own horse. To know someone who grew up on a ranch and owned her own horse was a novelty for many of the kids in Grand Junction. I connected socially even though we didn't have much money. I married a Grand Junction man whose father was president of a college and I could relate to him with no trouble. On the ranch the hired hands were always respectful. They wouldn't have been there if they hadn't been. Dad would have seen to that, but he never had to speak to any one of them. Ever! I must have learned something in that time, or being the way I was in all of my life; I've never experienced anyone being disrespectful to me. I learned to dance just by picking it up from friends, in church and at home. When we were little Dad and Mother wanted us to dance for visitors; there were lots of aunts and uncles around, and the grandparents. They all helped me grow up. It was part of our culture. Nowadays they call it a sense of community, helping each other. In fact, Frank Tidwell was telling me recently how sometimes when they used to come by, they would take another road to Green River that was just northwest of our ranch under Horse Bench and up the Dry Lake Wash. We used to go that way when the sand was bad and Horse Bench would get too sandy, so we'd try to go the other way. Frank said sometimes my granddad would ride up on his horse to help pull them out or he would stand on the car bumper so they could get through the sand.

Storytelling came naturally with all of those guys around talking man talk. With no electricity it went on all of the time. When they got to talking it was hard for the women to get a word in edgewise. I found in my later years I still have a hard time getting my voice heard when I'm out in crowds of people. I've tried to overcome that, but I still find exceptions. But that was the way it was. They all loved each other and the kids and they took care of us. They hollered at you if you did something you weren't supposed to do, and Dad spanked me a couple of times.

My parents had a really good relationship. I'd hear them talking late at night, just discussing things after everyone else was asleep. They always discussed things with us kids. There were no secrets in the family. Both of them readily asked my opinion about things.

We did have a radio that operated with a car battery. The Second World War was going on and we would turn the radio on every morning to get the news and the farm reports out of KOA and KSL. We never ran the radio for music or entertainment, just to get the news. Because of no electricity most of our lights were kerosene fueled. We had one gas lantern that we had to pump to get it started. We didn't use it much because we had so many kerosene lamps. We got up early and went to bed early. You followed the sun in the summer.

There were a few other ranches near us in the area of the San Rafael River. One was Frank Hatt's place. He was my uncle and had a ranch on the San Rafael River west of where present day Utah Route 24 is now located, just a few miles south of I-70. South of his ranch, downstream, was the Gillis Ranch. They ran cattle and farmed. They didn't come to our place very much because when they went to Green River they went up their own road. Because they were west of us it was easier for them to go that way than it would have been to come east and take the old Green River road. When you come out on top of Horse Bench, if you look to the southwest, that would be where their ranch was.

When I was a kid I used to have to ride bog to check the river to be sure the cows weren't mired in the mud. Bill Racy talks about the problems of riding bog. If I found one and if it was still alive, you had to get it out right away. I didn't get the cows out because I was too little and it was dangerous. If I found one, I would hurry back to the ranch house and get someone bigger to get it out. I used to ride upstream on the San Rafael River from our ranch and I would also ride up to the Dry Lakes west of the Green River and check the cows at the mouth of Dry Lakes to make sure there weren't any cows in the bog there.

Now the tamarisks have grown so there is nothing but tamarisks along the river banks. You can barely get to the river because they are so thick. In fact, many years ago my dad bought 135 acres of land at the mouth of Dry Lakes. He bought it for taxes and when he settled up with me and my sister and brother, at Mack, Colorado, we formed a partnership and I took the Dry Lake property as part of my share in the partnership. Later I sold it, except we kept three-quarters of an acre that we gave to Claire. Claire and I tried to find it in 1995, but it was all covered with tamarisks.

The families that I knew while I was growing up were mainly the Moores, the Tidwells, the Ekkers, and the Hatts. My best friend and second cousin was Dennavor Hatt Price. She was my Aunt Ruby and Uncle Frank Hatt's daughter. She still lives in Green River. I think one of the Hatt brothers still has the old Hatt Ranch out there, but they sold the water rights just as all the ranchers on the San Rafael did. I think that happened about the same time the Moyniers sold the water rights that they got when they bought our ranch to the Utah Power and Light Company. We sold the San Rafael Ranch to Leo and Pierre Moynier, Jr., of Price, Utah, on October 27, 1944. They were sheepmen so we sold our cattle separately.

When I was a kid on the ranch it was very lonely there. I was the only child for almost six years before my sister Claire came along, and my brother Steve never did live on the ranch. I was with all these uncles and they were talking all the time about horses and the cattle and being out working. When I was a little kid, maybe three or four or five, Mother would often pack me a lunch and I'd take my dog Sharkey and go along the fence line straight north where there were some big sand dunes next to a big rock formation, and I'd spend hours over there just walking and playing around. I had an imaginary playmate for a friend. His name was Fubbi. My parents thought I was talking about my Aunt Phoebe who was the wife of Arth Chaffin, Granddad Lou's brother. Arth ran the Hite Ferry for many years.

Fubbi always took care of me and told me stories. I kind of forgot about it and it was very interesting because when I came back from this year's cowboy caucus, the get-together of friends in Green River in May 1995, I was thinking about the trip we took out to Flint Flat and down the Flint Trail to the Under the Ledge country and Waterhole Flat. It was while I was at my home in Grand Junction, going over some tapes and pictures of that recent trip and I was longing to be back there again, that I thought of my current spiritual guide Fubbi Quantz, and realized he was the same one who had been my imaginary friend many years ago when I was a lonely little girl at the San Rafael Ranch. Fubbi still takes care of me sometimes, and guides me when I need it. This isn't unusual as I believe the soul is eternal and I've lived several lifetimes on earth. Anyway, it was a spiritual awareness for me.

At any rate, that was a real spiritual awareness for me being down there. It was only a day or so after I got back home and I could just feel the energy and felt it was just like when I was a kid and I was with my friend.

We rented places in Green River so Claire and I could go to school, or I stayed with my Aunt Ruby. Dad stayed at the ranch with the hired hands most of the time and took care of the cattle Under the Ledge. I also stayed with my grandparents in Payson, Utah, for the winter months when I was in the fifth and seventh grades so I could attend school there. My mother worked beside my dad because there wasn't much money to hire the help we needed after Dad's family left and he and Mother took over the care of the ranch and cattle operations. Bill Racy joined our family at age seventeen in 1938 and helped us so much. Dad taught us to work hard and play hard. We would work and then we'd have fun. One of the main fun things to do was going to swim in either the San Rafael or Green River. During the early forties my mother's brothers, Floyd and Rulon Hunt, helped us on the ranch after Ned and the other Chaffin brothers had moved away.

One interesting story that I had forgotten about came back to haunt me. It is a story that my cousin, Rulon's daughter Inez Hunt White, reminded me of five or so years ago. We used to go swimming in the San Rafael River a lot, until the river started going dry in the summer. There were big pools with water running through them and they were fun to swim in. She reminded me how I saved her life. The river was running pretty good and we were swimming and she got caught in an undertow. This happened south of the ranch and she said I was downstream and I grabbed her by the hair and pulled her out. It haunted me when I wondered five years ago if she still was glad I saved her because she was really crippled and hurting from a car accident many years before in which she'd lost a son. She died in 1995.

I'll mention an experience I had one time when I was riding bog on the Green River and had ridden up to Dry Lakes. I was riding a young mare and had gotten off to have my lunch as it was about noon when I finished riding bog. When I went to mount up she wouldn't let me catch her. She would trot just fast enough so I couldn't catch her and I had to walk back. It was about five miles and I got sun blistered because I had a short sleeve shirt on. My mother rode out and picked me up about a mile from the ranch.

One of the biggest joys I had was when Dad's sister, Twila Stark, came with her son Kirby and left him with us to work the summers of 1941 and 1942. He was a little younger than me, but much bigger. He was such a joy to be around. He was always playing pranks on me, and

Elaterite Butte.

we'd race our horses when Dad wasn't looking. Later Kirby worked for Ken Chaffin down in the oil fields in Louisiana and went over to Saudi Arabia to work in the oil fields there. He caught some kind of virus over there. I never did see him again, although he did visit Dad in Colorado, but I wasn't around at those particular times. He died of that virus and is buried in Louisiana. His mother, Twila, Dad's only living sister, is still living in Louisiana.

Sometimes the San Rafael dried up in the late summer and I would have to take the horses to water in the Green River every day or in evenings and, of course, any cows that were at the ranch had to be driven down to the Green. The milk cows were watered from a pond at the corral until it went dry. We never had many cattle around the ranch house as they'd be grazing around the hills. Once this big mule, Smokey, the best mule ever, kicked his heels up at the horse I was riding and laid my leg open. It was such a bad wound that I couldn't go to town to the doctor because the rough road would hurt too much. I was bedridden for about a month. My mother put Absorbine Junior on it. It smelled really strong and bubbled, but with the oxygen in it my leg healed. Since we lived so far from doctors, we had to take care of ourselves and tried not to get hurt.

As I recall, the brothers Ken and Clell left the ranch first and didn't help much after 1935. Then my grandmother and granddad and Ned left in 1936. Ned married Marjorie and lived in California, but they kept coming back and helped out. With Blanche and Earl Daniel, Marjorie's parents, and Ned and Marjorie, we had a lot of fun times. The guys would go Under the Ledge and work the cattle and hunt, and we women would visit a lot. Clell came back a few times, too, because he still had cattle there.

We never had sheep, not even around the corrals, because there was always a little bit of competition between the sheepmen and the cattlemen. I'm not sure I remember huge herds of cows. I believe the most cattle the Chaffins had at any one time was about 450 head, but they were always in small herds. I was always helping to move the cattle around down Under the Ledge. I remember taking them down to Big Water and later to winter some of them down on Spanish Bottom. We used to take cattle up the Golden Stairs Trail and over the ridge from Ernie Country to Big Water which was hard to do because of the narrow chinle stratum neck. We didn't call the area Elaterite Basin then. We just called it Big Water, and there was Ernie Country and Waterhole.

It was kind of interesting because we, Dad, Mother, Claire, and me, would take the cattle from Waterhole Flat, our main camp, over to Ernie Country and then down into Big Water. We would move the cattle to where the water was. In Ernie Country there were always these big potholes, you know, water hole tanks for the cattle. And then there were Lou's Spring and Clell's Spring, and that was always very beautiful country. Those areas are known as the Fins and Sunken Valley.

It seems like we went to Ernie Country and we'd camp there for not very long because the water always had mosquito larvae, so we'd have to boil the water. There was always a lot of grass, so you just took the cattle there and left them. But when we went to Big Water it was a long trek. It was hard to get cattle up onto the rim to cross over to Big Water from Waterhole. I remember getting tired and hot and thirsty and to get water you would just dig in the sand in Big Water and water would show up. I didn't like Big Water much. It was too open, I guess, and not many trees. I never went with the cattle out the North Trail. I've been all around it, but never did ride it. When they took the cattle to market they drove them up the North Trail, across The Spur, Twin Corrals, past Horseshoe Canyon, and past Tidwell's ranch to the San Rafael Ranch and on to the stockyards at Green River. I didn't go along on those drives from Under the Ledge because they happened in the fall and the spring and that's when I was in school. I understand the North Trail was a very bad trail, and it took larger people to handle the cows up there. Claire and I would help take the cattle from San Rafael Ranch, especially so we could show off our horsemanship as we rode into town.

Mother, Claire, and I often would go and meet the drovers in places like over near the Robbers Roost or just before they got to the San Rafael Ranch, but to get the cattle out of the Under the Ledge country and up through the North Trail and on to the Tidwell's ranch, they often would stay at Tidwell's on the way and rest up. That was how they got out of there. I don't recall ever taking any cattle down the Flint Trail. It was a very bad trail and it seemed to go straight up, not where the road goes now. It was so bad that you would have to get off your horse because you would have to pull the reins to help him over the big rocks. If he should lose his footing, it could be very bad. We packed everything in saddle bags on the horses or mules. It was always a long trek to go from Flint Flat down to the main camp at Waterhole Flat. We would stay at the flat by the cabins and early the next morning we would go down to Waterhole, but there were many times we left the ranch and many, many times you would come down off the Black Ledge to the White Rim and then you would follow along the White Rim as the road does now along to that trail into the long, big Waterhole Flat. It would be totally dark sometimes, and you would just let the horses have the reins because they knew where the water and grain would be, and they could see the trail in the dark.

I remember being so tired, and Claire always had leg aches and Mother rubbing her legs, but it was fun being at Waterhole. It was always the neatest time for me. Dad, and sometimes other guys, were always branding, and we would help. We had the spring developed and had all the good water we could drink. Years before, Dad, Granddad, and Ned, I think, was in on it, had built a pond there with an old Fresno scraper and plow and three worn-out horses and two mules. It pretty much always had water that I can recall, and enough water to swim the horses sometimes.

My mother said my dad amazed her with his rare ability to get out of unusual, drastic circumstances such as the time we were moving cattle around at Waterhole, and we got a hard rain that filled the ponds, so we decided to go home. Before we left we went to the big pond to water our horses, and Claire, who was about three years old then said, "Swim the horse, Daddy." Faun started swimming his horse, and when the horse was able to touch bottom, he started lunging. Faun had his feet up on the saddle to keep from getting wet and, when the horse lunged, Faun fell off. As he fell he caught his foot in the saddle strap, his hat came up, and the horse started kicking and lunging, but Faun was able to hold on to one of the reins on the bridle and turned the horse's heels away from him. Finally the strap broke and set him free. He took some water, but it could have been worse.

There were tanks, big potholes up from where the pond was, that the water would stay in. From there, about three times every summer, we would move the cattle around, sometimes through Sunset Pass from Waterhole over into Hatch Canyon. We could also take the cattle around Cove Canyon to Andy Miller Flats, and then later to Hatch. We had built a corral over there, and there were springs down in Cove Canyon where you could water the horses and cattle.

One or two times every summer we would go from Cove Canyon to my Uncle Arth and Aunt Phoebe Chaffin's place at Hite where the old Hite Ferry was. It was always a treat because they had early watermelons and cantaloupe and figs they grew down there. We would stay there and had a fun time for a few days, but it was a hard one-day trip to get there and go back. You would cross the Dirty Devil River upstream about a half mile from where it came together with the Colorado, and there would be those huge overhangs. Dad always told us if it starts lightning and thundering you ought to get out of there quickly because the flash floods would just take you away. That's all covered up now with the waters of Lake Powell.

Another time we were moving the cattle, it was a big herd, maybe fifty or a hundred. It was a hot summer day, and we were taking them from Cove Spring over through a pass to the north into Hatches. I got very ill from the heat, I guess, and because it was so hot, Claire, Dad, and Mother had to go on with the cattle. They told me to stay under a tree and gave me water and food and left my horse, and said to stay in the shade until I felt better, then come and catch up with them. They couldn't leave the cattle or they would spread out all over the country and choke from lack of water. They said if I didn't catch up with them, they would come back for me. I remember being alone out in the wilds. I was only eleven or twelve. You didn't think too much about it or you'd get afraid. Today I'm more afraid of cougars than I was then. There were snakes and things, of course, but I don't recall being afraid of anything too much when I was young. I never hunted deer or anything, and the only things I ever trapped were mice and fish. There never were a lot of coyotes. You would hear them; there was always one at the ranch that teased the dogs. There must have been more than one, but we always heard this one. He was off to the northwest where the natural water tanks were. They would howl in the little foothills and the dogs would bark at them. The coyotes never got the calves or anything.

They were bothersome to sheep, but I personally never saw sheep down Under the Ledge when we were there. They had different range allotments. We just never ran into them, although I remember the story of Dad saving the life of Karl Seely, Jr.

Karl and his family ran sheep Under the Ledge, and as Dad told it, it was in the winter or the fall of maybe 1941. The Seelys were down there and I was in school at that time and remember how Dad became a hero. I was very proud of him. Karl had gotten pneumonia and was really sick. The sheep people wanted to carry him out, and Dad wouldn't let them. He said Karl would die before they got him up the Flint Trail and out of there. Dad had been riding all day and his horse was tired so he took two fresh horses of Seely's and started out as fast as he could go. He rode the two horses on a long trip to the Roost Ranch where the car was, then on to Green River where they phoned and got a plane from Grand Junction to go out, and flew Dad back with them so he could show the pilot where Karl was on Waterhole Flat. They got Karl into the plane and up to a hospital in Price.

I know Karl Seely felt like Dad saved his life, but Dad didn't feel that way. He just felt when people were in trouble like that, you helped them. One of the things he reminded me of just before he died was that he stressed safety to his children and his grandchildren.

Sometimes at the San Rafael Ranch I would have to go by myself and take cattle over to Bull Bottom that is south of the ranch on the Green River. The trail into the bottom took off from the ranch through a gate on the southeast side and crossed the San Rafael River south of the ranch where the river was very shallow. You could cross the San Rafael farther north by the ranch house or upstream, but it would take longer to wind through the hills alongside of the river. The trail to the bottom was very bad, and I always got off of my horse and walked because it was a straight drop-off. I'd take only a few cattle because the bottom didn't have enough grass for a bigger herd. I'd get them over a ledge and trail them to the bottom then close the gate and leave them there to feed. Later Chad Moore put some bulls down in that bottom and it became known as Bull Bottom.

I could do a lot of things on that ranch, but I couldn't run it by myself. With no guys around—no way! I knew a lot of what had to be done administratively, but I'd need some guys around to do the stuff I was physically unable to do. From the very beginning I was taught to be responsible. They taught us to be responsible and ethical and to make our own decisions a lot of the time. I learned those things at a early age. When most kids were out playing games and things, I was out taking the part of a man because after the brothers all left there was just me and Daddy, Mother, and Claire. Claire was really young; she was almost three years of age when the brothers left. I had to take the part of a ranch hand. We had hired hands, but a lot of the time I had to tell them what to do, especially if they hadn't been there long.

I broke horses, not like Lorin Milton does, of course. What you'd do if you had a new colt is you would be gentle to start off. You would be on and around it all the time so it wasn't like you took a brand new horse and calmed him down. I rode some pretty rough ones, like that time I rode that mare up to Dry Lakes. I did get thrown a lot of times and got my toes stepped on, and kicked. I never caught wild horses, but we used to go on wild burro hunts over in that ridge of hills to the west and south of the San Rafael River. They'd try to catch a burro male, which was called the jack, and we would breed them to a mare. I remember one mare named Old Sue, and we would get mules as a result of the breeding. Sometimes you would get good leaders. We had one that was kind of a good trail leader. He would go along with the cows.

I don't know where the burros came from. Maybe they were left behind by miners or the Spanish explorers. I know they have been around for a long time. Sometimes we would catch wild horses and once in a while they turned out to be really good. I didn't go out on the wild horse chases because it was dangerous. The guys or neighbors would go out and start these bands of wild horses running and someone would be up ahead and steer them into a box canyon. They'd be caught there and you would pick out the one you wanted. I used to hold the gate open when they rounded the horses up and brought them to the ranch corrals, but I never actually went on the hunt itself.

When I lived on the Chaffin Ranch, I had favorite horses. My favorite, although not the fastest, was Tony, a medium-sized horse. I could go anywhere with him. He got bitten by a rattlesnake and died. I was in school at the time, and when I got home he was already dead and I cried for days. Claire's favorite was Rowdy, and she didn't want me to ride him. Dad bred Tickaboo, our registered thoroughbred stallion, to our blue mare, Sue, and got, I think, the first Appaloosa mare in Utah. He traded her to his good friend Ben Johnson, who bred some prize-winning Appaloosas in Colorado from her.

Some more things I remember at the San Rafael are that there was always lots of food, and lots of work to do. I really savored oranges, and Grandmother instructed me to eat the white part of the peel because it contained so much of the nutrition. We usually bought fifty-pound bags of flour, and one-hundred-pound bags of pinto beans or white navy beans. I don't remember grinding flour, so we must not have done that, but we had many bushels of peaches and apples to eat and can, and of course we had beef, pork, and chickens.

I have heard mountain lions at times, but I never saw one. One of the first summers I worked with the cattle at Waterhole, my mother, Claire, and I were going up the Flint Trail. Faun had gone on earlier to take cattle out North Trail. The trail was so rough we were leading our horses, and Claire was tagging along because she still rode in front of my mother in the same saddle. We were almost at the top when we heard a couple of awful screams, and we just knew there was a mountain lion up there. We got on our horses and were so scared we rode the rest of the way up making all the noise we could and watching every tree we went by. We hurried as fast as we could to the Flint Flat cabins, and got our car and got out of there, leaving the horses to take care of themselves.

When we went to Under the Ledge in 1990 with Claire and some of her kids, and Steve and his kids, and me and Bill Racy and a friend of his, we were camped out at Waterhole. My brother went up to the water tanks just above the pond and he said there were fresh tracks. Just fresh that morning. So that cat was close to our camp, and we were all sleeping on the open ground.

The thing was, while I was growing up on the ranch we worked hard and we played hard. There were always people around, but not often people my age. There was a lot of love and closeness in the family. Always a lot of horse stories and cattle stories, and always beautiful horses, well trained and fast. The guys would gather round the table with everyone talking at once. The neighbors helped one another, and trusted. Everyone trusted each other.

In those days we charged all of our groceries at the stores in Green River. The stores were owned by the Beebes and the Politanos. Malcolm Politano runs a store there today just as his dad did long ago. His dad's was just north of the bank. We would charge food and stuff all year, and when we sold the cattle, we paid off the bill. They trusted you. Nobody had any money. It was like Bill Racy told when Dad sold the cattle and paid his bills off, and he still had $485. He had never had that much money at one time before that. Bill Racy worked with us as a hired hand at thirty dollars a month and he made almost as much as Dad did.

Dad goes way back to 1899, and he told about meeting Zane Grey when he was researching the area for one of the books he was writing. He met him out at the Roost with Joe Biddlecome. Joe guided Mr. Grey around the whole area. Dad also had a lot of respect for "old Joe" as he called him in later years. The Chaffin boys grew up with the Biddlecome girls, Hazel Ekker and Pearl Baker. Pearl was Dad's very dear friend. Ken and Clell Chaffin were closer in age to Pearl and Hazel when growing up, and spent a lot of time at their ranch. They called themselves "the invincibles."

In June of 1943 mother insisted that we buy a house in Grand Junction, Colorado, so we girls could go to school and I could go to a larger high school there. She felt in that isolated place at the ranch on the San Rafael wasn't too good for two girls growing up. We still helped with the ranch and cattle when we could. I spent the last two years of high school in Grand Junction and graduated from high school in three years because I had so many basic courses in Green River before moving to Grand Junction. You didn't have any frill classes in those days, and I'd learned a lot with my mother's home teaching.

During all of those years on the ranch I thought I was doing the work of a man and of a woman too. I mean, I was very much into cooking and helping my mother, but my love was out helping Dad. I wanted to be out there, and I didn't think about whether I was a man or woman; I knew very much I was a woman. I always wore Levis or overalls and a shirt and a cowboy hat. I wore cowboy boots when riding so my feet wouldn't go through the stirrup. The clothes were often old and stiff, but when we went to church or to town I always dressed up. There were times, especially during high school, when I would want to go to a Friday night dance, or to a church function, but I'd be needed on the ranch. That really didn't bother me much because I wanted to be out on the ranch.

The grasses were so tall at Waterhole and Andy Miller Flats they'd come up to the horse's belly. We had more rain then than we do now. I still savor the smell of the rains on the desert and all the wildflowers in the spring after the rains, and the unusual plants on the Flint Trail we looked at as we slowly made our way up.

I remember the wymup bushes [barberry bushes] you could just ride up to and pick the berries from your horse, and how Mother hauled them back on pack horses to make jelly, and the petrified logs on the

Black Ledge, and the arrowheads we found once in a while, just lying on the ground. The Flint Trail and Flint Flats were given those names because there were so many chips of flint laying around. The ground used to be covered with pieces of jasper and flint, but starting in the 1940s people began getting into the area and picked up most of the artifacts. I remember how Bill Racy came to our ranch and became a part of our family, and his cowboy songs and stories, and Ned who was so close to me, and is still the best storyteller around, with Lorin Milton a close second.

I didn't resent doing housework or ranch chores, but I think Mother must have felt frustrated when she found out the day after she and Dad were married that he was so involved in the L. M. Chaffin & Sons family partnership. She didn't complain much about her work, but times were hard financially, and even though she was always treated with love and respect, it bothered her that they weren't on their own. When the major decisions were made, it was mainly the men who made them and the women went along with the decision. Like when the decision was made that my folks would stay to operate the ranch and cattle busi-ness and the uncles and grandparents would leave, it was a decision that everyone made. It was agreed that when Dad needed help they would come back, like the time he really needed help and Uncle Ned came back from California to run the cattle down Under the Ledge.

After high school and some college, I married Harry Wubben. We had a boy who looks and acts like my granddad Lou, and three girls. Harry was a good teacher and almost had a doctorate in educa-tion before he died in 1984. I also was married to Ralph Hills for four years and am divorced now. After working as a real estate broker in Denver and Boulder, I worked for City of Boulder Wastewater Treatment Plant and Water Quality for ten years. I retired in March of 1995 and moved back to Grand Junction to be closer to two of my chil-dren, and Utah, of course.

Claire married Bob Morrow. They had six children and live near Elko, Nevada. Claire is known all over the West for her old-time fiddling. Steve and his wife Maureen live in Fruita, Colorado. He's a rancher and fertilizer dealer, and they have four children, three boys and a girl.

When I left Grand Junction my folks bought this land near Mack, at New Liberty, Colorado. Mother bought an old schoolhouse that was put up for bid, and they remodeled it and lived there. Steve grew up there, and still has eighty-five acres there and I have five acres. Later, when Dad was ninety-four he decided he had better let somebody know that he had a lesion on his forehead that wasn't healing. He always wore a hat, and a cap in the winter. When we took him in to the doctor, it was a cancer. Although he underwent radiation treatments, the cancer had spread and he died nine months later. A month before he died we had to place him in a nursing home that was just a block from where my brother lived. He had always said he never wanted to go into a nursing home, so this was hard for us to do, but I was living in Boulder, Colorado, and working, and my brother was working and couldn't take care of him any more. Claire lived in Nevada on a ranch and couldn't help. There was no way we could give him the care he needed.

I would go over to visit him as often as I could. He would always ask me to sing to him. This would take me back to my childhood. When we were children growing up, he would ask Claire and me to dance and sing for the visitors. We always had some kind of music. Somebody could always play something, and Bill Racy was good on the cowboy songs. Grandmother Alice was always singing. She and I were very close. I spent a lot of time with her, and she often made me tea with cream, and pie, and talked a lot with me. She died in 1968. My mother died when she was seventy-eight in 1987 in Colorado. Dad was always in good health until he got the cancer. He was ninety-four when he died.

As I grow older, I am appreciating all the wonderful experiences I had growing up, and I am proud to be a part of that history. I am appreciating ever more the spirituality of that great land, and I have this longing to return as often as I can—and I will.

2

Ned Chaffin

Ned and his wife, Marjorie, live in Bakersfield, California. His folks bought what became known as the Chaffin Ranch in 1929. Ned was born in 1913 and spent his tender young years pushing stock around the desert and red rock canyon country that surrounded the Chaffin spread. He had a job most kids, who don't know any better, would give their eyeteeth to have. The ranch was located near the junction of the Green and San Rafael Rivers. Ned left the ranch in 1936, leaving an older brother, Faun, and his wife, Violet, to oper-ate the ranch, but Ned frequently returned over the intervening years to lend a hand when one was needed.

The Chaffin family had a prominent role in cattle raising on the San Rafael Desert and in the grazing areas Under the Ledge that became part of the Maze District of Canyonlands National Park. Many of the landmarks in the Maze District were named by various members of Ned's family. Clell's Spring was named for a brother; Lou's Spring was named for his father. Lizard Rock, Arla's Bottom, Harness-Up Spring, and other names originated with Chaffin family incidents. Ned recorded much of the history of some of those early ranchers and settlers. The inspiration behind these interviews came about when Ned organized a cowboy caucus on Memorial Day in 1994. Eight or ten mostly retired stockmen got together in Green River and relived old times.

Ned willingly shares his experiences with friends. He is all cowboy, not the Hollywood version, but one who is at ease in the saddle.

Ned Chaffin in Ernie Country, 1938. Photo courtesy of Ned Chaffin.

Cattle grazing near the rock formation cowboys called the Doll House, 1938. Photo courtesy of Ned Chaffin.

February 10–11, 1995, Bakersfield, California
May 30, 1995, en route to Hans Flat

I know very little about my grandparents except for what I have heard because they all had passed away before I was born. The one exception was my maternal grandmother who passed away when I was very young, and I remember little about her. My mother's father was named Daniel Gross Brian, and her mother's name was Ella Barnes. Mr. Brian was a good Mormon and a polygamist. He had a family in Utah and another one in Idaho. He was born March 5, 1835, in Harrisburg, Pennsylvania. He was the son of Thomas and Martha Wilding O'Brian. His mother had to go to work and he was bound out to two maiden ladies. They gave him the advantage of a good education and taught him refinement, but they were very stern and strict. He went to school until he was about seventeen years of age. He mastered three languages and was well trained in music and dancing.

When he was through with school he returned to his mother. Daniel heard of people coming west, and broke all ties and decided to come to Pikes Peak and become a doctor. Before going there he spent the winter in Salt Lake City and it was there he dropped the "O" from his name. He was converted to the Mormon church. He married Martha Elizabeth Ashwood on December 31, 1860. He was baptized on August the 24th, 1860. He worked in a sawmill in Mill Creek Canyon until 1861 when he moved to Cottonwood where he taught school. Later they moved to Salt Lake City where they attended many of the socials for Brigham Young and Heber C. Kimball and other church officials.

That is enough about my grandfather. I have four pages of history on him. My father, Louis Moses Chaffin, was born in Beaver, Utah, in 1874. He married Martha Elizabeth Alice Brian on June 19, 1897.

When Dad was a teenager he accompanied his father to the Colorado River where they placer mined for gold in several counties. Dad became a mining supervisor with a crew of ten to twenty miners. He spent quite a bit of time on the river from then until about 1915. At various times he mined most of the well-known sand and gravel bars upstream from Lee's Ferry on the Colorado River. His last fling at placer mining on the river was in the early 1930s when he and Billy Hay mined a gravel bar above Moab. They took a couple of teams of horses with them and built a sluice box and mined there for three or four months. When they finished and paid all of their expenses, they figured they had

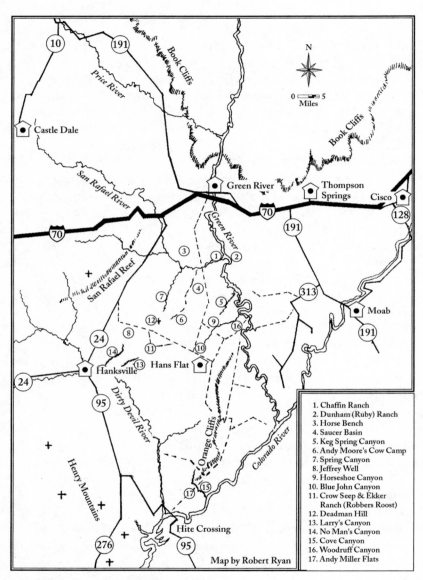

Ned Chaffin's Canyonlands.

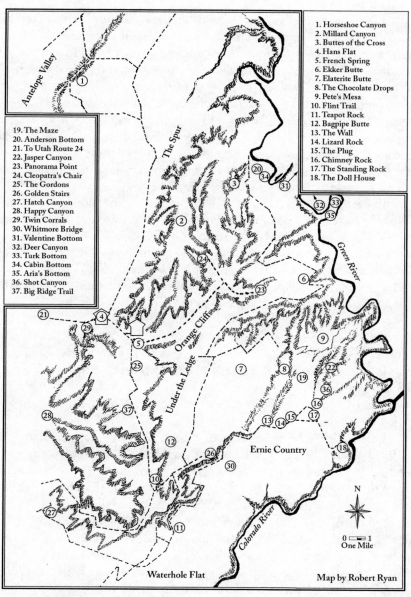

1. Horseshoe Canyon
2. Millard Canyon
3. Buttes of the Cross
4. Hans Flat
5. French Spring
6. Ekker Butte
7. Elaterite Butte
8. The Chocolate Drops
9. Pete's Mesa
10. Flint Trail
11. Teapot Rock
12. Bagpipe Butte
13. The Wall
14. Lizard Rock
15. The Plug
16. Chimney Rock
17. The Standing Rock
18. The Doll House

19. The Maze
20. Anderson Bottom
21. To Utah Route 24
22. Jasper Canyon
23. Panorama Point
24. Cleopatra's Chair
25. The Gordons
26. Golden Stairs
27. Hatch Canyon
28. Happy Canyon
29. Twin Corrals
30. Whitmore Bridge
31. Valentine Bottom
32. Deer Canyon
33. Turk Bottom
34. Cabin Bottom
35. Aria's Bottom
36. Shot Canyon
37. Big Ridge Trail

Antelope Valley

The Spur

Green River

Orange Cliffs

Under the Ledge

Ernie Country

Colorado River

N

0 ▭ 1
One Mile

Waterhole Flat

Map by Robert Ryan

Ned Chaffin's Under the Ledge.

made about one hundred dollars a month each. That gold was so fine it was hard to catch.

The Colorado River had a hold on Lou Chaffin. He just couldn't stay away from it. His brother Arth ran the ferry at Hite and did a lot of mining on the Colorado too, some of it with my father. He worked the Shock Bar and the Moki Bar, the New Year Bar, and over on Hanson Creek they sniped for gold. They would find a pretty good place and set up a snipe, a board about twelve feet long and twelve inches wide covered with gunny sacks. They would shovel the mud up on it and get maybe two or three dollars a day in gold with this simple outfit. The gold stuck to the gunny sack cloth. Most of the gold was fine flakes—so thin they would wash out with the black sand or would not amalgamate very well because they were so light in weight.

Robert Brewster Stanton, the engineer who had surveyed the Colorado River for a possible route for a railroad line to California, had formed the Hoskanini Mining Company. In 1897 he returned to the river and tested for gold with a Keystone Drilling rig. This was in Glen Canyon, but he gave up the idea of drilling further. J. W. Wilson was left in charge of what equipment he had and hired my father to sample the ground from Hall's Crossing to Four Mile. Then they brought in a dredge and tried that. But the gold was too fine. It just didn't pay, so they shut the dredge down and sold it at auction. Later a flash flood came along and sunk the dredge. The dredge was sitting in the river and now is under the waters of Lake Powell. The Keystone Rig later was taken up to Flint Flat by Dad and the crew. Then they hauled the rig down the Flint Trail to Elaterite Basin when Wolverton's Nequoia Oil Company drilled for oil down there.

Dad and my brother Faun first took cattle Under the Ledge in 1919. Dad bought the ranch on the San Rafael in 1929 from a Mr. Preston. It was farmland there where the ranch house is, and I think it was about two thousand acres. I don't know what he paid for it, but I'm sure it wasn't much because money was awfully scarce. He didn't record the deed until 1936. The Phillips Oil and the Texas Company were both starting in with drilling out in that country about then. Dad had a pretty good in with those people and he had a little money at that time. Of course, everyone would have said he had a lot of money considering the times. It would be very little now, probably enough to get you a hamburger at McDonald's.

My mother, Alice Brian Chaffin, was about as good a person as the good Lord could make. She was talented in many ways, a good musician,

Anasazi granary.

Pre-Columbian granary. Photo courtesy of Jack Reesy.

Get a horse! Dirty Devil River. Photo courtesy of Ned Chaffin.

Cabins at Flint Flat, 1919–1920. Photo courtesy of Ned Chaffin.

Desert cruiser, 1920s model. Photo courtesy of Ned Chaffin.

Working on the entrance road to Horseshoe Canyon, 1929. Lou Chaffin in road, Clell Chaffin on the truck bed. Photo courtesy of Ned Chaffin.

Faun and Violet Chaffin. The gentleman with the pipe is H. W. C. Prommel, engineer and oil geologist. Photo taken in 1928 near site of the Texas Oil Company well. Photo courtesy of Ned Chaffin.

Directional sign salvaged by Ned Chaffin.

The Great Gallery in Horseshoe Canyon.

a good cook, she was always a good mother and a good wife and a good grandmother. All the girls were taught to play the guitar by her, and they got piano lessons from a neighbor. A warm, wonderful person. You can imagine what raising a family in those days was like. When she, Aunt Josie, and Uncle George brought Grandpa Chaffin up to Bitterwater after he died, she was heavy with child.

I was one of eleven children, but by the time we moved onto the Chaffin Ranch on the San Rafael River, my younger brother Gay had passed away. He was only twelve and died of complications from polio. My eldest sister, Blanch, had died at the age of nineteen in 1919. She had a ruptured appendix and by the time they got her to a hospital in Salt Lake City it was too late. Another sister, Hazel, had died in 1888 when she was only three and a half months old. The other two sisters were both married and gone, but Mom and Dad, my brothers (Faun; Ken and his wife, Julia; and Clell), and I lived on the ranch at one time or another. Of course, Faun's wife, Violet, was there and Wiladeane, too. However, if there was a job open around in the country that paid over twenty-five dollars a month, it seems like one of us Chaffin boys was fortunate enough to get it, and most of the time one or two of the boys or Dad was out working somewhere when something came along that looked pretty good. This enabled us to hang on there at the ranch through some pretty hard times.

Down below the Ruby Ranch, on the east side of the Green River, Edwin T. Wolverton had a ranch. We fetched a house from that ranch. Dad dragged the house across the river on the ice. Of course, old man Wolverton never said anything about it if he was even still alive, but his son, I think his name was Ted, he kind of squawked, so Faun said he'd give him four head of cows just to keep his mouth shut. Of course, the fact that old man Wolverton—Faun worked for him for a year and when he got a check from him, it bounced—naturally that didn't count, you know, when it comes to the house. Anyway, Faun said he'd give him four head of cows and for him to keep his mouth shut, and Ted said okay. On the way into town when me and old man Marsing and Clell were driving the cattle in we lost four or five head of them, and one of the cows we lost was Ted's, so when we got to Green River we only had three head for him. So we took them across the bridge over to Elgin and a guy by the name of Carl Hunt put them in his field. When Ted came to get them and saw there was only three, not four, he accused Carl Hunt of stealing his cow. Anyway, to make a long story short, Faun told him to hell with him and that was all he was going to get.

That's the story of how we got the ranch house. They just took the abandoned house and slid it across the ice. Dad set it up on a foundation, and the first time I saw it was while I was going to high school in Green River and living in our Green River house. The ranch house was all set up and Mom was cooking biscuits on the stove.

In 1935 Dad and Mom sold the house in Green River and left the ranch to Faun and Violet to operate. Faun and Violet had two daughters, Wiladeane and Claire, and a son, Stephen. Dad and Mom moved to Payson, Utah, where he became superintendent of the lime quarry up there. They mined this rock for the Utah-Idaho Sugar Company. Five percent of your sugar is lime rock. This was very high grade lime rock and they used it at the Geneva Steel Company for steel fabrication. The last time I saw Dad at the ranch was in 1944. He was there helping with the corn harvest. In fact, at that time Millie Biddlecome took me from Green River out to the ranch. She was worried because the tires on her car were so worn and she didn't have a spare. These were war years—I was home on leave from the army—and tires were rationed and hard to get. Well, we made it to the ranch, and just as we did one of the tires blew out. Thankfully, Dad could always fix up something. He got an old tire, then he got another old tire that he got off the hay wagon, and he put that on top of the other one, and we made it back to town with that setup.

Dad retired in 1957 and died in 1962. Mom died in 1968. Faun and Violet stayed on at the ranch and took care of it and the cattle. All brothers had a share in the ranch and we gave Faun power of attorney so he could carry on the necessary functions of operating a ranch.

When we first had the ranch we used a diesel engine to pump water from the river. We bought it from George Franz; I assume he had gotten it from one of the oil companies he hauled freight for. It had probably abandoned the diesel and left it in George's yard. The irrigation ditches were dug with teams, plows, scrapers, and a lot of sweat.

It was strictly a cattle ranch. We raised some corn and alfalfa. Most of the original herd were Durhams or crosses, but we always ran Hereford bulls so we had a lot of brockle-faced cattle. I don't believe we ever ran more than four hundred fifty head. The only sheep we ever had would be strays that the herders would leave because they couldn't make the trip to the mountains. Coyotes were not much of a problem for us. They would go after the sheep, but not cattle. Maybe a calf once in a while, but seldom. Of course, the sheepmen had a problem, and almost every winter there would be trappers in the area. In later years the government paid men to trap. My old friend Lon Marsing trapped for the government for many years. Lon always packed a big tent, maybe ten by twelve, and I camped with him on many a cold winter night. He was good company, a nice guy, and like all the Marsings, a good hand around horses or cattle. He helped me on several occasions move stock from one place to another, in addition to caring for his trap line.

At the ranch Dad drilled the well that is now the cold water geyser. You can imagine his joy when he saw water coming from the well, and consider his despair when he tasted the water. It is so full of minerals all we used it for was cooling the food. We troughed up several springs. We would drag the planks on the sides of mules. This was a chore, but water was the most precious item in that country.

It was Faun's decision to sell the ranch and the cattle because the kids were starting to get big. That really wasn't the best place in the world to raise a family, especially in those days. Many times you couldn't even get to Green River in a car. He sold the ranch in 1944 to some sheep herders by the name of Moynier. They converted the ranch to a sheep operation.

There were a lot of sheepherders around those parts in those days. Many were French or Basque. I remember Henry Dusserre and his two boys. When I was there we only had one Frenchman come down Under the Ledge. He was Pete Masset. He was the only one who routinely ran sheep down there. Henry Dusserre would run sheep down into Happy Canyon once in a while. I remember one night I camped with him on the South Gardens. Today's maps use the word "Gordons," but according to old timers the area was named the French Gardens because it was so pretty and the French sheepherders grazed it a lot. Someone couldn't understand the French accent and "Gardens" came out "Gordons."

The next morning he [Henry] was going down into Happy Canyon. When he left camp that morning he gave his camp mover an injunction, he said, "Listen, you"—the trail going down into Happy Canyon was pretty rough in a couple or three or four places—well, he said, "I don't give a damn how many mules you kill, but you better make it down there with all of this wine!" Henry was quite a guy, big fellow, nice guy to be around. Good people, he and his boys.

The Seelys, Hy and son Karl, ran sheep Under the Ledge. So did a fellow by the name of Quince Crawford. Mr. Crawford had one herd of sheep; the Seelys had about three or four herds of sheep. I'll tell you a story about Karl Seely, and I mean old Karl. Young Karl is still alive and living in Phoenix, and he also has a place up in Colorado. He was just a few years older than I, so I imagine he is in his middle to late eighties right now.

Hy and old Karl were partners in the sheep business, and they dissolved the partnership. This was after the stockyards in Green River were moved south of the railroad tracks in the early 1930s. They brought the sheep into the stockyards, and they divided them and branded them, and they were heading for Under the Ledge. Leland Boline [sic] and Ike Huntsman were working for Karl Seely. Ezra Huntsman was working for Hy Seely. They all wanted to head Under the Ledge, and of course the first one down there got the best pickings. After you once go down the North Trail there is no place to pass, so they started to race from Green River to the head of the North Trail to get down that trail just because the guy that got down that trail first had it made. He didn't have to worry because there was no place they could pass him without mixing the sheep. This old dude Ezra Huntsman, they tell me he could move sheep faster than any man in the world, that he'd just make them go right out over the top of each other and nobody could keep up with Ezra. So Leland Boline, the camp mover for Karl Seely, said he'd watch Ezra's camp mover every night, and when his camp mover would set up camp, he'd look at his watch and he'd just go one hour from there to set up camp. He said the next night by sundown old Ezra would be right on their tail. Karl Seely and his crew won the race to Under the Ledge, but the reason they won it was because they used a little bit of chicanery there. They divided the sheep; Karl Seely's sheep were in the corral the closest to the desert and old Ezra Huntsman opened the gate to start Hy Seely's sheep down through this long chute. Leland saw them coming and he hadn't got his packs on yet, and he grabbed an axe and went up to the corral and he knocked all the sides out of the corral. It was made out of two-by-sixes about seven feet high. He just took his axe and went up there and he said they had to close the gate on him. They got about forty head of Hy Seely's sheep in and Ike and old Ezra were just standing there and Hy Seely, kind of a heavy-set guy, was there a-chompin' and a-cussin' and everything else and hollering, "Damn, that's not fair." Anyway, that is how Karl Seely got the jump on them. An interesting tidbit, when they came to the Spring Creek Canyon on that wide flat where the crossing of the San Rafael River was, old Ezra was right on old Ikie's tail with his herd. Leland said that old boy was really rolling those sheep. We barely beat him to the crossing. Anyway, that race gave us lots of good times talking about it, and they both, Karl and Hy, weathered the depression and made a little bit of money. When Hy died, his son Karl took over the herds.

The use of dogs in handling sheep is a very old and practical idea. Ezra Huntsman, whom we had referred to earlier, said that a good dog around a herd of sheep was worth one man and two boys. If anyone ever saw those good sheepmen use their dogs in that rough country, he would have no doubt about their value. Pete Masset always herded his sheep afoot and always had two or three dogs with him. Of course, dogs were company in that lonesome place. I would also observe that dogs are good company any place.

There was plenty enough feed and water for both herders in that county that year. Karl, neither one, ever took their sheep down the Spanish Trail to Spanish Bottom. Those steps on the trail, some people have foolish ideas about how those steps got placed in there.

The trail from what is now known as the Doll House down to Spanish Bottom drops about eight hundred feet in elevation. On two sections of the trail are found stone steps that appear to have been placed there to make it easier to get over rock ledges. Rumors abound that it was Spanish traders who used Indian slave labor to place the stone slabs. Some of the steps probably weigh in excess of three hundred pounds. Sheepherders have told various historians and authors that they were responsible for putting the slabs in place. Maybe so. Pete Monnet, a sheepman, told author John Hoffman he was the person who put them in place and built the trail. Mr. Hoffman interviewed Pete Monnet in 1973 when Monnet was ninety years old. Did he start from scratch? Did he add to existing work, or what? In talking to Mr. Hoffman I did not clarify these points; however, my father walked from Spanish Bottom to the mouth of North Wash and he said the steps were there at that time. I don't have any idea of the year, but I believe it was prior to Mom and Dad's wedding in June of 1897. There is something about Spanish Bottom that suggests mystery. Most of the old-timers I have talked to don't have much knowledge of the name or the steps. As I told Hazel Ekker, we might say the naming of Spanish Bottom has been lost in antiquity. If someone did come up with the correct answer, very few would believe it. So much for oral history. When I first went to Spanish Bottom, you could see where sheep had been; however, I don't believe any sheep ever ventured down while we were there. It was just too small an area to encourage anyone to put a herd of sheep down that rough trail.

I had a nice relationship with Dock Marston. He was primarily interested in things about the river. We exchanged letters and phone

Tibbet Arch.

The Standing Rock.

Bagpipe Butte, Under the Ledge.

The Maze.

Beehive Arch. Photo courtesy of Gary Cox, National Park Service.

The Sentinels at the Doll House.

calls, but we never met. My dad had guided him around and respected him. Dock wasn't interested much in the Chaffin Ranch or the Andy Moore Ranch or the Robbers Roost Ranch or the Tidwell Ranch. He gathered a lot of history about the river and his files and records are down at the Huntington Library.

There were only two black cowboys that I remember. One they called "Nigger" Bill. Bill worked for Art Meeks. Art Meeks was one of the biggest cattlemen in the country at that time. He ran lots of cattle in Wayne County and down around the Henry Mountains. This gentleman worked for him, and from what I hear he was an A-number-one dependable hand. I was just a small boy at that time. The other colored cowboy that I ran into, I don't know his name, but he worked for some outfit over on the other side of the river. Anything on the east side of the Green River is the other side in my vocabulary. Those people over there were strangers to me. I didn't know the area and I didn't know the people much. But on a few occasions he and his boss came to our house in Green River. I guess he was a hell of a good hand; in fact, I understand he was the foreman of this outfit. He was a well-respected cattleman and, once again, all I know of him is by reputation.

Bill, the one who worked for Art Meeks, the only association I ever remember of him—this was a long time ago in the early 1920s when the stockyards were on the north side of the tracks in Green River—anyway, they brought their steers in there to ship them. Meeks and his cowboys came down to the Chaffin place to stay. There must have been eight or ten of them and Bill was in the group. Mother fixed up a dinner for them as was the custom in those days, didn't matter if it was one or twenty. You fixed up what you had and made sure there was plenty for everybody. Bill filled up his plate and started outside and Mom said, "Bill, where you going?"

He said, "I'm going outside. I don't know if us folks ought to eat with white folks or not."

Mom said, "Bill, you get over there and set right down at that table. You are just as welcome in my house as anybody."

That's all I remember about him. But anyway, that's just the way it was at our place. There was no other way. When anybody came to our place, they were always treated with respect.

There was a Nigger Bill Canyon on the Green named by him or after him. There also was a Nigger Bill Canyon on the Colorado over near Moab, but that was a different Bill. He was a cattleman, too. Now I think those canyons, in fact I know they have, have dropped the word "nigger" and substituted something more acceptable in this day and age. The one near Moab is now called Negro Bill Canyon.

I think the most cattle we ever raised at one time was around four hundred and fifty. We never grazed on the North Spur. The Tidwells built a pond on the high part of The Spur. That is what they called the High Part. That is the area from Hans Flat, where you leave it you kind of come down into a big valley there, then The Spur starts to rise. At the highest part of The Spur is where the formation has risen there. In fact, that is one of the reasons why the geologists were very interested in that country for oil, was because of that rise that made the high part of The Spur. Outside of the sheep, or in the wintertime, the only people I know that ran any cattle in the summer there were the Tidwells. There are absolutely no running streams in that country except the Green River, which was either muddier than hell or alkaline as hell most of the time.

The people who built the cabins up at Flint Flat, and I don't give a damn what anybody says, were Mr. Wolverton, my father Lou Chaffin, my brother Faun Chaffin, Dubinky Anderson and Paul Saltgaver. They built the little rock cabin that Ezra Huntsman burned down in the early twenties, and they also built the cabin that was made out of the pine logs. Then after that Faun and Dad built the little rock cabin right along the side there in the winter of 1918–19. It was, as I remember it, just a little room maybe eight-by-eight or maybe ten-by-ten. That's who built the cabins. Some people claim Mr. Wolverton built all of the cabins, but that's not so. Anybody says they did it is a damn liar, and tell them I said so. Today visitors to Flint Flat, if they locate the remains of the old cabins, will find the name "Nequoia Oil Co." chiseled in one of the rocks on an outer wall of Wolverton's cabin. There are also many names written on the interior roof timbers, old historic names.

All the wells the Nequoia Oil Company drilled were in the Elaterite Basin. In my many years of musing over this area, I never thought to separate Big Water from the Basin. It could be that everything under the Red Ledge is the Basin, and Big Water is the area under the Black Ledge. We referred to the area as Big Water.

When the Nequoia Oil Company left, Mr. Wolverton took out what he could pack or take out with his teams. He left quite a bit of stuff there, like soft rope. Soft rope, to the novices that never worked around the oil, is soft-laid manila rope that they used to string their tools with. He left a great big coil of that rope and we used that damn stuff for tie ropes and hobbles for I don't know how many years. Some of the rope was three inches in diameter. That coil Wolverton left was inch-and-a-half and we unbraided it and used it for everything for many, many years. Today's visitors can view much of the rusted mining equipment in the area around North Spring. Faun worked for Mr. Wolverton for over a year down there, and when Wolverton paid him off, his check bounced, but you never heard Faun say one bad word about Mr. Wolverton. In fact, he said he was a swell guy and he knew damn well he would have paid him if he had the money, but he didn't have the money, so he [Faun] just charged it up to profit and loss. But Faun always spoke very highly about Mr. Wolverton. I can't remember anything about him personally. I know he went down to the Henry Mountains and started mining there after he pulled out of here.

In the fall of 1940—I was already married and living in Bakersfield—I took my father-in-law, Earl Daniel, and a gentleman by the name of George Whitmore back there to the Chaffin Ranch. We went back to help Faun do a little bit of cowboying. We met Art Ekker over on Twin Corrals and Art loaned me a mule. I jumped on the mule and went over to the Gardens and got our horses, and we took them over to Flint and pastured them. We went from there to Waterhole Flat. It had rained quite a bit on Andy Miller Flats, so we gathered up a bunch of cattle and moved them over to the Andy Miller Flats. I had to sign up for the draft, so I left them and went into Green River to register. The rest of them stayed there and went over to Anderson Bottom. In the meantime, before I left to go to Green River, we went over into Ernie Country. This was 1940 and it was the year we named that bridge in Ernie Country Whitmore Bridge. We didn't name it Whitmore Arch, we named it the Whitmore Bridge. The government changed it from a named bridge to a named arch. Anyway, that was named for George Whitmore, a hell of a swell guy. They stayed with the packs and, after I left Green River, I came out to Tidwell's and borrowed a mule from Tidwells and met them down on Anderson's Bottom where we were going to do a little bit of deer hunting.

Lorin Milton was there, Herb Weber and Faun, George Whitmore and Earl Daniel and myself—we were all there. We decided we were going to rope a deer, so we went over to Deer Canyon. Deer Canyon is the canyon that comes in just off the head of Valentine Bottom. We crossed over there on our horses, and of course we had a boat. We moved our stuff over there. Lorin Milton went up Deer Canyon and chased this bunch of deer down, and as they hit the flat down there—Faun was riding a horse we called Sailor, and he could really move it—and he roped a deer. Then we went on down Valentine and I ran this great big buck right

View of the Green River.

by my father-in-law. He took a shot at him and hit him high, right back in the loin. He wasn't hit enough to knock him down and, boy, he laid his horns back on his back and really took off for the river. Herb Weber was there with us, and he was a good roper, too, and he caught the deer just before he hit the willows at the Green River. He caught him with his rope. We cut his throat and hung him up in a big cottonwood tree, and that is the photograph I have of Herb, Faun, Lorin and the big buck.

Anyway, everybody calls you liars and says a horse can't catch a deer. Those people don't know what they are talking about. A good horse can outrun a deer and catch him right now. We had a good time, and that was the time we named the Whitmore Bridge and also named the canyon down at the head of Turk Bottom "Daniel's Canyon." However, that name didn't stick and I understand they renamed it Soda Canyon. Maybe Soda Canyon was its original name, I don't know.

We did name two places for my two guests, and those were the first tourists, to the best of my knowledge, that went down into that country. Now, there were a lot of people who went down Under the Ledge and down there hunting for gold, oil, rock, crooks, a place to hide, Indian artifacts, but to my knowledge those were the first tourists to go down there just to see the sights. They were a couple of swell guys, and really dear to me. I'm glad the Whitmore Bridge name has stayed. Wish they had left it a "Bridge" rather than changing it to an "Arch," and wish Daniel's Canyon, which I named for my father-in-law, had stuck.

I carried on telephone and writing discussions with Dr. Dean Brimhall for many, many years, but I never guided him and I never did meet him. I regret not meeting him for he was a joy to talk to and correspond with.

I did guide work for several other archeological expeditions. One was the Claflin-Emerson expedition. The Emerson participant was part of the family of Ralph Waldo Emerson. The Peabody Museum brought the expedition out, and a fellow by the name of Henry Booker Roberts was in charge of the two archeological surveys in 1928 and 1930. He was working on his Ph.D. at Harvard University at that time. He was a real smart cookie; his father was a retired professor from the University of Denver, and he was a super brilliant man. Faun, Clell, and I pulled up on Waterhole Flat; of course it was after dark, as usual. We were going to camp up there at the Point of Rocks because it had rained that day and there was water in the little potholes there. However, we saw a fire at the Claflin camp down by the pond at Waterhole Flat, so we decided to go down there.

There was Dave Rust, Doctor Roberts, Alfred Kidder, Jr., and Les McDougal. Alfred was a student at Harvard and his father was a very famous Southwest archeologist. Mr. Roberts wanted Faun to let me guide them around that country. Faun said, "Sure, but you got to give us a day here tomorrow because we have to round up and brand these calves. We'll use him tomorrow and then you can have him." That night after we came in after branding, Faun looked around and said, "Where's Les?"

Mr. Roberts said, "We let him go and sent him back to Hanksville."

Well now, old Faun had red hair and a temper to match and he really flipped his stack and he said, "God damn it, if I'd known—what did you do, let him go?"

Mr. Roberts said, "Well, yes. We don't need two guides with him and Ned both."

Then Faun said, "If I'd known you were going to let Les go, I wouldn't have let Ned go with you. I don't like this. I didn't mean to take anybody's job away from them. Les has got a family and needs the work. Hell, I'm madder than hell. I wish you had told me. God damn it, I guess I ought to leave you down here on one of these rims."

Anyway, I went with them. We went over into Ernie Country, we went down on the Spanish Bottom, we went over into Big Water from the Nipple Trail, and went up the North Trail and came down to the Phillips well. Art Ekker was driving the jitney for the Phillips Petroleum Company at that time. The jitney driver in the oil patch is the guy or gal who does all the running around primarily to get supplies such as fuel, small tools, and such. The jitney was a flatbed, maybe a Ford or Chevy. When the Phillips Petroleum Company abandoned the well on The Spur, they sold or gave the jitney to the Tidwell boys, and they had it in use when I left the country. This one was larger than a pickup and smaller than a truck.

A guy by the name of Bob Vance was a tool pusher for the company and he told Art to crank up his jitney and take Mr. Roberts to town to get some supplies. They all jumped on that old jitney and rode to town. When Art got to town and loaded up the supplies, they came back. When they came back, I found out that he who lives by the sword dies by the sword because I found out I had been fired. They had hired Leland Tidwell to take them down Horseshoe Canyon and up the Green River and back up Horseshoe.

Old Bob Vance was an Indian from Oklahoma. He was working as a tool pusher for the Phillips Oil Company and, here again, he blew his stack and he told old man Roberts's butt up one side and down the other something fierce. You wouldn't believe the things he said to Mr. Roberts. "God damn it, I bring you here, I feed you. I send my truck to Green River with you. I did that to help Ned, I didn't do that to help anybody else. I sure don't like this!"

That is the sum of my association with the Claflin-Emerson team in the summer of 1929. This was all reconnaissance work. We didn't do much digging. The next year we met them, and we went down Under the Ledge and we went over to Red Seeps and to Sidewalk Spring where we dug that cave out. We found some interesting artifacts there, including a robe that was made out of some kind of fur. I guess it was buffalo. It took us about a week to dig that cave out. We had a different crew. We had Don Scott, Jr., whose father was later the curator at the Peabody Museum. There was James Thurber Dennison, his father owned the Dennison Manufacturing Company back in Framingham, Massachusetts, so we called the kid the toilet paper king. Also, there was Waldo Emerson Forbes of the poet's family. He was a student at that time and a hell of a swell guy. We did mostly digging that year.

Then we went over to Cottonwood Spring over at Waterhole Flat. The ruin just below the spring there, we excavated that. In fact, there was about three feet of silt in there. If you go over there now, they tell me you can still see the old fire bed where they did their burning and everything. We found a bundle of corn cobs. I believe there were six cobs tied up with a piece of bark, and holes had been bored through the cobs. Mr. Roberts said this was used in ceremonies. Another interesting piece was of red ocher that was used to paint on rocks. As I remember, it was about eight inches long and about one and a half inches in diameter, and it had some etchings on it. It was slightly tapered to the ends. We also found some points and lots of pot sherds.

We went up to the willow tank and dug out a ruin up there. After we got through there, we moved down to Horseshoe Canyon. We camped at the mouth of Spring Canyon. We dug out a couple of caves there. We were joined by a couple of professors from the University of Utah. Also, along came Don Scott, Sr. We stayed there. Don Scott, Jr., was accepted by the California Institute of Technology for his graduate work and he left us early in September. About the fifteenth of September, Dennison and Forbes both left because they had to get back to Harvard. It seems to me it was about the middle of October before we wound that deal up. They all went to town, and I took Dave Rust's mules over to Hanksville. I was going to take them over to Rabbit Valley where he was going to winter them, but he came over and said he'd take the mules up there because he didn't have anything else to do. I got back on my horse and went back to the Chaffin Ranch. That was the end of a very, very pleasant and, I might say, a very profitable summer for me. They paid me ninety dollars a month. That was for me and my horse, and that was more money than any kid in southeastern Utah ever dreamed of making at that time. This last instance was the summer of 1930. I worked for them for two summers.

From that camp, Hanksville was the nearest town. It was a good, hard day's horseback ride. The trail I rode was from the canyon up over where Chad Moore has his cabin now by the old Texas well. Then I took the trail on the south side of the Flat Tops and hit the road over to the Tasker well and straight on to Hanksville. A pretty good little jaunt, about thirty miles, and it was toward day's end when I got there. In those days you didn't push too hard. I had a nice time in Hanksville. That's when the Webers were running the hotel and the livery stable. Mrs. Weber had a big garden and in that big garden were tomatoes that were six inches across and red-ripe and full of juice. I'll never forget how good those tomatoes tasted. After being out and living and eating out of a can or eating Dave Rust's rice and beans all the time, those tomatoes were something we just didn't get.

It was a very happy time, a wonderful association, and a long association with my old friend Dave Rust. We kept in touch for a long time. Dave sent me a bunch of photos. I came on the bus from California to Green River one year, and my suitcase got lost or stolen, and I lost all of those photos except one. I still have that one.

I want to tell a bit about George Franz. His name keeps popping up in articles by historians like Barbara Ekker or Pearl Baker. He was quite a guy, all wool and a yard wide. He liked to drink, he liked to laugh, and he liked to have a good time. I guess he liked to work, because if he wasn't drinking or laughing or telling jokes, he was working. George Franz was in the transportation business at the old garage on the west side of the main street in Green River. That's where I first knew him. He was running the garage at that time.

The movers and shakers in Green River, Utah, at that time were W. F. Asimus, George Franz, and Lou Chaffin. One day W. F. Asimus came down to our house and he had Dad call George. George came down. W. F. Asimus had a letter from T. C. Conley. T. C. Conley wanted W. F. Asimus to send him three hundred dollars, and said if he did he would run two million dollars through Green River. So they sat there and they had a few drinks. Dad always had a jug handy, and they talked about a bunch of pros and cons about Conley's request. Of course, there were no jobs available then. Nobody had any money and times were really tough. Well, old W. F. Asimus said he would put in one hundred dollars. George Franz would put in fifty dollars and Mr. Asimus would put fifty dollars on Dad's bill up at the store because Dad didn't have any money. So they decided and they sent two hundred dollars to T. C. Conley. That is when T. C. Conley got the Continental Oil Company and the Texas Oil Company to come out there, and they did all that surveying work. This was prior to the Texas Oil Company drilling their well and Phillips drilling its wells. These wells were the result of this endeavor by T. C. Conley. George did all the trucking for these companies.

T. C. Conley was a promoter. He would go out and hustle venture capital for oil prospecting. All the work done at French Springs, the Texas well, the Phillips well and some wells on the east side of the river were the result of his money raising efforts. Dad and Mom always spoke well of him. George Franz did all of the freighting for them and for my dad. Dad outfitted and took care of the survey crews, and he and Uncle

Arthur built the road across Horseshoe Canyon. All the older Chaffins worked around the drilling rigs and on the roads. The work these people did and the money they spent was a real boon to Green River. When T. C. and H. W. C. Prommel. et al., came early in 1926, the town of Green River was almost dead. When they left we had all survived, and several people made a lot of money.

In 1929 the Phillips Oil Company abandoned its well. It was on the east side of Horseshoe. It went to a depth of over 5,000 feet, but never produced in commercial quantities. The Tidwells salvaged a lot of the timbers from the wooden derrick and built some sheds and corrals with the lumber. We Chaffins bought the ranch on the San Rafael. That same summer George Franz bought out Eph Moore, Bill Tibbetts, Kenny Allred, and maybe some of the holdings of the Daltons. These people were all from Moab. He bought their cattle and their water rights on the Big Water and the lower Green River.

That summer we branded all the cattle. Of course some of those old cows had been stolen a hundred times, and they had a map on them that looked like the map of Mexico, they had so damn many brands on them. Nobody could tell who they really belonged to. Old Eph Moore had been crippled up in a horse accident and he wouldn't never ride a horse off a slow lope. There were a lot of wild cattle there, and Clell was breaking three horses for Hazel Ekker.

To make a long story shorter, those cattle were really wild and we went down there to brand those cattle. We branded in a corral in a side canyon just between Big Water and Meat Hook Spring in Big Water. I don't believe there was ever such wild cowboying ever done as there was then. We had me and Clell, we had Albert Weber and Warren Thompson and George Franz, of course. It took us five or six weeks to round those damn cattle up and get them rebranded with George Franz's brand, which was the three bar slash. There were a hundred fifty to two hundred head of cattle.

The next year Clell and Goldie Franz got married, and George had Clell run the outfit, and I didn't work for George. I graduated from high school in 1931. Right after I graduated from school I went out and went to punching cows. In the winter of 1931–32 George bought a bunch of calves from us and we took them from the ranch down Under the Ledge. I went down there with them and stayed all winter. I fed his cattle and those calves and I fed them cake and made sure they had water through the ice, and took care of the whole bit. It was just after New Years when we got down on the Green River. I stayed there and never came to town.

I got to town the sixteenth of April, so that was a pretty long hitch. For my pay I got my board and clothes. George said he couldn't pay me nothing, so that was all right. That was just the way things was. I heard people say in those days if a guy didn't have any money, what the hell was he going to pay you with?

During the four winter months of 1931–32 we took care of Mr. Franz's cattle on the Green River below Millard Canyon. When we first arrived at Anderson Bottom, the small cabin was there and that is where we stayed. It was small with only one room with a bed and a stove. Outside there was a metal granary. We had a battery operated radio that we played for a short time each evening. We killed a beef and hung it out under a big rock where it remained frozen. When you wanted some beef, you would take the axe and cut off what you wanted. We also had canned food and potatoes and onions. We ate a lot of rice and beans. We also killed a deer for venison steaks and jerky, and of course we had tea and coffee and those good old baking powder biscuits. We ate good.

We moved the stock from Anderson Bottom down to Valentine Bottom and put some cattle over the river into Deer Canyon and on Tuxedo Bottom. We had a tent on Valentine Bottom and lived there for about a month. We then moved down to Cabin Bottom, cleaned out the log cabin, and stayed there until we moved out in April.

Anyway, I finally got paid for it because when George sold his cattle he sent me a little note that he'd also sent to Art Ekker. He gave me his brand and said when they gathered and sold his cattle, if they missed any they were mine. Well, they missed one cow and one yearling heifer. So they were mine, and Art Ekker took care of them until I had nine head. Art said, "Hey, Ned, what do you want me to do with those cows?" He said, "You want them? Do you want to come and get them, or what do you want me to do with them? They're getting to be quite a few. I've been glad to take care of them for you and furnish you with the bulls and all, but after all, it's time."

So I said, "Sure, go ahead and sell them." Well, I got more money for those nine head of cattle than I ever dreamed of having in my life. This was after World War II and the price of cattle had gone up quite a bit.

The winter I worked for him down on the river, George came down and stayed for three or four weeks, and then he went out, but said he'd be back before too long. Well, too long was after the ice went out and he and Arla, that was his wife, came down the river in a boat. Arla's Bottom is named after her, of course. Clell and I were camped at Cabin Bottom and they came down there and we kind of fixed things around there.

I went to town, Green River, for about a week, and when I came back, George had leased some ground up in the Book Cliffs, up above Woodside, up in what they call the Little Park, and in the Big Park. He thought it would be a good idea to take some cattle from the dry country and take them up in the mountains where all that grass was. We trailed them damn cattle from Anderson Bottom clear up into the Book Cliffs. If we didn't have a time! There was Clell and I, and Warren Thompson, Vas Howland, and George Franz. We had about one hundred and fifty or two hundred head of cattle. What a crew! We came up over Devil's Slide over to the Tidwell's Ranch, across the desert, up the Salaradus Wash and over to Woodside and then up to what they called Little Park. After we got those cattle up there, that was the last time I ever worked for George Franz. He was a great guy. He was a promoter; he knew how to do things and he was a very dear friend to my father and my mother.

[Ned Chaffin shared additional recollections on May 30, 1995, while en route to Hans Flat. Also participating in the discussion were Bob Ryan of Georgetown, Colorado, driving his Hummer; Bill Foreman, district ranger for the Maze District Canyonlands National Park; and the author, Dick Negri. Ned begins talking about the Great Gallery of pictographs in Horseshoe Canyon.]

Ned Chaffin: My father wanted to cut the big gallery out of the rock and take the rock and the gallery to the World's Fair in New York. He considered this very seriously, and the bank even offered to lend him the money to pay the freight to haul the gallery back to New York, but then they got digging into it and found out it wouldn't be advisable to do it.

Bob Ryan: The story about the oil crew wanting to dynamite part of the gallery off of the panel to make a coffee table for the president of the Phillips Oil Company is quite a story.

Ned: I don't believe it.

Bob: Well, the story as it was told to us was that someone at the Tidwell Ranch heard the dynamiting and rode down and held the oil crew members off at gun point. That's the story that we heard.

Dick Negri: I'll try to remember to ask Frank Tidwell about it. He just might know. I doubt if it really happened. It couldn't have happened and been kept quiet. Bill, have you heard this story before?

Bill Foreman: I've heard that story . . .

Ned: I'm not going to believe that story and I'll tell you why. If you had been out to the Phillips well working twelve hours a day seven days a week for a year, you couldn't get that fanny of yours out of there fast enough. Believe me, the day they shut that well down, they left, and I mean they left in a hurry, and all you could see was a cloud of dust.

Bob: That may be, but the story has to do with when they closed it down, and before they left; this is what they were alleged to have done.

Ned: I am not going to believe that because I don't think it is true. Number one, it would take somebody like my father who knew how to get that thing out of there without ruining it. You had to know what you were doing and you had to have the proper equipment. For those guys to go up there to that big gallery, they would have to drill the holes by hand. They didn't have compressors, unless they went to town and rented one, which is something I know damn well they didn't do; and number two, if those guys had planned to do that it would have been gossiped all over the country.

If one of the guys told me he did it, I would have believed it, otherwise I couldn't believe that story. We all know what oral history is. Oral history is what I want to tell you and the way I saw it. We're riding along Horse Bench in this Hummer right now and a year from now if each one of us wrote an essay about going from Green River to the San Rafael, you would think we were on different planets. I think this story might have been made up by someone trying to sell the story to a magazine.

The boss out there was an Indian, Bob Vance was his name. I don't believe, in fact I know, when you got that Bob Vance mad you had better watch out because he had no control of himself. A hell of a swell guy right along with it. I just don't believe Bob Vance would have stood for anyone messing around those pictographs. I'll bet my bottom dollar against your fifty cents he wouldn't do that. I don't believe it!

Bill: I've thought about that a lot, and there are some pictographs that are busted off and that is supposedly where they blasted the rock away. But if they blasted the rock, then you would see where they blasted because if you put a mark on that wall it is going to last for the next five or eight thousand years, or ten thousand years.

[*On the evening of June 7, 1995, Frank Tidwell told me he had never heard of the confrontation between cowboys from the Tidwell Ranch and the oil crew. Frank said they had drilled and operated that particular oil well during the years 1928 and 1929. He was born in 1930, so if it happened, it took place before his birth. His family abandoned the ranch in 1946 subsequent to a sustained drought that made it too tough on the cattle. They simply couldn't make a decent living there with little or no rainfall year after year.*]

During our conversation I told Frank that I would send him a copy of
Barrier Canyon Remembered, *an essay about the pictographs written by
Robert M. Jones.*[1] *The essay describes a trip into Barrier Canyon (Horseshoe
Canyon) by a group of artists selected by the Utah Art Project administrators.
This project was a federally funded WPA project of 1940 to create a life-size
mural of the Great Gallery on canvas.*

*An incident described in the article may shed some light on whether or
not the panel was dynamited by members of the oil digging crew. According
to Mr. Jones, Lee Tidwell, assisted by his brother Delbert, was the guide for
the artist group, and at one point Lee told of a trip made by engineers and
geologists from the Phillips Oil Company. The chief engineer said he
planned to blast out a fragment of the mural on the canyon wall to take
back to old man Phillips. The response by Lee was, "Just try it and you'll
take a couple of 30 calibre slugs in your hide back to Oklahoma!"*[2] *The point
was taken.*

*Subsequent to this discussion I, on November 27, 1995, conversed by
phone with Elzy J. Bird of Midvale, Utah. At the time of the incident
referred to, Mr. Bird was the director of the WPA Utah Art Project. He was
responsible for assembling the team to produce a full-sized reproduction of the
Great Gallery of pictographs. Mr. Bird was present throughout the project.
The Indian Arts and Crafts Board of the U.S. Department of the Interior, in
cooperation with the New York Museum of Modern Art and other museums,
was gathering material for a collection of American Indian arts. This mural
was to be an important part of the art in the exhibition.*

*Mr. Bird confirmed Jones's description of the sequence of events pertain-
ing to the engineer's desire to blast out a piece of the pictograph panel and the
guide Tidwell's threat to put a couple of 30 calibre slugs in the engineer's hide
if he tried to harm the pictograph panel. Bird stated that the oil on canvas
mural was actually two canvases, one twelve feet by sixty-six feet and the
second twelve by twenty. These dimensions differ from those in the "Barrier
Canyon Remembered" report, but I am convinced they are accurate. One of
the murals is on display in the Utah Museum of Natural History in Salt
Lake City. The other is on display at the Eastern Utah Prehistoric Museum
in Price. Visitors to the Great Gallery in Horseshoe Canyon may notice chalk
marks in one-foot increments along the bottom of the panel of pictographs.*

---

1. Robert M. Jones, *Barrier Canyon Remembered* (Stamford, Conn.: Glad Hand Press,
    1989).

2. Lee Tidwell was Frank Tidwell's uncle. Delbert Tidwell was Frank's father.

The "Holy Ghost" group, Horseshoe Canyon. Photo courtesy of Canyonlands National Park ranger Gary Cox.

These were placed there to assure accuracy in the proportions of the canvas reproduction. Mr. Bird was one of several persons who placed those marks on the rock wall. Mr. Bird kindly mailed me a summary of his report, "The Barrier Canyon Mural," which is his account of the expeditions to reproduce the pictographs.[3] In a footnote at the end of his report, he stated:

> *Those of you who are familiar with the beautiful panel of pictographs in Barrier Canyon will remember the large figure called the "Holy Ghost" with the attending smaller figures. At the time we worked there, and many trips later, I found shattered pieces of stone with the red pictograph paint scattered at the foot of this panel. Lee Tidwell told me the following story:*
> *"Once when I was ridin' in the canyon I heard a loud explosion. I gave my horse the spurs and wound up at the big panel. There were a couple of oil men there and they had just blasted off a piece of the*

---

3. Elzy J. Bird, "The Barrier Canyon Mural," on file in the Western Americana collection of the University of Utah's Marriott Library.

wall with dynamite—just to the left of what you call the "Holy Ghost." They had destroyed several of the figures and you can see what's left of 'em scattered there on the ground. I'd brought my old .30-30 saddle gun with me and I jerked it out. I told 'em to get the hell out of there or I'd let them have it. They left without any trouble."

Readers should note there is no mention of the name of the oil company referred to in Lee Tidwell's discussion. It should not be assumed that the dynamiters were from the Phillips Oil Company crew. In fact, Ned is ada-mant that Bob Vance would never have permitted such a thing to go on. Furthermore, no member of his crew would have dared to do so behind his back. Mr. Vance's approach to a disciplinary action in this case would have justified the ACLU's existence. Ned will attest to that!]

Ned: I'll tell you something about the marks on the wall. You never saw Lou Chaffin's name on the wall, did you?

Bill: No. We have found many, many names, historic names scratched on the canyon walls, but never Lou's.

Ned: The reason Lou never wrote his name on the walls was because an old Indian medicine man who treated him for some blood poisoning he had told him, and the words were something like this, "The man who leaves his mark on the canyon wall leaves his soul there, too." I know that's the truth from personal experience. I've got my name on those walls down there, and if part of me isn't down there, I'd sure as hell like to know where it is at. It always will be; there is never a day goes by that I don't think about those canyons down there. Not one single day of my life. My dad told me, "Never write your name on these walls. Never cut your brand in the rock!" And I paid as much attention to him as I did to the wind blowing, and I'm sorry. I'm sorry my name is on those walls down there.

Dick: Ned, have you seen those pictograph panels in Sego Canyon up north of Thompson Springs? There is a slab there that looks like it was cut out with tools. If that is what happened, perhaps that slab is in a museum someplace.

Ned: My father worked in the coal mine up there in Sego Canyon in the winter of 1922. He and my older brother Kenneth worked there and we lived in the company house. They only operated the mine in the winter when coal was used for house fuel by everyone, and for the railroad. They would stockpile the coal in the winter and shut it down in the summer.

I knew Pearl Baker from the old cow punching days, and of course she was older and more intelligent than the rest of us, than Hazel and Clell and I, and she lorded it over us all the time. She came up there to teach school and she taught us who was boss real quick.

You know, though, if that slab is in a museum, maybe that is for the better. We all know the day will come when somebody will come along up the canyon with some high quality spray paint and ruin them.

[Later on May 30, 1995, while crossing the San Rafael River:]

Ned: This is a new experience for me. I've never crossed the San Rafael on this new bridge. Look at all the tamarisks. I can't believe how the channel has changed. There is going to be a flood come down here one of these days that is going to clean this whole place out including this bridge. When it rains up in the Blue Country around Castle Dale and rains hard on the San Rafael Desert you get a lot of water coming down here, and that channel won't handle it. It is too thick to drink and too thin to plow.

This country, and now we are just west of Keg Spring Canyon, it looks like there is more foliage than there used to be. There aren't any sheep here any more and I sure don't have any objections to that. In the winter when you had snow, the sheep liked to come down into this area because all this brush here, every bit of that is very, very strong feed. Sheep are browsers, anyway, where your horses and cattle go more for your grasses. They covered this country with sheep, made three or four swipes at it. Go this way once, then across that way, then back again. In a place like Waterhole Flat, the good Lord knows how many swipes they took at that.

The trail down into the head of Shot Canyon is a good one. Whoever built that did a good job. They built it just to get down there. Bill, have you ever been down it?

Bill: Yes. I have. It is still there. It's fallen in a little bit, but it is in good shape. Somebody put a lot of work into it.

Ned: I don't have any idea who built it. I saw the build-up from the bottom of the canyon. We had some cattle in there. I rode up the canyon and I could see that build-up that goes up to the rim, you know, those steps. That was a way out of there. It was a year or two before we had any occasion to go back in there. Clell took the packs and went around the old way and told me to go around and see if I could find my way down into Shot Canyon. I had just about given up when I found the way. I was riding Smokey, an old mule that was sharp shod, and I'll tell you, I looked at that trail two or three times before I decided I could tackle it. But old Smokey just inched his way, and away we went. That was the only time I ever used that trail. We never did use it for stock. I don't have any idea how that trail got built. Probably built by some old hoot-owlers planning to use it as an escape route.

Bill: You guys used to take your horses and mules on some incredible trails. Have you been on the Devil's Slide Trail?

Ned: Oh, sure. That's what we used all the time. You should have seen it before the government had a project there. My name is on a rock there in January 1935 or late '34. Anyway, the government had a range improvement project. Built trails, troughed up springs, the whole bit. Working on the Devil's Slide was one of those projects.

Bill: Was that CCC?

Ned: No, it was separate from the CCC. I don't know what they called it. George Franz, due to certain political connections, personal associations, and friendly disposition or whatever, was the boss. My father was the foreman. He was in charge of the crew and I did the packing for them. Packed on mules all their camp gear and did the cooking for them. We must have worked there three or four weeks. I got so much money working for the government on that job I couldn't count it. They also paid me for my mules.

The same year they troughed up the Two Pipe Spring up on the Big Ridge, and they put little troughs in at the Lou's Spring at the Maze, and troughed up Clell's Seep over at the Chute in the Maze. They went over to the San Rafael Swell, but I didn't go over there with them. That was all this same project. They not only improved the range, but they gave people some employment and jobs so they wouldn't starve to death. I can't convince anybody who wasn't here at the time how hard times were. I believe if you had two hundred dollars cash, you could have bought half of Green River and taken a mortgage on the other half. There just wasn't any money. Those jobs we had only paid two or two and a half dollars a day, but it sure looked big then.

Bill: Did you go up and down the Devil's Slide Trail before the government worked on it?

Ned: Oh, yeah.

Bill: Geez, I hiked that a few weeks ago and I went up where the old trail was and came down where the second trail is, and I was astounded when I saw where you guys used to go up and down that trail. There are some old bones there.

Ned: You better believe there are some old bones there. Some of those old wild cows were unmanageable. We had one old cow, boy she was wild, wilder than a deer, and she come down to that big jump right there near the bottom, that rim, and she just went right straight off of it. She never slowed up. And her calf followed her. That was the end of them. I think my brother Clell called that the Devil's Slide first. It doesn't matter who called it that, but whoever called it that knew what he was talking about. It is a dangerous place also because it is loose. I'll bet it is a son-of-a-gun by now.

Bill: I don't think a horse could go up it now, but maybe you could do it.

Ned: I hope I never have to again, but it is amazing. You put those good shoes on those horses, and they get to where they know where they can go. Those sharp-shod shoes had notches that stuck up on the heel and a bar on the toe, and when you got on the rock the weight would get on those notches, and on that soft sandstone they really gripped.

You know, if my old friend Dave Rust was here right now, he'd still be cussing the railroad at the Grand Canyon. It seems that when he was a kid, he was one of the instigators of that mule trail going down the canyon. He and three or four other guys decided to build a mule trail down there. About the time they started, the railroad decided it was a good idea and kicked Rust and his friends off. In those days the railroads were all-powerful. If it weren't for the railroad, Dave Rust would still be down there. Some say he built the Bright Angel Trail, but I don't know if that is true. I heard a lot about the railroad from him. He was pretty bitter and felt he had been treated unjustly. And he probably had.

Clell and I camped at night on that slickrock over there near Keg Spring, and in the morning when we got up, it was a beautiful morning. The sun was shining; it was wintertime and there was about eight inches of snow on the ground. By the time we got here to the lower end of Antelope Valley, the south wind started blowing right straight down the valley. It wasn't very long until the snow started kicking up. Boy, we were just covered with snow. It turned cold and we took the cattle over to Horseshoe Canyon down the trail, and we headed for the Tidwell's ranch.

That was a night out; every cow puncher in the country was there. Andy Moore was there. He had been heading for North Spring and got his car stuck in a drift. He was lucky. There was a sheepherder camped not too far away, and Andy saw the light in the sheepherder's tent and he went over and stayed with him. Paul Herron, Pearl Baker's second husband, he got stuck in a drift and darn near froze to death. Stayed there all night and burned some cedars.

Clell and I started the cattle down into Horseshoe, then we took off for Tidwell's. About two hours later here came George Franz and his truck. He was so drunk he couldn't get his hat on. You know where the gate is going down the last rim going down the canyon into Horseshoe? Well, George's truck had dual wheels on it and we could see where his outer wheels had gone over the edge of the rim. It was a darn wonder old George didn't turn off. He got to Tidwell's ranch, and there were three cabins there. We were staying in one and we had a roaring fire going in a pot-bellied stove, and old George came and sat on the stove. That is true! I saw it with my own eyeballs. What a character! Everybody in the country was out there that day. The Tidwells came out, it was right after Christmas, but they got out before the wind started blowing the snow. Andy Moore, the Chaffins, the Tidwells, everybody got a taste of it.

One time Andy Moore got caught here in a vicious hailstorm. It laid the brush flat and old Andy was right in the middle of it. He told me his old horse tried to buck him off. All he was trying to do was get his saddle off the horse so he could put it over his head to protect himself from the hail, but that horse didn't want the saddle off because it protected him somewhat. He about beat Andy up. Andy was a great guy and a good cowboy. In fact, he was the foreman for a guy by the name of MacMillan. MacMillan owned two ranches. He had the Hatt Ranch on the San Rafael, that was the upper MacMillan Ranch, and he had a ranch above the Gillis Ranch. That was the lower MacMillan Ranch. He ran cattle all over the desert here. He was one of the casualties of the post-World War One depression that hit here.

When MacMillan paid off Andy Moore, he gave him nine head of cows and a bull. And that's what Andy started with. He lived out here with those damned cows and that one bull and he built himself up a hell of a nice operation. He did it by hard work. You didn't have the fancy automobiles to run to town every night. You came out here and you stayed. That's what he did, and his family. They had the old man Wheeler place, and that's where they stayed. When the boys got to be seven or eight years old, Bill and Chad, and got big enough so they could get on their own horse, why, he had them out here helping, of course. He was a good cowman and a good neighbor.

[Later during the drive toward Hans Flat, as we were driving by pasture land where A. C. Ekker's cattle were grazing:]

Bill: Those cattle A. C. is raising aren't for beef, they are rodeo stock.

Dick: Ned, when you were riding out here did you cowboys carry rifles?

Ned: What for? What does anybody want to pack a gun for? All a gun does is get you in trouble, that's all. Nobody ever solved any problems with a gun. We kept a rifle in the pack in case we wanted to get some venison. Slim Baker is the only one I ever saw packing a gun. Some of those old boys traveling through had rifles on their saddles. That old Art Murray, he was one of the toughest guys in the country as far as being a hard man, but I don't think he even owned a gun. Joe Biddlecome always had a .30-30 around handy. But he never packed it. In those days you had to rely on what feed was here. You had no use for a gun.

Bill: Didn't you have to worry about if you had an injured cow or horse you'd need to shoot him?

Ned: No, you always had a pocket knife and you cut their throats. One time down on Waterhole Flat I wished I had a gun. We had an old horse, old Piddle. I'll always remember how traumatic this was to me. In this instance, Faun couldn't do it and there was no way we could save him, so I took my knife and cut his throat. Faun, as tough as he was, he couldn't do it. He skinned the horse, though, and took the hide. That was a sad time.

Hazel and I had these two wild cows and their calves, and we were holding them up to where they couldn't run. Here comes Pearl, screaming her head off about something. The damn two cows got scared and run off one way, the two calves ran off the other way. About that time along came Joe Biddlecome, and he shouted, "Damn it, I told you guys not to run them cattle and to hold them up!" And he came up to me and hit me over the withers with a hard twist and hit Hazel, too. Old Pearl never said a thing—we had them held up till she came along and spooked them. We had some wild cattle, wilder than antelope.

You know, Pearl was such an intelligent human being, real smart. Had a quick mind. Sometimes too quick. She lorded it over Hazel and Clell and I because she was older than we were. She always wanted to make sure we did everything she wanted us to do. We would play mumblety-peg. She would play with us until somebody beat her and then she'd get mad and quit. Hazel, Clell, and I used to gang up against Pearl, but Pearl could hold her own. Hazel and Pearl were both well educated. Joe and Millie Biddlecome saw to that. He couldn't even . . . he signed his checks with his brand, diamond and a half. Some people might call it a running diamond, but he called it a diamond and a half. That's the way he signed his checks, and if you had one of his checks, you could bet your bottom dollar you were going to get your money.

[That concludes the conversations that took place on the trip from Green River to down Under the Ledge and on to the abandoned Chaffin cow camp in Waterhole Flat. The February 1995 interview with Ned Chaffin resumes:]

I moved to Bakersfield in 1937 and worked in the carpenter trade for a year or two. My sister Gwendolyn and her husband lived here, and I came out to pay them a visit and work for a month or two; however, I met a beautiful young lady at an old-timer's dance and decided the best thing to do was court this lady, which I did. As luck would have it, I was successful. We were married here in Bakersfield on November 4, 1938. Marjorie is the only child of Earl and Blanche Daniel. She attended local schools and is a graduate of Taft College. She is active in several local organizations. Her special love is her family, and she loves to work with school youngsters in regard to Americanism and loyalty.

Then I worked for Marjorie's father. Her father was a wholesale distributor and he manufactured soda water. I worked at his plant. He retired in 1950, and he and I went to Nevada and bought a ranch, but he really wasn't cut out for ranching and he decided to sell out. He kept the ranch just a year, and then sold. That is when Faun came over to Nevada. He had come to run the outfit for Mr. Daniel.

When I came back to Bakersfield, I went to work for the National Supply Company. My first job was sweeping up. The boss gave me a broom on the first day and told me my job was to clean this place up, which I did. At the end of the first week he said to me, "I like the way you work. I like your attitude. You can hang up the broom. I want you to be the shipping and receiving clerk." So I did that for a few months. This was in 1950, so I was about thirty-seven then. I had various jobs with the National Supply Company, and I was manager of our store over at Taft, California, and I ran the store here in Bakersfield after that. We got onto computers very early on and it took several years to get it running smoothly. I was promoted to warehouse supervisor and had the responsibility for buying all of the supplies for California and the distribution of those supplies to the other stores. I retired from National Supply Company at the age of sixty-five in 1979. I've been enjoying my retirement with my beautiful bride, Marjorie, ever since. We do a lot of work for the Freedom's Foundation from Valley Forge. We also do a lot of volunteer work with the schools and the Veterans of

Foreign Wars and the Kern County Museum and the Kern County Historical Society.

We have two daughters, four grandchildren, and two great grand-children. Marjorie and I are both happy, we get along fine, and we are in good health.

[Postscript: a letter from Ned, August 10, 1996, that expresses a transition that is remarkable for a rancher who has mistrusted environmentalists, espe-cially due to threats to close public lands to grazing:]

To Dick, Barbara, Et al.,

I've had a hell of a time writing this and have found it very difficult to put my thoughts on paper, but here goes.

On June 1st, 1996, the few old timers at the Cowboy Caucus in Green River melted away and left town for home. However, my grand-daughter Regina and wife, Marjorie, wanted to go over to Dead Horse Point, over to Moab, and up to Arches National Park. I especially wanted to show Regina some of the old spots where I punched cows in my wild and misspent youth and assumed the Island in the Sky overlook in Canyonlands National Park (Grand View Point) would give us a great opportunity to see part of my old stomping grounds. I had told Regina that Mt. Ellen in the Henry Mts. was a great landmark, visible from a great deal of South Eastern Utah. I had also told her about the Navajo Mts. and the old Indian legend about the mountain, however, shortly after we turned off the highway heading for Dead Horse Point I woke up to the fact that something was wrong. Where were the Henry Mts? We couldn't even see them! Anyway, we proceeded to the overlook! I couldn't believe my eyes. I thought I had lost my mind. I was looking at more smog and dirt in the air than we have here in Bakersfield, (which is saying a lot!) Also, we could not see Navajo Mts. The Blue Mts. and the Elk Ridge were just a blob on the horizon and the deep Canyons enter-ing the Colorado River from the East (Dark Canyon), Etc. were not distinguishable thru the haze. Ekker Butte, due to its prominence, was standing there and, of course, we could see Arly's Bottom, Turk's Bottom, No Name Bottom and the Lower End of Cabin Bottom, where I spent the Winter of 1931–1932 feeding cattle for George Franz. Of course we could see the White Rim and Dead Horse Canyon and I showed Regina where Bill Tibbetts and Kenny Allred and Ef Moore gave me the last of the water out of their canteens on a hot summer day, in the early nineteen twenties and how we chased a couple of head of really wild cows into that little cove and got them back to the herd.

I could not get over the shock of the pollution and my thoughts turned to the "old days." Regina and Marjorie asked some pertinent questions and several tourists gathered around and seemed to enjoy some tales about the old days.

I hate Environmentalists. Let me rephrase this. I hated Environmentalists until I looked off into one of the most beautiful vistas in the world and saw a beautiful, colorful scene diminished in no small measure by a blanket of dirt that is made by man. I do not have any education or experience for a solution to this problem, even though everyone should be very concerned.

Food for Thought

Since moving to California in the late 1930s, I have made many trips back to my homeland and each time I have returned with some of the colorful Red Rocks from the area. I have observed that the rocks, if left outside, lose their beautiful red color. Is this loss caused by the smog? Could be. We can all hope that the dirty air in the Southeastern Utah area will not cause the Wingate Sandstone to lose its beautiful red hue.

To sum up my feelings, I have felt frustration, helplessness, and the whole bit, but most of all a feeling of deep sadness for my Beautiful Homeland!

Very Best Wishes,
Ned Chaffin

3

Lorin Milton

*Lorin Milton is a cowboy's cowboy. Though born in 1918, he continues rop-
ing steers in rodeos and raising cattle on his spread in Torrington, Wyoming.*

*In his younger days he cowboyed in the Book Cliffs, at Art Ekker's
spread at Dubinky Wash, and in the nearby Ten Mile Wash area located on
the high plateau north of the confluence of the Green and Colorado Rivers. He
also covered the west side of the rivers, where the members of the Wild Bunch
once took refuge in the canyons of the Robbers Roost area, and ranged
throughout the San Rafael Desert.*

*He speaks of Dubinky as an area rather than just a wash. Driving the
Dubinky Well Road, today's visitor will discover a nonfunctioning windmill
and a stock watering tank that has been vandalized with guns and graffiti.
The windmill and stock tank are located alongside a dirt road some six miles
from Utah 313. Three-quarters of a mile before reaching the windmill, the
road crosses Dubinky Wash. The Ekker Ranch was located down the wash
about a mile and a half south of the road.*

*The wash runs into the head of Hell Roaring Canyon, and it was at a
seep in the wash that Art and Hazel Ekker lived in a house constructed of
railroad ties. Neither the windmill nor the stock watering tank was in place
when Lorin cowboyed there, but the remains of a shed and the picket corral
that he helped build still stand. No trace of the ranch house can be seen.*

*The Levi Well Road north of the Dubinky Well site goes past the
Dripping Spring cow camp that Lorin mentions. We stopped at the camp in
the spring of 1996 and were pleased to note that the ladder and pail used to
collect water were still in place at the Dripping Spring. Lorin stresses that
this camp and Dubinky were important centers of cattle raising.*

Lorin Milton, 1995.

A word of caution to visitors to the area: numerous dirt roads intersect; most are unmarked and impassable when wet. A compass and a decent map are essential, and it is always wise to carry emergency supplies in the vehicle.

Lorin is full of tales, never shy about telling a joke or two, and hence always welcomed at gatherings. He is a cowboy poet and can make up stories faster than most people can read them. A fellow with many skills, he is well known for breaking horses and famed for using "the gentle touch" with the stock. No written description can complete his portrait; he has to be heard, preferably around a campfire.

July 28, 1994
Torrington, Wyoming

Father was born in Georgia in 1868, and went to Texas when he was six. He gradually went clear up through Texas and ended up working for big cow outfits in the panhandle, near Dalhart, all through that area where the XIT cattle outfit was later. He finally ended up in western Colorado and eastern Utah. In eastern Utah, not far from the Colorado border, he

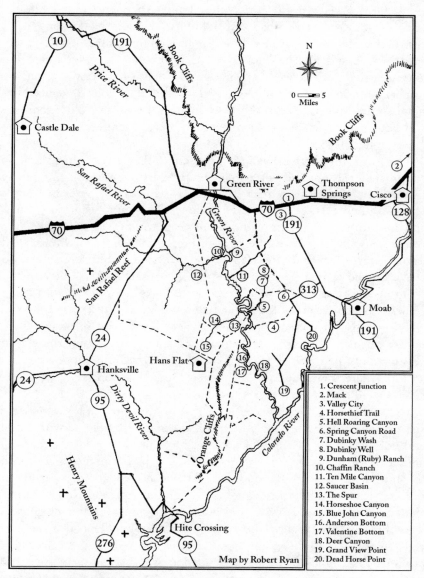

Lorin Milton's Canyonlands.

Map labels and legend:

N

0 — 5
Miles

10
191
Price River
Book Cliffs
Book Cliffs
Castle Dale
San Rafael River
2
Green River
Thompson Springs
Cisco
128
Green River
1
70
3
191
70
San Rafael Reef
10
9
12
11
8
7
313
5
6
Moab
24
14
13
4
191
15
20
24
Hanksville
Hans Flat
16
18
95
Dirty Devil River
17
19
Henry Mountains
Orange Cliffs
Colorado River
276
95
Hite Crossing
Map by Robert Ryan

1. Crescent Junction
2. Mack
3. Valley City
4. Horsethief Trail
5. Hell Roaring Canyon
6. Spring Canyon Road
7. Dubinky Wash
8. Dubinky Well
9. Dunham (Ruby) Ranch
10. Chaffin Ranch
11. Ten Mile Canyon
12. Saucer Basin
13. The Spur
14. Horseshoe Canyon
15. Blue John Canyon
16. Anderson Bottom
17. Valentine Bottom
18. Deer Canyon
19. Grand View Point
20. Dead Horse Point

ran an outfit for Harry Bogert years ago. Eventually went to work for the Preston Nutter Corporation in Utah. He was the cow boss there for years. He worked for Preston Nutter longer than he worked for any other person. Nutter also had vast holdings down on the Arizona Strip, and Father put in two years down there straightening things out. He used to hire and fire; he had his own checkbook through Nutter. He never married until he was forty-five years old. My mother was a school-teacher, born in Iowa, but raised in Nebraska, and was out there teaching school when they met each other. I had a sister who was older than me and Father was fifty years old when I was born; therefore, he was more like a granddad to me.

Father and Mother lived on a ranch in Green River, Utah, then he bought out the holdings of a man named Mirt Tomlinson out in the Book Cliffs area east of Green River in Horse Canyon. Later he proved up on all the waters. They were all springs, no running water in washes, and he took up a stock grazing homestead which was 640 acres. We summered our cattle up at the head of Horse Canyon (which was called Tom Farrer Valley and Cub Valley) and wintered in Horse Canyon. To prove up the waters he fixed the springs so that stock could water at them at any time of the year. Some were troughs of wood with some cement up against a rock ledge. He had them located by a surveyor so he could get title to the springs. That's where I got a lot of early riding. Father ran horses there first for years. He ran his cattle up the Green River and on the Price River. That's where I followed him on many a hot mile up there. Later he moved them to Horse Canyon. The dust dang near choked a kid to death on those old rims on the Price River.

I was born in Green River in 1918 and grew up and lived there for sixty-five years. My first job outside of working with my dad with cattle and horses was for Arthur Ekker out at Dubinky. He needed some help gathering weaners. He weaned his calves and drove them to Thompson to ship them out on the railroad. Arthur had a grazing permit at Dubinky. It was after this that he bought the Robbers Roost Ranch. Walt Smith from Green River was working for him, and then he got me. The three of us corralled those cows at Dubinky. He had a big, old cedar-picket corral there, and cut the cows away from the calves that evening. That took a while, but we ended up with the calves in the corral and the cows were outside the corral. There were no fences in those days in that area; there might be now. At daylight we got saddled up and we got rolling with the cows that were hanging around outside the corral bawling. Drove them down Dubinky Wash, and really herded them. In

Fur trapper Denis Julien's signature, 1836, in Hell Roaring Canyon.

other words, made them go as fast as we could to get them away from the calves. Drove them dang near to Hell Roaring Canyon. Then we went back at a fast run on our horses. We threw the gate open on the calves, pushed them out of the corral, and headed for Thompson.

Mrs. Ekker, Hazel, said we were just barely out of sight with the calves, headed up Dubinky Wash, when the leaders of those cows hit the corral behind us. They didn't know which way their calves had gone. We drove them up to Valley City and corralled them in the rock corral that night. The next afternoon we got them to Thompson and shipped them out.

Then I had some work to do in Green River, and when I got done with that I went back out and hired out to Arthur again. That is the time we had some stragglers we had missed. Maybe ten head, not being weaned, so we sort of gathered them up and we had them pretty well in line, and we knew where everything was. Arthur and Hazel had to go to Salt Lake City to a meeting of some kind, so he took me down to the Hell Roaring Trail which wasn't too far from there, and showed me what to do. Well, I worked on that trail for four days fixing it up. That's a bad trail. Hell Roaring Canyon is maybe ten miles long from the Green

River going east, mostly. Dubinky Wash runs into the upper end of it. We were going to gather all those weaners we missed and push them down this trail and leave them down there. There is a little bit of running water down there, and they'd do good. Good feed there, too. So that is what we did. But that trail is so bad at the start that you have to have a little corral right there where we corralled all the cows with their calves. If we had ten calves, we had ten cows, and we cut every cow out of this little corral but one. We kept her for the leader, and then we put our bars up. There was a bunch of cedars there, and brush. Good stout corral, but we had one big old weaner that had gotten out of the corral by getting on a rim of rock. I grabbed him by the head when he came by. We were trying to make that cow get started down the trail so the rest would follow her. Arthur came running up and grabbed this calf by the tail. I got shook over the calf's shoulders and Arthur grabbed him by the head. Finally, we got him down and Arthur, who was a lot bigger and stouter than I was, held him down while I ran and got his horse. We had to get a rope on him, and then we got our bars back down and got him back into the corral.

By that time we finally made that cow that was our leader see the light, and down she goes, and we whoofed the rest off right behind her. That was an awful trail at the start to get something off the rim. It was not that dangerous if they stayed on it, but if they ever got off of it, they could get killed by falling over ledges. It's been known that there were several head of cattle killed on it. We had it rocked up and brushed up all the way on both sides of the trail dang near to the bottom. That is where my four days of work came in. While they were in Salt Lake I did the trail work. Made the trail practically a lane lined with rock and brush walls. It had been done before, but you had to redo that trail every once in a while.

Out in that country the weaners weighed four to four hundred fifty pounds. Up here in Wyoming where there is lots of grass and hardly any rocks, they will weigh lots more than in that rough country. That's desert country. They did good down in the canyon. I went down and checked them a time or two. He sent me down on horseback; actually, you walked and led your horse down that trail. I cut all those cedars for a new corral he was building at Dubinky. Used some oil well cable that was lying around an abandoned well site for fencing. It was an inch or more thick—tough stuff.

Soon after that I went to work for Budge Wilcox up at Florence Creek forty miles up the Green River, and I worked there all winter.

At Dubinky, Arthur and Hazel Ekker lived in a little house made out of railroad cross ties. The living room was also their kitchen. They had a bedroom for the kids and a bedroom for themselves. No electricity, of course, and they got their water out of Dubinky Wash one hundred yards above the house. You had to dig down to get the water. Arthur had cemented it in, right in the bottom of the wash. If a flood came, and they did when it rained hard enough in that sand country, it would fill it up. He housed it in with a wooden lid so it wouldn't fill with sand and put in a pitcher pump and water trough—good water, too. He'd water his saddle horse there. He and Hazel had the two older children there, Eddyjo, and Evelyn Mae, who everybody called Tissy. Eddyjo was the older. He was about six then and had started to school. Two good little kids.

When Arthur and Hazel bought the Robbers Roost Ranch in 1939, he moved his cattle out. I wasn't working for him steady. He had a hand named Don Dowd from Grand Junction. One time Arthur came and got me at Green River and we went out in his pickup to Dubinky where Don was. The three of us men loaded his heavy furniture on the pickup to get ready for the move over to the Roost. Early the next morning the three of us saddled up and went over to Spring Canyon Point and gathered his mare herd. Arthur got Don and I lined up and we went to the Ruby Ranch with them. Arthur rode back, unsaddled, and took the pickup with its load of furniture up to Green River and spent the night there. Don and I had a pack horse with us with our beds on and all. We knew somebody was living there at the Ruby Ranch; in fact, that's the first time I met Bill Racy. Bill was there alone. He was working for Legs Dalton, and Legs's dad was Earl Dalton, but Legs was the main one who Bill Racy was working for. We pulled in there in the shank of the evening with the herd of horses, watered them in the Green River and corralled them that night. Then Don and I threw our bed rolls out and slept at the Ruby.

The next morning Arthur drove the pickup down to the Chaffin Ranch on the San Rafael. He had lined up Faun Chaffin and they saddled up a couple of horses and swam the Green River. Then the five of us crossed his mares over to the west side. One mare got disconnected and broke back. She wasn't broke to lead, and Arthur roped her. Don Dowd had his own private horse which was a good old gentle horse, but not much else. Up in years, too. Don took the lead rope and had his horse cinched up pretty tight with that mare right in behind. When he hit the swimming water, he had to have that mare snubbed up tight because she wasn't broke to lead, and she was bigger than his horse. She could have pulled his saddle off, so he had it cinched real tight and maybe that's why his horse couldn't swim. He just swam a few licks and then went downstream and drowned. Old Don boiled off, and his nose barely broke above the waters. We got the saddle off, but it ruined that saddle. It got soaked with water, and that wood and rawhide under the outside leather warped. It ate every horse he rode with it, and he had to buy a new saddle.

I rode up to the Chaffin Ranch with Arthur, and we took the pickup out to the Roost and unloaded the furniture. I was out at the Roost numerous times after that helping Arthur a little bit. I worked at the Roost most of one summer.

After the war, I got back to Green River and worked for Alton Halverson. Alton and his younger brother Harold lived there. Harold did the farming and Alton was the cowboy, and they ran their cattle out at the Ten Mile area. That is thirty-five miles south and east of Green River, between the Green and Colorado Rivers. It's in the upper part, not way down by the Island in the Sky. Ten Mile is the drainage that all of Thompson Canyon clear to the top of the Book Mountains goes down through. He had a camp there that was called Dripping Spring. It had good, but little, water that dripped out of a seam in the rock. It was culinary water for our camp. The horses' water in the wash was a little bit alkaline. I worked off and on for Alton for several years, until finally I went to work for the Cunningham Cattle Company up in the Book Cliffs. Out at Ten Mile I built a branding corral out of cedar posts and cottonwood logs that were native there. We used a team of horses to haul the wood in. Alton had a bad heart, but he did a lot of riding. He hired people like me to help brand the calves. When we branded calves, before I built this corral, and this went on for several summers, we would just have to corner cattle out on a point between two washes where the banks were straight up. The firewood was greasewood to heat the branding irons. It isn't real good wood. I tied my horse over on one edge to keep the cattle out on this point, and watched the other edge. We had the fire in the middle, and Alton would rope a calf and drag it up. I'd throw it down and tie it, and he'd go get another one. I'd tie it down and then he got off and we'd go to branding and vaccinating and all that. Then we'd let them up and get two more. We'd rope and brand them here, yonder, and everywhere. Out on Spring Canyon Point there was a big sand rock dome with a split in the middle of it. There was a jump-off in it part way through. The cattle couldn't go through, and we would corral the cattle in there. It was a natural corral. We branded there

Richard Seely at the cowboy camp at Dripping Spring.

Windmill at Dubinky Well.

numerous times. But Alton's cattle roamed all over the area, clear up to Crescent Junction. I was working for him when we found out the service station was being built at Crescent Junction. This was close to 1946 or 1947, somewhere in there.

In the meantime, while working for him, I'd break whatever horses he had to get broke to ride. He even had a pack mule that someone had partially broken to ride, and I finished that mule out so you could ride him. We had no feed for our horses, only grain—oats. We grained them in the morning and at night, and hobbled them out at Ten Mile at Dripping Spring. I was lucky he had a little bell as we were always in the dark. Working for Alton you never got into camp in the daylight—never, not ever! We'd feed the horses with nose bags and tie them up so they couldn't get away with the nose bags on. Then we'd take the nose bags off, hobble them and turn them loose.

We hit camp in the dark. There was no electricity there, just a shack with a bed and a stove in it, a cupboard on one wall. Flour we kept in a tin so mice and rats couldn't get at it. It was a pretty good little cow camp though, right there handy and in a bunch of cottonwood trees. We had that good Dripping Spring water up there beneath a ledge.

One summer I went out to the Roost. Must have been in the late '40s. Arthur Ekker talked me into coming out to rough out a bunch of horses. He had four that had never been ridden, and maybe a fifth one he started once, but never got out of the corral on. So I rode out to the Roost on my horse. I stayed one night at the Chaffin place, the Moyniers owned it then. Harve Marsing was living there, and I stayed all night with them. June Marsing was his brother; he is the one June's Bottom is named after. My mother taught all those Marsings in school when they were up at Woodside before she was married. I made it to the Roost the next day on my horse. We turned my horse loose at the Roost, and I never used him until summer was almost over and I rode him back to Green River.

When Arthur asked me to come out to the Roost, it was early summer. He hadn't started branding, and he wanted me to rough out those horses, that is, break them to ride. We had made a verbal deal because I had worked for him before at Dubinky. He would help me get started with some of them. He'd lead me out on some of them, snub is the word. He did on some, and some he didn't—whatever we worked out. Then we started branding calves. Of the two oldest kids, Eddyjo was the oldest boy and he was over sixteen then, a big stout kid that knew how to throw down calves to hog tie them to brand. I would throw in with him and we would get busy and do the calf wrestling. We branded all over the Roost country. If I remember right, we started at home base at Crow Seep and branded them. Tissy, I think, was fifteen, did the roping. She'd rope them by the neck and dally them to the saddle horn. That is not being tied to the saddle horn. She'd gotten in trouble with a rope tied to the horn once, with a calf and with a horse stepping over the rope. I think Chad and Billy Moore were there when it happened. She had quite a wreck without being hurt. I think Arthur had to cut the rope. Anyway, no one got hurt, but that's the way we branded then. Then from the Roost house at Crow Seep we went over to Roost Spring area on Roost Flats and branded up those cattle. There is a big old picket-cedar corral upstream from the Roost Spring, somewhere in the vicinity of that chimney of old Cottrell's. We branded there more than once, for it was there that maybe the bulk of his cattle were running over on the Roost Flats area.

From there, it seems like, we moved. When I say moved, Hazel drove the chuck wagon—we called it that. It was a Diamond T pickup and we had all of our plunder and our bed and groceries on it, and we went to Hans Flat. That was before any of the ranger's stations or anything was there. We branded down there. First we did Twin Corrals, branded there, then Hans Flat. Then down into the head of the Spur Fork country. There is a corral down there we branded at. We went to Frenchie's Seep and we branded there, and around North Point and the Gordons and branded. I never did get to the Flint Trail, and never did go to Under the Ledge country because the Ekkers weren't running any stock under there. The Chaffins had, though.

Then when we got done in the Roost country, we dropped back and went over to North Springs and Andy Moore's. They had him lined up, and Andy's got one cabin there at his camp. It's on top of the bench where there is some horse feed, and cattle don't run that much up there. Andy had developed a spring down in a canyon at the head of it. Had it cemented in, and the cattle watered there. We branded his calves in his wire corral there, and Ekker's too. Ekker had quite a few cattle there at North Springs. They had drifted over there.

I'm riding these broncs during all this time and punching cows, and that's the way it should be. If you're breaking horses for a cow outfit, the horse should be rode behind cattle, gathering them up. If at first the horse is quite rank and is quite bucky or ornery with you, you might stick close to someone. I followed old Arthur quite a few miles gathering cattle and I'd be loose on a bronc horse, but he'd be there in sight of me if something bad happened. If you got to where you got one under your thumb, you could get out on your own and get away from everybody. That's when you're really getting him. A horse will always follow others and behave more or less, but when you get him on his own, he may look back at you and get startled and take off.

In between runs when we were branding and back at the Roost house the Ekkers were doing their thing, but I was always riding those colts. I'd ride one for an hour or two at least, and come back and get on another one and go. I rode up on Deadman Hill and all over the place to get them all rode. I wasn't going to break that last one, but after I had gotten through the first four, Arthur said, "Why don't you tie into that last one?" We called him Magee. "He ain't no rougher than anything." So I did, and had done five out there that summer while we were branding. I never did get bucked off, but I came awfully close. Right there at the Roost house corral I had a horse come uncorked with me. Hazel had been out getting her eggs from a few old hens. She was walking alongside this picket corral when that horse bunched up after making a bucking turn at the end of the corral, and he threw sand all over her. She thought I got bucked off, and ran back to the garage to get Arthur, but he came out and saw I was still in the saddle. "Don't look like he's off to me," he said.

When finished at North Spring we went on to Saucer Basin, closer to the San Rafael River going towards the old Chaffin Ranch. We branded there. On the flats there at Saucer Basin we had quite a group of cattle. No corrals, no fence nowhere. Maybe we had two hundred head gathered there, I'm not sure. Andy was getting older then and in sort of ill health from the rugged life he had lived, and he did most of the roping. I'd hobble my old bronc, and we worked together and got everything done in a couple of days. This was probably in '48. That's close to it. I finally wound up with Arthur, run in my horse and went back to Green River.

I went back to the Roost after that. Seemed like Arthur could always talk me into going back there when he really needed help. He sold his steers one spring to Budge Wilcox. Don Wilcox, Budge's oldest boy, had taken three broncs out there to help gather. He had been there a month when Arthur got me. They had them mostly gathered, but not all of them. They were in a canyon off of Blue John Canyon. Thinking back, it must have been a prong of Horseshoe Canyon. We gathered some more and camped down there. We had a bunch of his steers when we came out. Hazel met us with the truck, the chuck wagon deal. We came out past Blue John Spring. That first night there was a little rim of a canyon place that he had fenced off that we could hold them in. There was some water there. Early in the morning we headed for Saucer Basin. We stayed in yet another little blind canyon in that reef of rocks between Saucer Basin and the San Rafael. I think it was called Moonshine Canyon or something like that. He had a woven wire gate right in the mouth of that little blind canyon. A little canyon, wasn't a quarter of a mile long, but you could stick them in there, put the gate up and camp there. The next morning we'd cross the San Rafael and head towards Green River to the stockyards. Then Budge took over and took them up in the Book Mountains to graze.

Coyotes were not much of a problem. I've seen coyotes that lots of times would get after little baby calves. Once in a while they would kill them, but not like wolves. They were a problem. I was too young to be of the wolf days, but I'll tell you I've set and listened to my dad and other oldtimers tell wolf stories and, damn, its true—wolves are bad for cattle. Gee whiz, they'd hamstring a cow. My dad, when he was running Nutter's outfit there on Range Creek up where there was snow at higher elevation, they run across tracks of wolves chasing a steer and they had a lot of big steers, two and three years old up there. Dad and another hand hurried up and followed those tracks up in the snow, and the wolves heard them coming and left. But here was a steer down and couldn't get up. He was ham strung, and they had been eating on his hind quarters. He was still alive, so Dad pulled out his six shooter and shot him in the head and put the poor thing out of his misery. They were a problem, the wolves were. I've seen a few stump-tailed calves. Coyotes get to chasing little calves and bite their tails halfway off. Sometimes they get right up on their little old bodies and dang near get them. Maybe the calf would run to its mother and she'd scare the coyote off just in time. I was working for Gary Ekker when he was running some cattle up on the Price River up where it runs into the Green. We crossed Price River one day; we had to rope most of the calves and drag them through the water to get them over. The calves wouldn't take it; the cows would, and there was one little spotted calf, red and white calf and, by gosh, we went back up there two days later and the coyotes had gotten him. Just about had him eaten up. That was about twelve years ago. They could be a problem, you bet, but out where we were with our cattle with my dad, they were never a problem there. Maybe there was too much other stuff like rabbits and deer and everything.

As a kid I'd just sit in awe listening to old-timers. They came and stayed all night or a week at our ranch in Green River. My dad was fifty years old when I was born, so that put him way back there when the wolves were bad, and I listened to many a wolf story. I knew one guy and his kid who stayed at our place for several days and he, instead of being a good cowboy, was more of a hunter and a trapper, my dad told me later. This old guy told about catching a wolf. He could tell by his tracks the wolf had been caught before. He could tell by the front foot and he had a toe or two missing. He had gotten loose. He got to be a real killer, but that guy finally caught him, but it took two years to lure him into a trap. What got him was the use of a scent on an old cow carcass, and the wolf would make his rounds about once a month. There was an old pole corral there, and the trapper said he noticed the wolf would wallow in that old cow's hide and bones, and he'd put a little scent there every time the wolf came through. Finally, he set a trap, and he was very careful to get rid of any man scent on the trap. He smoked it with sage brush and handled it with gloves. Each trapper had his own tricks, and they were all secretive guys about what worked for them. He'd never tell you what the formula for his scent was. Well, his name was Roe Carroll. He finally set his trap and caught him. It was that old three-toed wolf, and he was responsible for killing many a cow whether they were big or little.

They are talking about turning wolves loose in Yellowstone National Park. If they haven't, they are about to do so. Part of the effort to reintroduce them in the park. Boy, they don't know what they are getting into. It took those old cowmen and sheepmen years to get rid of them. Albert May, who was mayor of Green River in his older days, for instance, was raised over on the north slope of the Book Mountains at Meadow Creek. Those are long winters over on the north slope. They run a lot of cattle, and the wolves were a horrible problem in those days. He said one time they took four teams and four wagons to Mack, Colorado, to pick up straps and cowbells to bell cattle to try to keep the wolves from killing them. Took the gear back, a three-day trip, to Meadow Creek, gathered cattle and got them through a chute where they put the bells on them. I asked old Albert how it worked. "Pretty good for a while," Albert said, "but the wolves got used to the tinkle, tinkle and they went back to killing." He'd laugh and he said, "About all the good it finally turned out was the bulls could sure tell where the cows were in that rough country." Wolves were a bad problem whereas coyotes weren't. Mountain lions were never much of a problem with cattle, but more with colts. If you were running mares and colts on the mountain, you better look out because lions like horse meat. They would be reluctant to attack a grown horse, but they were damn sure rough on colts. They had to be in rough country where a lion could get up where they could pounce on them and get them quick.

I got married in 1950 and quit working for Halversons, and I went to work for the Cunningham Cattle Company. Bill Cunningham and his folks (this was before Bill was married), they were running cattle up in the Books—the Book Mountains, the Book Cliffs. They summered on the mountain and wintered on the desert between Grand Junction and Green River. They had an allotment for grazing on that land. I worked for them for several years, then I quit and leased a bunch of cows out on the San Rafael Desert from Mrs. Lilly Denny. I stayed with her cattle until I saw that was a losing proposition. She had these cows out at Garvin's Wells, out near Temple Mountain. Chad Moore knows all about her and that country. I stayed there several months until I saw I couldn't make it with her or the cattle, so I went to work mining uranium at Temple.

Cunningham paid better than anybody, really. He had a good outfit and you ate better, you had good horses, good corrals and fences, and everything when you summered on the mountain with Cunninghams. The elevation on the mountain was between seventy-five hundred and ninety-five hundred feet. But if you are a cowboy, when you get a family— and I married a family, my wife had some girls—by gosh you have to get more money coming in. I stayed punching cows for two or three years after I was married, and finally gave it up. Went to work in the mines and got three times the money I did punching cows. But maybe that's one reason why my lungs are the way they are now, probably from that unmerciful air in those mines.

I then became one of the better weekend cowboys. Cunningham could get me most any time. After the mines, I went to work for the Utah State Department of Transportation patching roads on the maintenance crew. I stayed so long they finally made me a foreman the last five years, and I retired as a foreman.

I spent a lot of my vacations at Cunningham's helping to gather cattle off the mountain and bring them down to the desert. I'd take two of my own horses that needed riding and I always had a green horse or two. I'd be up there on the mountain in the fall two whole weeks and three weekends. That mountain was rough country, and you had to know what you were doing. It takes quite a while to learn about that kind of country. If you missed cattle, if they are left there in the fall, when you are riding up there the next year you will find their carcasses for they will snow in and die on you.

Maybe the last act we would do was to fly over the area. Bill Cunningham couldn't stand to fly in those little planes where you dive-bombed around. We had one of the better pilots in the whole country, Jim Hurst of Green River. I flew several falls with him hunting Cunningham cattle in the slowest airplane he had. You want a slow one so you can see good. It didn't have a lot of power to get elevation quick. You have to watch, you fly those side canyons. The ridges are high, and if you fly up one of those canyons in those soupless airplanes, you can get trapped. You can't make the circle to get out. Hurst was a wonderful pilot, he knows all that stuff. He'd fly up the main canyon gaining eleva-tion all the way and get out on top, then you'd circle around and dive-bomb, literally dive-bomb, right down into the head of the side canyon and out. If there was snow, you could pick up a cow track quick, or you'd see the critter. There are lots of trees on the Book Mountains and we'd find cattle dang near every fall. Bill had a corral and a drift fence right across the mouth of the main canyon right above his ranch. We branded there every spring.

You counted all the cows as you took them up on the mountain in the spring. Then you counted them when you drove them down in the fall and you would know if you were out some. Once in a while you were short. That was rough country up on the mountain, and we had many an adventure getting them back. After you flew, then you'd get back there on horseback as quick as you could. Sometimes you couldn't get back quick, and they'd move on you, but you'd find them somewhere.

Now they have sold out to the Nature Conservancy. Between the BLM and Fish and Game and the nature boys it was still run as a cattle operation. Besides, the elk situation on top of the Book Mountains got awful in the latter years when they were running cattle. There might have been a thousand elk summered in his summer country, and they will eat dang near as much as a cow. You couldn't save a canyon to come out on in the fall. When they sold out, his boy Greg moved on and has a ranch up north of Kaycee, Wyoming, and south of Buffalo over towards the Big Horns to the west. I've been up there several times, and when Bill comes through here he stays with me.

Now with Halversons out in the Ten Mile country, Alton had died from cancer, and Harold, his younger brother, took the cattle. He and his wife, Cleo, ran them several years. Then they sold to Gene Dunham. He has the Ruby Ranch down the east side of the Green twenty miles below Green River at the mouth of the San Rafael River. Gene bought out the Halversons and wanted me to come out and work for him, but I didn't. I knew Gene good, and used to shoe his horses. In fact, I was the horse shoer in Green River for years.

Went down to Sam's Mesa a couple of times. There was a narrow spot at the neck where Arthur Ekker had a brush fence of cedar across the neck. It was pretty far from the Roost Ranch, but there was a good spring down there. You had to know where it was under a ledge. Pretty fair water as I remember it. We did not camp there, but could have if needed. We had cattle down there. Another time Arthur had Ruben Hunt, friend of mine, same age as me, working there one winter and in the spring he conned me into coming out for a little vacation, so I went out there. This was before I went out there to break those horses. One reason Arthur wanted me out there is he had about a dozen head of big old yearling bulls that needed to be branded and worked over. They were running right around the Roost ranch house. We gathered them and dehorned them and made steers out of them. It took a day or two to do that. They were here and there and it took some time to gather them. After that we packed up our beds, grub and everything, and went down a trail from the Roost ranch house and got down in the bed of the Dirty Devil River.

We had to shoot out a rock that had slid in the trail. We went off a slickrock at Larry's Canyon, downstream from No Man's Canyon. No Man's Canyon is downstream from the Roost Canyon, so that's where you are. All of those canyons run into the Dirty Devil River. Arthur put his bulls down there, but this rock had slid in the trail. Arthur knew about it and sent us down there with a single jack hammer—that is a light sledge hammer you can handle with one hand—a short drill, and a stick or two of dynamite. Most of the cowboys, especially in rock country, could shoot dynamite. So we drilled a hole about eighteen inches deep or so, set in a stick of dynamite. This was a big sand rock, no way could we get around it. The way we got the sand out of the hole so we could place the dynamite in was to crush the end of a stick of cedar. We'd wet it with canteen water and stick it down the hole where its wet end would take up the sand. We kept this up until we had the hole cleaned out. Then stick the dynamite and fuse in and let her go.

I never got down into Happy Canyon, though I looked off at it a few times. We camped on the bottoms of the Dirty Devil River, good bottoms with good grass. Those bottoms were never grazed much. He put his bulls in there because they are so much stouter than a cow and that is an awfully quicksandy river bed, the most quicksandiest place I've ever been in. You could stand out there in places and jump up and down and see the ground shake for thirty feet around you. It was awesome. Old Arthur Ekker was used to that; before we'd cross in a certain place, for instance, that was damn boggy, he'd get off his horse and cross afoot. We'd traipse across on foot leading our horses. If it had water, a scum of water on top of that quicksand which is real wet, he said, "When you get that scum of water standing on top like that, you can probably go right across on a horse. It won't sink you. If you don't do that you might sink, then you flounder and then you're bogged down."

In the late '40s we went up No Man's Canyon and on the left going up was a cliff dwelling up in an alcove on a ledge. It was hard to get up in there. Arthur doubted if anyone had ever gotten up there. I was the littlest of the three, so they got a cottonwood pole and I had climbed up as high as I could on another cottonwood post that was leaning up against the rock wall. They got this pole they had found, it was longer than a fence post, and those idiots pushed it up right into my hind end and shoved me up to where I could get a hold of the rock ledge and get up on it. Then I turned around and lowered the pole to where they could reach it and hauled them up to where they could make it on to the ledge. We got up there looking around. You could see where the old fires had been and everything. We thought maybe we were the first white men to ever get up there. Then we saw them: everybody's name in Hanksville was chiseled on the rock wall of that alcove. They all had been up in there.

On another trip we got through branding calves for Ekker and Andy Moore out at Saucer Basin. We went back to North Springs and gathered the country. We brought back all of Ekker's cows that we could get, and herded them back to North Springs and held them in that canyon that night. The next morning we gathered the Moores' and all of Arthur's cattle that we could. We pulled them together and started for the Roost with them. We turned them over to Tiss Ekker. She took them over; we had maybe eighty head of cows that were over on Moores' and she was taking them back to the Roost Flats. We went part way with her, and we had packed up one pack for us (us was Eddyjo, Arthur, and I). We cut through and went down into Horseshoe Canyon where the old road went when they drilled that oil well at the Tidwell Ranch. We went down that road and up Horseshoe Canyon past those Indian pictograph panels, and on up out into the Spur Fork country, and finally got back to the Roost.

Arthur showed me a place where the wildlife people had turned some buffalo loose there about in 1941. It was before I went to the army. Arthur showed me a fence up in Horseshoe Canyon, and there was a gate right in the trail. There is no road there, just a trail. He showed me where two cow buffalo had jumped that from below going uphill and had cleared that brush fence. A cow couldn't have done it in a hundred years, but those buffalo cows did.

I'll never forget we were branding calves and I was breaking horses down in that Spur Fork country, or maybe it was Horseshoe Canyon, and there was a little picket corral down there that we used. It was near a big natural tank of water. The drainage in the wash went over a ledge that was maybe twelve to fifteen feet high and formed a huge pool of water. The cows watered out of that. Two bulls got to fighting during our gathering of the cows, just above the ledge. One bull pushed the other right over the rim into the pond of water. I mean, he went clear over. I was right there, so was Eddyjo and Tiss and Arthur. What a splash! That big old range bull went clear out of sight. He came up snorting, I'll tell you. He started leaving the country. He'd had it, and we had to head him off and get him settled down. That other bull had him whipped good, but we held him there and he turned out all right.

One thing I want to tell you about was the fun we had deer hunting. That is, hunting deer "Chaffin style" down on the Green River. In the fall of 1940 Leland Tidwell invited me to go deer hunting with him. We were to go down off of The Spur (Tidwell Ranch) to Woodruff Bottom (later called Tidwell Bottom) on the Green River. He had some cattle down there he would check, and also hunt deer. So I bought a deer license, but something turned up and he had to go to Salt Lake City on business. He felt bad because of my license, but just before he left he ran across Ned Chaffin. Ned had come out to this part of the country to hunt deer and had his father-in-law and a friend with him. They lived in Bakersfield, California. Ned was raised at Green River and down in the Under the Ledge country where they ran cattle, but had recently moved to California. His older brother Faun was running the cattle. Ned had to come up to Green River town to register for the one year military draft. Remember, this is October 1940. Leland and Ned looked me up, and Ned said to come on and hunt with them. He drove me down to the Chaffin Ranch on the San Rafael River, and got me a horse of theirs and I rode it to Tidwell's ranch on The Spur. Next morning Ned and I saddled up and he had one or two pack horses, and headed across The Spur country, and went down the Devil's Slide Trail and to Anderson Bottom on the Green River. Faun and the others got in that evening from Under the Ledge country. Faun had Herb Weber working for him.

Next day we went by horseback down to Valentine Bottom. We found a big buck up in a short little blind canyon, and when he ran for the river, someone shot him through the middle, but he could still run good. Some trees were there between us and him, so Herb ran to his horse, jerked his rein free of a bush, jumped on, took after the deer while making a loop, and roped him just, and I mean just, in time before he hit the willows or tamaracks at the river. You know, a deer will take to the river easy. Their hair is hollow, therefore they swim high and easy. We dressed him out and went on down to Turk Bottom and then back to camp. No deer there at Turk.

Next morning we went back to Valentine and swam the horses over the river. That put us on the east side. There was a little blind canyon there called Deer Canyon. Faun said it generally had a few deer in it. It was less than a mile long. Ned had a movie camera and took pictures of what he could get. I was the one to run the deer out to them. Faun got first throw and Herb second if Faun missed. I would bring one deer at a time, if I could. More then one would foul it up. There were maybe four deer in there. When I got one coming out, I would make noise enough so deer would not turn back and also the noise alerted the roper and camera man.

The roper would be on the right side (going up the canyon). This is near the mouth of the canyon. When the deer saw him, it would run over on the opposite side on a little rocky hillside, maybe fifteen yards wide. Then the ledge would be straight up, one hundred to two hundred feet. Then it would come to some big rocks that would force it to get back in the wash bed where a horse had a good chance. In the meantime, when the deer went by the roper, he started his horse and when the deer hit the wash bed, the roper was right behind it and on the run—a real natural place to catch one with a horse. I think Faun caught two and, if I remember right, two deer came one time that I couldn't separate, and a big doe ran on through, Herb gaining, but she hit the brush before he could throw. When Faun caught them, after three big jumps were out of them, Herb would heel them and that was it. Oh, what a day! Talk about excitement!

I've hunted deer many times later and a lot of those times I've clean forgotten, but I've never forgot the time when the deer were roped Chaffin style across from Valentine, way down on the Green River.

Now, for the rest of the hunt. Ned and his party had to go home. They rode up to Tidwell's to pick up the truck. He took my deer in and turned it over to my folks. There was a little surveyor crew there at

Tidwell's, and one of them came down to hunt. In the meantime, Faun and I went up Millard Canyon to chase burros. We got after a bunch, but they made their escape down through some awful rocks.

Next day we go down and swim over, but no deer in Deer Canyon. So we rode on down a way and ran into the Howlands from Green River. They had boats. After no success on deer, we headed back up to cross the river. We had taken an extra saddle horse over to bring deer back, so Faun talked Sammy Howland into having his dad pick him up at our camp with a boat in the morning, so Sam came with us. When we got to the river it was dark—I mean, pitch dark. So dark you couldn't have stuck your hand in your pocket—couldn't have found it. There was a willow jungle to go through before the river, willows thick as they could grow, and a lot of big ones. We went in single file, first Faun, then Herb, then Sam, then me, and then the surveyor. Sam started lagging behind Herb. Then I got to egging him on. "For heck's sake, keep up. If we lose sight of them, we won't get out of this mess till daylight." We finally busted out of them and plunged in the water and across to camp. Another good big day.

Them Chaffin brothers and Herb Weber were all "sons of the soil." All born and raised in that desert, rimrock canyon country. They were, above all, cowboys—cowmen who knew how to run cattle successfully and to survive in one of the ruggedest out-of-the-way places I know of. And when a chance or a break from cow work came, they knew how to have fun.

I retired from the state roads and I worked three winters after that at what we call Willow Bend, the farthest farm up the west side of the Green River from the town of Green River. I worked for Gary Ekker up there. He has a big farm put together there. The first winter there, after retiring, we had over eleven hundred head of Cunningham cattle there. We had all of his weaners and a bunch of his old cows and all of his bulls to winter there. We had the calves in the feedlot and ran the cows all over the country and up the river. I'd work for Gary Ekker off and on, riding and roughing out some horses, mainly fall, winter, and spring up on the Price River.

I had only one child, Jake. My wife had several girls. She died four years ago and is buried back at Green River.

In Wyoming, I think the future of ranching is solid. This is grass country, the old buffalo country where there were lots of buffalo is a darn good place for cattle. It rains enough here so the grass is good. I bought 240 acres of grass, that's just a little old dab out here; I'm maybe the smallest cowman in Wyoming numerically, physically, and financially. Right now I could dang near double my money on it. I've owned it nearly four years and the price of cattle has come up. There are lots of cattle here in Torrington. They sell them here by the thousands in the fall and in the spring. The trouble down there in Utah is that it seems like it's been dry there forever.

I'm seventy-six years old now, but I'll never forget that trip. I'm very thankful for Ned and Faun to have me down there. Herb died several years ago. Faun just died last year at ninety-four. Ned's still going strong out there in Bakersfield at eighty-two.

Now up here in Torrington I take care of my acreage and stock. My son, Jake, is a rodeo roper. He's won lots of awards and used to travel quite a bit on the rodeo circuit. He is an all-around good hand and I'm glad to be with him. I do my daily chores and keep up with things. I was glad Ned held that cowboy caucus and I know he is thinking about another one in the spring of '95. I'll be sure to make it. Gives me a chance to tell some of those "Two Black Crow Stories." One of them . . .

There were two black crows. One of them says, "We bought pigs in the fall for four dollars. Fed them all winter and sold them in the spring for four dollars."

The other black crow says, "Well, you can't make no money doing that."

The first crow says, "So we found out."

Another . . .

One crow says, "We had black horses and we had white horses. And we found out the white horses ate more hay than the black horses."

The other crow asked, "How come?"

The first crow says, "The only thing we could figure out, we had more white horses than black horses."

Now you can turn off that infernal tape recorder!

4

Harry W. (Bill) Racy

Bill Racy, unlike the others interviewed in this book, was an import to Utah.
He was an Indiana boy who learned to be a ranch hand in those hard, hard
years just prior to World War II. In 1937 sixteen-year-old Bill hopped off a
freight train in Green River. He was cold, hungry, and flat broke and even-
tually found work as a ranch hand on the Chaffin Ranch. He worked on var-
ious ranches in southeastern Utah's canyon country, but also found his way
through most of the other western states.

He is one who encouraged Ned to organize the cowboy caucus because he
hadn't seen Ned for fifty-six years. Bill has written autobiographical sketches
of his early life. Portions of those sketches have been incorporated and
expanded upon with this interview.

May 30, 1994
Sun City, Arizona

I was born in Oaktown, Knox County, Indiana, on May 31, 1921. My
parents separated when I was three. I went with my father until I was
eight years old. After that things just went to pot, and I never lived with
my parents again. I just spent time with this aunt or that uncle or neighbor or what have you. I don't remember my father too much; I knew
him, but I don't really know him, and the same way with my mother.

Well, after years of that, until I was fourteen, I did everything you
could think of, you know, like working on the farms, killing rabbits,
picking blackberries, anything I could do to make a quarter. I had a
paper route once, but came the winter of 1935 and '36 and I had hit rock

bottom. I didn't have any place to stay, and I didn't have too much to eat, so the principal of the high school there got me in a left-handed manner and turned me over to the authorities, and they put me in an orphans' home. I didn't like that. You know, I had two mothers, two fathers, three brothers, two sisters and me there in the orphans' home. I didn't like that, so I ran off. Well, the first time I run off they caught me in Terre Haute, Indiana, and a woman that was in charge of the juvenile jail there, she and a she-gorilla would have been twins. I never met such a hateful woman in all my life. The State of Indiana must have dug three feet below the bottom of the barrel to dig up something like that.

Well, they got me back to the orphans' home, and I went willingly. The mother at the orphans' home was a real fine lady. She said, "Why did you come back?" I told her it was twenty below zero out there, I don't have any money, and I don't even have enough clothes to keep me warm. I said I'm going to go again, and she said, "Well, if you do, go alone." I said all right, but I stayed there another six weeks or so and along about in March I left again. But she made it possible that I had some good warm clothes, a good pair of shoes, a good warm hat, and everything. Well, I'm fourteen years old, and I'm hiding out now from the orphans' home and the law because school was not out. As a kid I hid out here, there, and yonder with this farmer and that farmer, working for my room and board, doing their dirty work. Poor kid, they would say, we have nothing else for you to do today, so you have to find yourself somewhere else to stay. Well, I got to this other place to stay down on a farm in Carlisle, Indiana. That guy said, "Well, it will be just room and board and I'll send you to school, buy your clothes and everything, but you have to go to church." Well, I didn't object to that, and another thing, he didn't hire me just to do his dirty work. You know, I was just there. And I worked for his brother-in-law for several days and made a few extra dollars.

Came Mother's Day in May I said, "I'm not going to church with you today. I'm going down to my mother's for Mother's Day."

He said, "No, you come on to church. After church I'll drive you down to your mother's." I said all right. If I had gone out to the highway, I could have been to my mother's in an hour. By going to church with them, going across the country eight or ten miles, I was about seven miles from my mother. His brother came up to him and said, "After church we are going over to Mom's for dinner. Come over there."

And I said, "He is taking me to my mother's right after church. It will be a few minutes."

He looked around to his brother and said, "What do you mean you're taking him to his mother's? You don't owe that kid nothing. If he wants to go to his mother's, let him walk." And that's exactly what the man did, and I walked the seven miles. Well, I only got to spend a couple of hours with my mother, and when I got back to the farm that night I packed my suitcase, and in the morning I said good-bye, and here I am.

I had three brothers and two sisters. One brother and one sister are dead now.

For the next eighteen months I just wandered all over the West. From Indiana I went to South Dakota and from there up into Washington, Oregon, and California, and then back to Arizona. Finally I went back to Oregon just to look for a job on cattle and sheep ranches. It was still 1936 and I was fifteen years old, but I was getting nowhere fast and I didn't know what to do about it. Of course in that day you didn't get ahead very fast working for a dollar a day. Anyway, one day I gathered up what little bit I had and headed out. I got on a freight train and after a few days I was crossing Utah on the Denver & Rio Grande Western Railroad. I wasn't going anywhere in particular, just looking for a job. In October of 1937, I was sixteen years old, I went through Green River. I got off the freight train and went downtown to see if I could find work. Now it was getting cold and I was hungry, scared, and broke.

I went down to the Silver Dollar pool hall where I bumped into Daff Thompson. Daff and his dad, Henry [Bishop Thompson], offered me a job for my room and board, spending money, and tobacco. I didn't have anything, so I thought that was better than nothing, at least I could have something to eat. So I went to work for them. They ran a few cows out in the San Rafael River Valley.

When I speak of the San Rafael Valley, it runs along the river. Not very long to start with. They just had a cow camp out on the San Rafael River. The camp was located on the north side of the river and the west side of Highway 24 in that corner. Of course the highway was not there in 1937. It was a dirt road that ran west of this camp over through the Hatt Ranch. I worked for the Thompsons for my room and board and spending money. My work was well cut out for me. I rode the San Rafael, up and down, every day for the next five months digging cattle out of the bog.

The cattle wouldn't drink the muddy water in the river if there were any clear pools around. While drinking from the clear pools, they would sink in the quicksand and bog down. In the morning when the river would rise the critter would drown or would be bogged down to

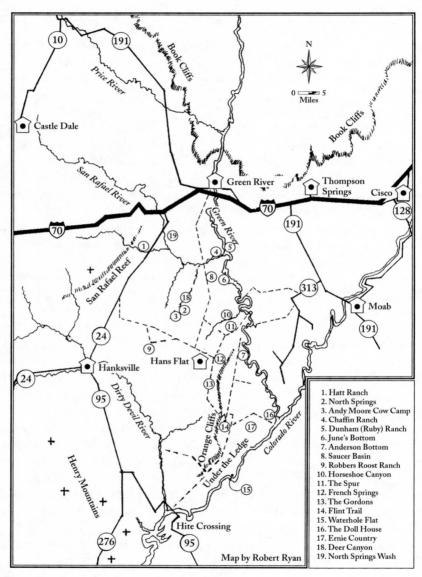

Bill Racy's Canyonlands.

1. Hatt Ranch
2. North Springs
3. Andy Moore Cow Camp
4. Chaffin Ranch
5. Dunham (Ruby) Ranch
6. June's Bottom
7. Anderson Bottom
8. Saucer Basin
9. Robbers Roost Ranch
10. Horseshoe Canyon
11. The Spur
12. French Springs
13. The Gordons
14. Flint Trail
15. Waterhole Flat
16. The Doll House
17. Ernie Country
18. Deer Canyon
19. North Springs Wash

Map by Robert Ryan

one-half her body in the quicksand, with her head and neck stretched straight out and her nostrils only an inch or so out of the sand. So the river didn't have to rise much to drown the animal.

Digging a cow out of the bog was no simple chore. You would dig all four legs out one at a time, fill the hole full of weeds and sticks until all four legs were out. Then you would stretch the two front legs up along her neck and head, put your rope around her head and two front legs and pull her out. This was done to keep from choking the cow, and to pull the cow out to solid ground with your saddle horse. This was quite a job for a horse to pull the cow, just dead weight, out of that sand. Once my cinch broke and me and my saddle landed about ten feet behind the horse. Now I know what a rock feels like when it leaves a slingshot.

Well, while you were digging her out of the quicksand, sand would get loose all around for quite a ways and she'd get back into loose sand and she'd just sink in pretty fast, so you'd have to dig her out again. In other cases, they would turn and fight you. If she had horns she would try to horn you, but in most cases they were too weak to even get up. They would lie on solid ground until they could muster up enough strength to get on their feet by themselves.

I'm not the only one riding the river. There were Frank Hatt and the four Gillis brothers from the Gillis Ranch, which was located down-river. Also, Andy Moore. Andy's ranch was located next to the Gillis Ranch. I would only ride down the river to the Gillis and Moore Ranches about two miles from camp, and up the river to the end of where the cattle grazed.

One day shortly after I went to work for the Thompsons, Daff and I went to town for supplies. We returned to the cow camp the next after-noon. We left town the next day about two P.M. We stopped at Howard Anderson's Texaco service station to gas up. Daff had an old Model T Ford; I'll try to describe it. It had no lights, no bumper, no fenders, no hood. Just a radiator with two brace rods, no windshields, no doors, no running boards, wood boxes for seats, and a crude wooden flat bed, but it would run. That was the only car Daff had.

While we were gassing up, a 1937 Buick from Ohio pulled in for gas. A man, his wife, and two teenage girls all got out of their car and were just looking at that old Model T. We were ready to go. I guess we were two of the most crude men they ever saw, half-wore-out faded Levi pants and jackets and rough out-boots. A big chunk was torn out of the brim of my hat. As we climbed up on our box seats, Daff let out a yell, "Ahhh Hooo! Two more payments and she'll be all mine," and we headed for the cow camp. I looked back as we pulled away; those people had not moved. They looked as if they were frozen. I'll bet they never forgot that incident.

On the way to camp Daff sang his song, and it went like this: "I bought myself a Ford machine, filled it up with gasoline, cranked it and the darn thing got away. It didn't wait till I got in, now I own a pile of tin. But I walk right up each month and pay and pay. So much down, so much every certain day. It didn't wait till I got in, now I own a pile of tin. But I walk right up each month and pay." Those of you who might read this story in the future, and you remember the Model T Ford, this song says it all.

In November my two brothers came through Green River. They were making a tour through the West. Don got sick in California, and they went broke paying doctor bills. They lived on what Bob could make boxing. They were on their way home to Indiana, but they were broke and so was I. Don signed his car over to me, a 1932 black Chevrolet coupe, all decked out in chrome with spare tires on the front fenders. It was quite a car in its day, but to me, I had a little white elephant. I never put a gallon of gas in that car for the next four months. Don sold the horns off the car to Howard Anderson at the Texaco station for ten dollars.

Don and Bob left Green River on the same D&RGRR freight train that I arrived on, on their way home to Indiana. To me this was a sad incident when my brothers came out to the cow camp and in just an hour or so were gone. Bishop and Daff Thompson were pretty well shook up. They thought I was going to quit. All three of us were broke. When they figured out I was staying, they gave a sigh of relief. "Well, we've still got our boy to care for our cattle, horses, and camp."

Dafton was the assessor for the county that year. The sheep were assessed for their numbers, and the sheepman had to pay so much to run his sheep on open range. It cost a cowman five cents a head a month to run cattle on open range, and calves up to a yearling could run free. It was the Taylor Grazing Act. We were going to the desert with pack horses to assess the sheep, but now Daff said, "Let's go in the car."

I said, "Okay." We would just be on desert roads, and it was bitter cold. So we left in a week or so to assess the sheep. We drove to Andy Moore's camp at North Springs, and camped in his cabin that night. I backed the car up a hill as far as it would go so as to start it the next morning by rolling down the hill. It didn't start. I got three burlap bags, rolled them up and tied them with haywire and set them on fire. I put it under the motor and under the transmission and under the differential, and warmed up the oil. In a few minutes the car started on its own. We went out on the desert, found the sheep where Daff assessed them, and drove back to Green River.

I could read Dafton's mind now. He's got him a car to run around in, and Bill can't do anything about it because Bill was broke. We used my car to go back and forth the rest of the winter, which was okay. I got to go each time because it was my car. Later on, I believe it was January now, Dafton's wife had a new baby. Daff asked me if he could take my car to Price to take his wife to the doctor for her six-week check-up. Under the circumstances, I said okay. He went to Price and wrecked the right front wheel of my car. He put a used tire on it, but the front end was out of line. Not bad, but in the summer the front tires wore slick. After that I made up my mind that Daff Thompson was not going to drive my car again. He didn't, but things became worse for me in camp. One day I was talking to Frank Hatt. I told Frank about the whole deal and that I would like to quit the Thompsons and what would I do with my car? Frank owned several acres, and he said I'm sure I can find a spot big enough for you to park your car on and come back after it. So I got a complete new lease on life.

I stayed on at that cow camp until March, this was in 1938. I had worked for five months for the Thompsons and had been paid twenty-five cents spending money, one pair of Levis size 36/31. I wore 31/31. The Levis were worth about one dollar. That and the twenty-five cents spending money and about four dollars worth of Bull Durham was all I got for five months' work. I also accumulated maybe seven gallons of gas in my car, enough to drive to the Chaffin Ranch and back to town. During my stay with the Thompsons I made many good friends, such as Andy Moore, Orson and Marion Adams, the four Gillis brothers, mainly Bob Gillis. Bob and I rode the river together many times and so did Andy Moore and I. I met Horace Ekker, Art Ekker, Frank (Slim) Baker, and Frank and Vail Hatt, Hap Wilcox, and of course Faun Chaffin. That winter a bunch of horse chasers came to Green River. J. E. Wetherington and Ralph Wetherington were brothers, and David Lee and Buck Cavender were there too. These men dealt in wild horses, good or bad, and they broke a lot of horses for ranchers around the country. Their bad horses they probably sold to a rodeo for bucking stock. J. E. was one of the finest horsemen that I knew.

In March I went to work for Faun Chaffin. The Chaffin Ranch lay at the mouth of the San Rafael River where it runs into the Green about twenty-three miles south of the town of Green River. There were Faun and his wife Violet and their two daughters, Claire and Wiladeane. Wiladeane was about nine and Claire was about four. They had a hired hand, Shorty. I don't remember his last name. There was peace and quiet, love and laughter on the ranch and plenty of work too. In a sense it was one big family. Violet raised a flock of turkeys and the two girls. She worked as hard as we did, just a different type of work. She canned and washed dishes for a total of six of us. I helped Violet anytime I could in the evenings or when the work was slack. I did anything she asked. One time she made some cheese. It didn't gather the way it was supposed to and she was going to throw it out. Just then I came by and I said, "Well, what have you got there?"

"Oh, some bad cheese. It isn't any good." she said.

Well, I sensed something was wrong and I said, "Let me see." The bowl was full of marbles. I ate one of them and it was the best tasting cheese I can remember. I didn't let her throw it away. In time I ate every bit of it.

One day Shorty was doing something that Violet didn't like, and she told him to quit. He stuck his face in hers and said, "What will you do if I don't?"

She said, "I'll slap your damn face." She didn't do it. Shorty was a total illiterate. Violet hated that man with a purple passion. Shorty couldn't do anything. On one occasion Faun went to town and told me to start mowing hay. He told Shorty to ride out to the old Dry Lake bed area to move some cows out. He saddled up old Slats and led him across the ditch to where Violet was standing. He tried to act like Gene Autry. He crawled on Slats like a big boy scout, and Slats bucked him off. On the way to the ground he was hollering, "Help, Violet." So I got Slats and I went and moved the cows, and came back and started mowing hay. Shorty nursed his sore spots, due to the sudden stop when he hit the ground, for the next few days. He couldn't handle a team of horses, he couldn't handle a saddle horse, you couldn't trust him and you couldn't depend on him. To this day I don't know what the bond was between Shorty and Faun, yet Faun kept him on to the bitter end.

Faun ran about four hundred head of cattle, maybe some fifty head on or near the ranch. The rest he ran some sixty miles from the ranch in the country known as down Under the Ledge. The country is now known as Canyonlands National Park. No cattle run there any more. I made three trips Under the Ledge with Faun during that summer of 1938. We would be gone approximately three weeks each trip. The trips were made by pack horse and saddle horses. We would tend the cattle and do the work that had to be done—move them to better grass, clean up water holes, repair corrals, take care of calves, brand, dehorn, etc. Now, each trip was just about the same, and yet each trip was different. The ledge country appears the same as in the Grand Canyon down from the confluence of the Colorado and Green Rivers some two hundred miles. The country was absolutely beautiful, more so than any artist could ever paint. It was so quiet and peaceful down there—just looking around everywhere. Nice fat cattle and horses grazing on the grassland under approximately twelve hundred feet of ledge. You couldn't stop looking at the beautiful rock formations. I am still amazed at what God can do.

I would go to town while working for Faun as I had some money. I would always buddy up with Alvin Drake. I met Alvin in 1937, and we became good friends. We'd chum around Green River any time I got to town and we got together. One time Alvin and I were going to Price. All of a sudden we heard a loud clatter. I thought the motor was going to fly out of my little car. We stopped to see what had happened. The car had a four-bladed fan. One blade broke off the fan and went through the side of the hood leaving a gash about six inches long. "What are we going to do now?" I cut the fan belt, and we went back to Green River. I drove up to the mechanic and told the man what happened. He just broke the blade off the opposite side and put on a new fan belt, and all was well. Well, Alvin and I felt a little silly—we didn't know what to do.

One trip I made to town that summer, of course Alvin and I were together again that weekend, J. E. Wetherington, Ralph Wetherington, David Lee, and Buck Cavender were in town. These four men were doing whatever they could do to earn a few dollars until winter. They said they were going to catch some wild horses on the San Rafael Desert as there were plenty of wild horses on the desert then. Alvin and I were talking about those guys catching wild horses. Just in conversation Alvin said, "You know wild horses chasers eat beef." I said, "Yeah, I suppose so."

Of all the wild horses on the desert, I never did catch one. I've chased them just to see them run. These ranchers weren't about to let you burn up their saddle horses just to catch a wild horse that was only good for dog food. As of now, I've only known of three wild horses that turned out to be good horses. Of course, there's probably more, because I know we read about the wild horses. If you can catch a suckling colt, it probably will be a fair horse, but if it runs with the wild bunch until it is

Bill Racy on Slats. The riderless horse is Captain Kidd. Photo courtesy of Bill Racy.

Bill Racy on Captain Kidd and Ned Chaffin on Cheyenne, 1938. Photo courtesy of Bill Racy.

Bill Racy on Slats with pack horses, 1939. The Sentinels are in the background. The area is identified as the Doll House on modern maps. Photo courtesy of Bill Racy.

a yearling, then chances are it will never get over that wild life. When you turn it loose, you have to run it down again.

The summer is about over, and I'll have to find me a job elsewhere. It is time to harvest the cantaloupes in Green River. Some of the world's best cantaloupes are grown in Green River, Utah. So I went to town and got a job picking cantaloupes. I bought some clothes for the winter, and bought my first pair of cowboy boots, and did a lot of partying. Of course, me and Alvin Drake at this time were together and worked together. The town was overrun with people who were in town to harvest the cantaloupes and watermelons. So it was just one big ball. After the cantaloupe season was over, I went to work for Alton Halverson for about six weeks. We gathered his cattle up and got them ready for winter. I was out of a job again.

One day I bumped into Andy Moore and asked him about a job. He had two men, Orson and Marion Adams, working for him and he didn't need a third man. He said I could work for him for my room and board and spending money, and that's all that was available. So Andy bought me tobacco and clothes, and about ten dollars a month spending money.

It's about the first of November, 1938. Sometime earlier Andy had taken about fifty head of calves to a bottom on the Green River just below the Chaffin Ranch. I think they called it June's Bottom. There was a lot of grass in there, and he just put the calves in there to eat the grass off. There was plenty of water, and right by the river. The calves couldn't get out once the gate was closed.

Orson Adams and I made a pack trip on the San Rafael Desert where Andy ran his cattle. We were gone about two weeks. We rode to Hanksville and rode out the Dirty Devil River. We pushed any cattle we found back to the desert. We'd try to move any cattle we found back to better water, and drive the poorer cows toward the ranch. We'd camp wherever night caught us. We packed plenty of oats for the horses, and plenty of food and water for our camp use. Often we would melt snow for camp use.

In December we did a lot of work around the ranch. Everyone was cheering up because Christmas would soon be here. We went to town a couple of times. We were in town on Christmas Eve. Alvin and I got together again, and J. E. Wetherington was in town. That night we went back to the ranch.

On Christmas morning, Andy said for me and Orson to go down to June's Bottom and bring that bunch of calves to the ranch. It only would be a couple of days, so we packed light. Christmas Day was a nice warm day. We were working in our shirt sleeves. We left the ranch about ten A.M. for a five-hour ride on horses. Like dumb fools, we left without our winter coats. We had long-handled underwear on, and our Levi pants and a shirt, and our chaps and a Levi denim jacket. We arrived at June's Bottom about two P.M. I got down off my horse and opened the gate, and Orson went through the gate with the pack horses. As I was closing the gate, Orson said, "Bill, there's riders in this bottom." We looked around—four sets of tracks going in, and none coming out. Well, they were in there somewhere. We unpacked our horses, put the gear in the cabin, and then got back on our saddle horses and went down the bottom, but found no riders. We found a campfire still warm. We looked around and found nothing but some disturbed ground. Why would they camp here when there was a cabin in the upper end of the bottom? So they must have killed some beef. We got a pole and dug in the campfire, and sure enough, there was the dressing of at least one beef. We found where they left the bottom—out up a ledge that was almost impossible.

There was hair and blood on the rocks where the horses had scraped their knees. They really spurred their horses over that rough, steep ledge.

We went out the same place, but we led our horses and pulled on the reins to help them get footing. Our horses never slipped once. We tracked those horses south to a rock cabin. They had stacked flat rocks up under an overhanging ledge to build a cabin. The rock cabin was about eight by fourteen feet with a fireplace in one end and canvas hung for a door and canvas hanging over one opening for a window. We rode up to the cabin. They asked us in. The men in the cabin were Ralph Wetherington, David Lee, and Buck Cavender. Just to pass the time of day, they said they were chasing wild horses, but hadn't got any. The beef was not mentioned. So we left and went back to June's Bottom for the night. We talked the deal over and went to bed. This was Christmas Day in 1938.

It turned cold that night. I would guess fifteen to twenty below zero. The next morning we got up real early to get the calves started. When we went outside, I'll tell you, it was too cold to leave a crowbar outside. We gathered up the calves, and started for the ranch. Normally, we could have made the trip in six or seven hours, but it was so cold the calves just didn't go. We beat those calves almost every step of the way to the ranch. We wrapped ourselves and our bodies up in our saddle blankets to keep the cold out. I guess we built fifty fires in the next two days before we reached the ranch late in the afternoon on the twenty-seventh of December. Our feet, hands, and face were not frozen bad, I don't know why. We just lucked out. Today I think the beating of those calves every step of the way was the reason for our surviving the trip.

We put our horses up, went to the cabin. We were about froze and dead tired. We were okay in a couple of hours and ready to go again. We were both young men. I was about seventeen and Orson about twenty. After we recuperated, we sat down with Andy and told him about those fellows killing his calves. Andy was pretty mad. Andy was a cattleman and he always had horses to be broke to the saddle. These men were horsemen. Andy would have gladly given them all the beef they could eat to break horses for him, but they chose to steal from him, and that was a large pill to swallow. So Andy, Orson, and I went to Green River to get the sheriff. The four of us then headed for the Chaffin Ranch. We arrived at the ranch about midnight. Chaffin only had three saddles, so Andy, Orson, and the sheriff went out to the horse chasers' camp, and I stayed at the Chaffin Ranch.

They came back about three A.M. with the three men—Buck, Ralph Wetherington, and David Lee. They put their horses in the corral. Violet Chaffin had prepared something to eat. All six men sat down and ate. Afterwards, the seven of us, Orson the sheriff, Buck, Ralph Wetherington, Dave Lee, and I loaded up in Andy's pickup and headed for Green River. That was a pretty cold ride to town. It was still twenty below. When we got to town the men were put in Green River jail for a day or two, and then transferred to a jail at Price where they stayed until their trial some six or eight weeks later.

Now back to the ranch and back to the desert to tend the cattle. Before this winter was over I made seven trips to the desert, about three weeks each trip, four with Orson Adams and three with Andy Moore. Andy and I on one trip rode to Hanksville and rode out the Dirty Devil River. Each trip was the same yet different, always pushing cows to better grass and better water, some poor cows to the San Rafael River Valley. This was the bad winter of 1938–39; it got to be thirty degrees below zero. I'm told that winter repeated itself in 1988–89. Each of these six trips were made by saddle horse and pack horse. We had an A-frame tent six by four by six feet high. We would pitch that tent each night. In the tent we would have beds, food, and a small stove. It took very little sagebrush to warm up the tent and cook our meals. The stove was about eight inches high, fourteen inches deep, and eighteen inches long, approximately. The first stove of this type was built from a Ford Model T gas tank, then some tin-bending outfit started to make them better and more compact. You had a firebox about four inches square and twelve inches deep with a ten-inch-wide oven. A telescope stove pipe fit in the firebox. That stove would run you out of that tent even at thirty below zero. You can't stand up in the tent, only on your hands and knees, or you could sit down.

As long as you were in the tent, all was well. You were warm and comfortable, but come morning, boy, that's the blast. You crawl out of that tent at minus thirty degrees and go wrangle the horses. That was my job. We always put a bell on a horse that we would ride bareback. You would listen for that bell. If you were going away from the ranch, the horses would only be maybe a hundred yards from camp. We fed them oats night and morning in a nose bag.

This held true as long as we were going away from the ranch, or south, but when your trip was about over and you headed for the ranch, the horses knew it, too, and they would be as much as three miles from camp headed for home. They would go that far hobbled. We would have to go get them and that was quite a walk at thirty below zero, and it was also dark. You would build a couple of fires to warm up before you reached the horses, but in any case you had a horse to ride back to camp. You'd ride him bareback. When I'd get back to camp Orson would grain the horses and saddle up while I had breakfast. Then I would throw the stove out to cool, we'd strike the tent, pack and go. Repeat the same thing each night.

Andy had a cabin on his allotment at North Springs and at the far south edge of his range some fifty miles from the ranch. While riding out the south end of the range, we would camp at North Springs maybe two or three nights. One day Andy and I arrived at the camp at North Springs early in the afternoon. Andy said, "Bill, I'm going to ride over south here to check something out. You can cook up some rice for supper. I'll be back before dark." So I got in some firewood and got everything straightened out, and about an hour or so before dark I cooked the rice. I had never cooked rice before, so I figured one bowl of rice for Andy and one bowl of rice for me. By the time Andy got to camp, I had every pot, every pan, and even the empty tin cans in camp full of rice. Boy, we had rice for two or three days. Andy got a big bang out of it. This concludes my work for Andy Moore for about five months of the winter of 1938 and '39.

At the horse chasers' trial, Orson Adams and I were the only two witnesses. Orson was called to testify first. He was excused, and I was called to the stand. I was sworn in, and at this time the three men changed their plea from not guilty to guilty, and I was excused. Buck got one year in prison. This was his second offense, and he was prosecuted by the county or state's attorney. Ralph Wetherington and David Lee were given two years probation, and they were to work out the calf for Andy Moore. David Lee worked a month for Andy Moore and fulfilled his obligation. Andy ran Ralph off.

The state attorney went to Faun Chaffin and asked him if he'd work Ralph and David. Faun said he would work David, but not Ralph, and I'm back working for Faun Chaffin. I'd been on the ranch a month or so when David came to work, so Faun, David, and I made a trip down Under the Ledge.

This trip was the same as any trip, just tend the cattle and move some cows around. We went down the second ledge on down to the Green River. We were going to kill a deer for some fresh meat. Faun had his .30-30 Winchester rifle, but only one shell. We found a deer. It was standing broadside to us. Faun leveled down on that deer. *Bang!* and he missed. Of course, then the deer was gone. So we went back across the river. After looking over some old cliff dwellings, we were going to rope a deer. I'd broken my rope a day or so earlier on some horses, and I didn't have a rope, so I rode up the head of a box canyon to chase the deer out. There must have been twenty deer up the canyon. Faun and David were at the mouth of the canyon. They were to rope one of the deer. Ropes were flying, but no deer. But we sure had a lot of fun that trip chasing those deer. I think that was Anderson Bottom. This trip came to an end, and we went back to the ranch. I stayed on till fall, and Dave left.

Now we were building a dam across the San Rafael River just above the bridge. One day Slim [Frank] Baker came by on his way to town. He said, "Faun, some of your cattle are out by Saucer Basin." Faun told me to get on Smokey and go run the cows back to the river. On the way I went to roll a smoke. In my pocket was a six-inch piece of dynamite fuse. I wondered what would Smokey do if I lit it.

Well, Smokey was a mule. I lit it. I found out. Boy, he whirled and he didn't stop bucking until we got to the corral gate. I saddled up old Slats and headed for the cows. I didn't get back until after dark. Faun was pretty mad. He said, "I told you to take Smokey and ride bareback, not to come to the ranch and saddle a horse." So I had to tell him what I had done.

The next day Slim came through late in the afternoon on his way back out to the Robbers Roost Ranch. It was time to quit for the day. I'd smashed my finger prying on a rock and it was hurting and throbbing. Slim stopped to say hello. He had a gallon of whiskey. He offered us a drink. Faun and I just took a small drink, but Shorty tipped that jug and took five or six swallows. By the time we'd got to the ranch, which was about a mile down the river, Shorty was so drunk and rubber-legged he didn't know if he was on the San Rafael or in St. Louis, Missouri. Just one more time he made a total fool out of himself, which was about every day.

Now Faun Chaffin was dead set against smoking. I smoked Bull Durham, and so did Shorty. Faun and Violet, neither one smoked, and we were discussing smoking one day. Faun tried to get me to quit. Shorty said, "I'll quit. I've quit several times, there's nothing to it." So he quit, but he didn't.

It's time to make another trip Under the Ledge. The work at the ranch is caught up, the hay put up, and the corn is in good shape, and all is well. Faun was going to town for supplies. He said, "Do you need anything?"

I said, "I'm out of tobacco. Get me a carton of Bull Durham." He said okay. Faun came back from town, and we got our gear ready. The following morning we left for Under the Ledge. We were gone about ten days. In a day or two I went to get me a sack of tobacco. In the pack there was only a half a carton. I said nothing—maybe that was all they had at the store that day. This trip was about the same as any trip. We're done now, and we're headed back to the ranch. When we reached the ranch, crossed the river, went up through the trees, there was no ranch. There had been a fire. All was burned but the house. We took care of our horses, and went to the house to find out from Violet what had happened.

Well, Shorty hadn't quit smoking. He'd stolen a half-carton of my Bull Durham and was hiding from Violet to smoke out behind the haystack, and he caught the hay stack on fire and couldn't get it out. The fire burned the summer's hay, the shelters for the milk cows and horses, and the corrals. The saddle shed burned, the extra saddles, pack outfits, harness, and many tools with wood handles, all excess leather goods, and some sacks of oats. The only thing that was saved was Shorty's saddle, and Violet got it out of the shed before the fire got too big. Well, our work was cut out for us now to build new corrals, shelters, and whatever.

We built a dam across the San Rafael River, it was located just thirty to forty feet above the old bridge site, downstream from where the new bridge is found today. We chopped down some cottonwood logs, built some cribs out of those logs, and filled them with rocks.

The dam was only three or four feet high, just high enough to divert water to the irrigation ditch that we dug down to the Chaffin Ranch. This is the ditch we shot. That's why I had dynamite fuse in my pocket when I set the mule to bucking. The dam didn't last very long. Cottonwood rots pretty fast, and they washed out pretty soon. But the ranch needed irrigating, so there was a lot of work on that ranch just then. This was in 1939.

To build the irrigation ditch from the dam we dug it mostly by hand, but we shot it through the rock in a place or two—dynamited it to tie it in with the old irrigation ditch because they irrigated before the new ditch got built. We tried a pump from the San Rafael River, but the pumps didn't work too good. They clogged up with silt.

That's when Ned came home. He gathered up that little herd of cows, and with no help from me, no help from anybody. He gathered them all himself out of the San Rafael Valley, and when he got them ready, well, by then we had the ranch irrigated, and that's when we headed out with the cattle.

The ranch wasn't a great big ranch, maybe over three hundred acres, if it was that big. All we had was alfalfa, hay, and corn. And that was just to feed the stuff on the ranch, the horses and milk cows. He didn't feed his cattle. They ran down Under the Ledge the year round and ate natural grasses.

Ned and I went down there about this time of the year—about May or June. We were all ready to hit the trail. We got our packs ready, and horses. The next morning we packed our horses and headed to the Under the Ledge country. It is now included in Canyonlands National Park.

We drove the cattle about twenty miles to where we entered Horseshoe Canyon from the west. This was also the same entrance Delbert Tidwell used to enter The Spur country when he run cattle up on The Spur. We took the canyon trail because of water. There was no water on the desert trail.

After a couple days in the canyon we came out at Hans Flat. There we drove the cattle around the rim to French Spring. Today the park's ranger station is located at Hans Flat. We camped our last night on the trail at French Springs. That night it rained, which was good so far as the cattle and horses were concerned. We stretched a rope between two trees, draped a tarp over the rope and built us an A-frame tent to sleep in. There was one little hole in the tarp and, of course, that's where I set my boots. The next morning one boot was full of water. It seems as though I beat, tugged, and pulled for an hour before I got that boot on. Now we're ready to go.

We gathered up the cows and horses and started down the North Trail. This trail is a narrow horse and cow trail down a twelve-hundred-foot ledge. You had to pack your horses tight as they couldn't pass a few narrow spots with a wide pack. These ledges range from a thousand to twelve hundred feet high. I took the first half of the cows and pack horses and started down the trail. Ned brought up the later half and was last.

Ned's horse, Captain Kidd, had run all winter down there free with the rest of the horses. Of course, he was a broke saddle horse, but when we caught him he didn't want to be rode. He liked that freedom, and when you top off any saddle horse that has been running free three, four, five, six months, he'll jump up and jump around some. Some of them will buck pretty hard, but for the most part a saddle horse doesn't really buck. They might make a jump or two and crow-hop around for they are not a bucking horse. You will find your bucking horses in a rodeo.

Ned topped old Captain Kidd off, and just to watch him you'd think he was drawed up like a coiled spring just ready to explode. But he didn't buck, he just finally got the kinks out of his back and he was just old Captain Kidd in a day or two. Captain Kidd was a good horse, fast as the wind and smooth as a rocking chair to ride.

We took those forty head of cattle down to a country we called Sweetwater in Waterhole Flat, which I didn't remember, but the last time I talked with Ned he said that's where we took them. Once we got them there, we just turned them loose and they grazed. We had other work to do with other cattle and checking out the water and the grass and what have you. We checked the horses all out and run them in the corral at Waterhole Flat. Caught up the one we was going to ride down there and caught up the one we were going to take home back to the ranch. The cattle we took down there, well, they was just there. We just checked out the country, the water and the grass, and did whatever had to be done to anything that we seen. We didn't run into any sick cattle or anything, so that was it.

I don't know for sure how many cattle they run on the ranch. Faun Chaffin told me when he left there he came out of there with 650 head of cows and calves and possibly bulls. Well, if you come out of there with that many cows and calves, I'm just assuming he had about 350 to 400 head. I never did know exactly how many head he had.

Faun had other cattle down there in Waterhole Flat when we got there with the forty head. We didn't break our herd up in the sense that we put two hundred here and two hundred there. Doggone, you look at a range—well, you figure, well the range I'm talking about might be ten to fifteen miles wide and ten miles long, you know. That's good enough for a couple of hundred head or a hundred head and you try to get that number in there. Then you leave them there for a month or six weeks; you go back to the ranch. In a month or six weeks we come back. If you lucked out, you got a couple of good rains and you got a lot more grass, then your worries are over with and so is your water problem, but if you don't, like one time with Faun Chaffin, he and I gathered up maybe two hundred head and took them up into what he called his winter range 'cause there was no feed or water down below. Now, that's the trip when I thought I was going to die, the only time in my life I thought she was all over with.

I was bringing up the rear of those two hundred head, and I had all calves. And my water bottle come open and my water drained out and I didn't have a drink of water. I was so dehydrated that I was almost too weak to get on my horse. I went back to the spring, and no water there. Well, a seventeen-year-old kid ain't got any sense anyway, so I didn't have enough sense to panic. I hobbled my horse and dug a ditch out in that spring in the wet sand and laid down. I don't know if I went to sleep or if I passed out, and I don't know how long I laid there. I didn't even have a watch, but when I woke up I wasn't even thirsty. My body had absorbed enough moisture out of that wet sand that it quenched my thirst and I wasn't a bit thirsty. I got back on my horse and went back on the trail.

Now, had I gone on, there was plenty of water, but I didn't know that. Boy, when I got back up there and found Faun, I got into a water hole and I laid in there and stripped off and washed my clothes and drank all I could drink. I just washed the salt and sweat out of my clothes and laid them up on a rock. In 110 degrees they dried in five minutes. I put my clothes back on and got back on my horse, and away we went just like nothing ever happened.

The cattle can find water at a certain distance, but those cattle ran there year round and they knew exactly where every water hole was. Every spring, too, but when they got there, if there wasn't any water, then you had a problem. You had to be there or you're gonna lose them. They would just stay there and choke to death.

As I said earlier, Daff and Bishop Thompson didn't have a ranch, they just stayed out there on a cow camp. They only had about 125, maybe 150, head of cattle, and they just run them in the valley. That was under the Taylor Grazing Act. They paid a nickel a head a month to run them cows there. A calf can run free up to a yearling. When I worked for them all I did for them was ride that valley to see to it the cows didn't bog down in the quicksand. There was a lot of quicksand, and I took care of the cabin and the horses.

While I was there I built a corral, a round corral about thirty feet in diameter. We used it for a lot of things. We'd top our horses off in there, for one thing, if they were a little bit raunchy. The corral is all gone now, rotted away, but I swung the gate in a wagon hub, and twenty or thirty years ago I stopped here and dug up the old wagon hub and took it home with me. I got it painted black now, setting out in front of my house in Sun City.

Most of the time when we were trailing cattle we packed our food and meals. We didn't kill game. Some did. Oh, if you did run out of food, you can be sure we shot a deer, but mostly we had our tinned food.

Where June's Bottom is on the Green River there used to be a wagon road in there. Somebody went down there and farmed it. There used to be a cabin there. I understand the river has changed course and

Notice at French Spring.

most of the bottom is gone now. I don't know if you can make it in there by four-by-four or not. Somebody who lives around here might know, if you could find that somebody.

After that night at French Spring when the rain filled my boot, we started down the French North Trail. I took the lead with the pack horses. The cattle followed them. Down the trail we went.

Now, from the edge of the rim, before it was converted into the ledge, there was a little cove there. One of the cows took a little blind spot and got stopped there. I threw rocks at her, but couldn't get her turned, and she got in there. She went in there about twenty or thirty feet, tried to turn around and fell over the ledge and she broke her back. Ned was bringing up the tail end of everything. When he came by, there was nothing I could do about it. I couldn't get down to the cow from where I was, so Ned came by, climbed down, and cut her throat to put her out of her misery. So we lost one cow.

Ned's horse went on down the trail and mixed up with the other horses. When Ned caught Captain Kidd, he threw an absolute perfect throw. I'll never forget that. It was as perfect as any professional cowboy ever threw a rope. He threw that loop over the other ten or twelve horses, and it dropped right dead over Captain Kidd's head right in the middle of that bunch of horses.

After a few days of working the cattle down there, we were done and we headed for the ranch. We were gone about a week. During this time we lived strictly off the back of the pack horses, and we were probably eighty miles from home. When you make a trip such as this, you really take care of your horses. These horses are your livelihood. They get you there, and they get you home. You better take good care of them; eighty miles plus or minus is a long walk across that desert.

After a few days Ned returned to his home in Bakersfield, California, and I stayed on the ranch. This was in 1939. It is now 1994, and Ned and I haven't seen each other in fifty-five years. I've not seen him since, but talked to him on the phone and exchanged cards and letters with him. I'm looking forward to a reunion with Ned on my seventy-third birthday on the old ranch.

I just rode whatever they gave me. On that trip I had old Slats. I had a little black mare that we were breaking, and I had a little stud that we were breaking. They were pretty well broke, but that's the three horses I had with me—Slats, Tickaboo, and I don't remember this little black mare's name, but I rode her, Slats, and Tickaboo.

After I left the Chaffin Ranch I came up to Green River, Utah, to work the cantaloupe. Of course, everybody came to town and worked at picking the melons. That was just a common thing that everybody did. The clutch went out on my car; it needed other work, too, so I traded it for a horse and saddle. I sold the horse and saddle for a hundred dollars. Then I went to Idaho and worked the beet and the potato harvests.

After I left the state of Idaho, I came back to the Green River area. I went to work then at the Ruby Ranch. This ranch lays across the Green River on the east bank at the mouth of the San Rafael. I'd cross the Green River every week or so to go over and visit with the Chaffins. I found a sand bar that I could wade the river.

One day Art Ekker, Faun Chaffin, and Art's hired hand came through the Ruby Ranch with Art's saddle horses. Art was moving cattle and horses back to the Robbers Roost Ranch, as Slim and Pearl Baker had sold out. Pearl and Hazel were sisters, daughters of Joe and Millie Biddlecome. Joe settled in the Roost country in 1909, so Mrs. Hazel Ekker was actually going home.

We corralled the horses and had something to eat. Afterwards I told Art I knew a trail across the river where the horses could walk. I'd lead a couple of horses and maybe we could just walk, as I'd made about six round trips over to Faun's the past month or so. So all was set. We went into the river. The two horses I was leading went to my left. They walked off the sandbar into swimming water, drug me off my horse, and for a minute or so I was hung up in the lead ropes. My horse was standing out in the middle of the river.

By now all horses were in swimming water, Art, Faun, and Art's hired hand. The hired hand's horse panicked and drowned. He got the saddle and bridle off, but he was okay. Art gave him the pick of the herd for the loss of his saddle horse. Why this happened, I don't know. Seems as though when you plan something, something always goes wrong. I went back across the river and waded all the way. And back to the Ruby Ranch. This incident bothered me for many years, and that was the last time I ever saw Art Ekker or his hired hand.

In a few days another man came to the ranch. A lot of cattle were coming in for us to take care of, and I couldn't handle them by myself, so they sent in a second man. When their drive was over with, that was the end of my job. So in a few days, J. E. Wetherington delivered a horse to this guy. He led the horse out of a window of his car. There was J. E., the driver of the car, and his wife. The rancher's son had ten gallons of grape wine set there, and I was taking care of it. J. E. and the driver of the car and his wife and I had some wine. I killed a couple of chickens and we cooked us a good meal. By this time we were all feeling pretty good.

On this ranch was a mule, a big mule. He could be rode, but boy, could he buck. I asked J. E. to ride him; J. E. said he'd ride him first if I'd ride him second. Come my turn, and I got on. The ride began. I was riding that mule hands down. The stubbing broke on the saddle; my saddle and all went over that mule's head. I hung my spurs on the top of a corral pole, whipping my head and shoulders against the ground. I'm still in the saddle. Somewhere between that mule's back and the ground I quit bronc riding, at least for the time being. I never really quit, but that was the last animal I ever got on just to see if I could ride it. My work is done at the Ruby Ranch.

Then I went to work for Hap Wilcox, a sheepman. I was tending camp for his herder, Tom Cottrell. I was cooking for him, tending the camp, taking care of the horses and the pack mule. I'd take the horses to the river every morning, and from where we are right now in Green River, it was only out there about ten miles, out in the hills. Bring back a couple of loads of wood on the pack mule, and I'd cut it up into stove lengths and rick it up there beside camp because winter was going to be coming on. I had a pretty good supply of wood built up there, but it couldn't end because the winter was pretty long and you were going to burn a lot of wood.

Some guy came through there that I met out on the Roost range one time. He was a prospector. Just a young boy, he come out there looking for me. He talked me into going with him up into Idaho and maybe even up into Oregon prospecting for gold. That sounded pretty big, so I quit Hap and went with him. Then I got to thinking about it when we went into Price. Going up into those mountains prospecting for gold when it was thirty-five below zero, or twenty-five or twenty, whatever it is, it gets cold up in those hills in Idaho. I decided I wasn't going to do it, but I had messed up. I had quit my job in Green River, and it would do me no good to come back here because Hap would have replaced me. He had to have somebody. So while I was thinking about it, I just went down to the bus station and bought me a ticket for Vincennes, Indiana, and I went home. There was a lot of talk about the war then, and I couldn't find a job, so I joined the army. I was in the army for four years and nine months.

Well, after the war all of my circumstances had changed, and shortly after that I got married. I never got back out west again as a ranch hand or a cowboy—only as a construction worker. Then I worked as an iron worker for thirty-three years. In that time I worked all over these United States. I've been in forty-nine of the fifty states. I've been in thirteen foreign countries, and while I was in the army I crossed the Pacific five times, crossed the United States six times, and made one trip completely around the world. But I never got back out here as a ranch hand or a cowboy, which was and still is (of course, it is all over with now) my first love—cattle and ranching.

Most of the small ranches are gone, those that were strictly cattle ranches. Those that were family owned and operated, they're about all gone all over the whole world, or the whole West. Just like the Chaffin Ranch, it's gone. Well, of course, Faun and Violet, they're gone, too. The ranch has just reverted back into the desert.

Now, when you see the ranch, you may not think that because it's right on the very northern edge of the desert, and right along the Green River and the San Rafael River, which is a lot of humidity, and there are some trees and brush, but right south of there a couple of miles then you got fifty miles of desert. The old ranch, it's just converted back into brush. But along with the ranchers and the horses and the cattle, they are all gone. But so is the cowboy. He is gone forever. Right now and in the last twenty years there have not been enough American cowboys to fill the demand. They come up from Mexico and South America. Well, that's a pretty sad statement when you think about it, when you consider the part the cowboy played in the building of the western half of the United States. There was no work out here in the early days. It was all ranch work. Cattle, some sheep, but mostly cattle. So you had to be a cowboy, or you just didn't work. Money went a long ways. You didn't have to have a lot of money to do something if you had any at all. So from the cowboy your towns sprung up, all your business in your towns, from your blacksmith to your general store, your marshals, your sheriffs, your outlaws, your politicians, your governor, and in one case the president of the United States, Teddy Roosevelt. And then, of course, let's don't forget old Will Rogers. There will never be another Will Rogers. He was the cowboy of all cowboys.

Well, then come the movies. Good and bad man, the romance of the range and what have you. Even that is gone now. We got actors and actresses, but we have no writers. There is not a good writer left that can write a good western story like *Buffalo Bill, How the West Was Won, Shane,* and *Red River*—those guys are gone forever. But the actors and actresses, they can act anything if they have a script. But when you think about this romance of the range, now that is something to look at. You go out here on this range as we did here. You go out for a week or two at a time, no water; you may go three or four days without a bath. It is a matter of opinion who smells the best or worst, whichever way you look at it, you, the horses or the cows. Well, I never run into a blond with her hair flying back there two feet on a runaway pinto going across that desert, and had I run into that situation and caught her, she'd have probably preferred the runaway horse to that stinking cowboy. So all this romance that they portray in the movies—that didn't happen because this was a rough life. The only ones that know it are the ones that did it.

Cattle and sheep graze over each other. There are lots of stories that cattle won't or can't graze where sheep have been. That's just to keep the fighting going. They can graze over each other; they may not like it, but they can and they do. One thing about a sheep, a sheep eats right down to the ground and a cow can't get it. That's the only difference. The sheep sheer the grass off, they don't pull it up. They'll break it off right next to the ground, but if it's high enough, the cow, she'll eat up at top and get along fine. But they will graze together. The old stories was years ago just to keep the fighting going between the cowman and the sheepman. There has been that hatred between them.

I got another story of the sheep up in Oregon, it didn't apply here, that will give you some idea. I can't get it authenticated, so I can't give you the name. I've tried to research it, but haven't gotten the answer. Well, I was working for a sheepman up in Oregon, and I noticed this one man never said a word. An old man to me then, I was only fifteen, but he was sixty, sixty-five, possibly even seventy. I was night-herding the sheep this time, lambing time. All I do is ride around the herd to keep the coyotes shoved back from getting any lambs. I was talking to the herder one day, and I said, "Do you know this fellow?"

He said yes and told me his name.

And I said, "Well, what gives with him? I've known him for about three months now, and I have never heard him say a word."

So then this herder told me the story. Now, this was back years ago, back during the days of the cattle and sheep wars. He was running his sheep up on this high desert in Oregon. Three cowboys came through, and they caught him and they beat him half to death. They got him on his hands and knees and made him walk around his herd of sheep and baa like a sheep. When he got to the farthest side of the herd, they'd had their fun and turned him loose.

Well, he crawled back through his herd and got back to his camp. He revived himself as best he could, and he got his saddle horse and his rifle, and he went after them. He caught up with them and he killed one, wounded one, and captured the third one. When they had the trial he was acquitted with self-defense. But they went back out and got the wounded man and the dead man. The wounded man told him (they got sent to the penitentiary), "When I get out of jail I'm gonna kill you, boy, for sending me to the penitentiary."

Well, right then the herder was a young man, only in his late teens, maybe twenty or so, and he didn't think too much about it. As time went on that bore on his mind and he pulled some strings, and he got the man paroled. Then as time went on it started to bore on his mind of killing that man, and he turned into a vegetable. And that is what he was when I knew him. So you see, even in the rough days of the cattle wars you can't kill a man and brush it off like a sore throat. On the range that's a pretty serious offense.

While I was on the ranch for Faun and Violet and for Andy Moore and all those places out there on the desert, I was continually singing. As a layman, I guess I could sing all right. I never learned to play a guitar, but I sang for Faun and Violet every night.

Once Violet told me that her favorite song was "Empty Cot in the Bunkhouse Tonight." Well, of course, that favorite song could have changed over a period of years, but then that's what it was. I guess I sang that song for Violet fifty times. In fact, when I was working in Saudi Arabia back there in 1976, 1977, and 1978, sometime in there, I cut a tape and sent it to Violet and recorded that song on that tape. As far as I know, Violet still had it when she passed away. Faun probably still has that tape, or maybe Wiladeane. It was still at the house in Mack when her mother died, so it's around there somewhere. Of course, that's many years later, and the song may not be as new as it once was, but that had no bearing on the song, anyway. It was just that Violet loved that song, and I sang it for her.

Otherwise, nothing spectacular happened to me. This is just sort of the life of a cowboy and a cattle rancher. It could have happened to anybody, but if this ever gets into a book, or anybody hears a tape or reads this in a book, and they go to a restaurant and have a steak dinner, and after reading this in a book and after hearing this on a tape and seeing what a cowboy or a cattleman goes through within the run of a year (because the work is the same—rain, snow, or sunshine 365 days a year—the only difference is you take off clothes in the summertime and put them back on in the winter) I truly hope that they enjoy that steak just a little bit more when they learn what it takes to produce that beef. That is, of course, if they are eating American beef. Why this country imports foreign beef, I don't know. If the government would let us, the cattlemen in this country could surely produce enough beef for this nation, but they choose to buy foreign beef.

Another little item: before the war when I was just a teenager, I worked on farms, cattle ranches, and sheep ranches. I hoed corn, I picked cantaloupe, I picked strawberries, I picked gooseberries, I picked apples, I picked pears, I picked watermelons, I picked potatoes, and topped sugar beets. I did everything there was, and I was glad to get it because I just thought it was a job. Then, in those times, if you didn't work, you didn't eat. Today in 1994 and for the past several years, that's stoop labor. All my life I've done stoop labor and didn't know it. Of course, they didn't have welfare then. You either worked or you didn't eat.

But then, you know, back then in the late thirties you could buy a new car for less than a thousand dollars, and buy a good used car for less than a hundred dollars, and you could buy a pair of Levis for less than a dollar. You could buy a good hat for three fifty. The pair of boots I bought for seventeen dollars and fifty cents, and they were tailor hand-made boots made to order. Of course, when you figure that up, seventeen fifty for a pair of boots was half a month's pay. But everything was much cheaper then, but so was the wages. Now, you can't hold it against the ranchers that I worked for thirty a month or even my room and board, because they didn't have any money, either.

There isn't much future for the cowboy of today. Back then a cowboy worked for thirty dollars a month, or a calf a month and five dollars, or a calf and a half and five dollars. It all totaled thirty, thirty-five, or forty dollars a month. I was talking to a doctor that was raised on a cattle ranch back during the Great Depression, and he was also a bronc rider. I was talking to him about the cattle today, and he stressed to me like it was really something that you have to pay a cowboy six hundred dollars a month. He said it ain't no wonder there aren't any cowboys if you have to pay them that much. Well, think about that for a minute. They sell a calf nowadays for six or seven hundred dollars. Why not pay that cowboy a calf and a half a month and five dollars for every twenty-five dollar increment in the value of that calf? He'd be making two thousand dollars a month compared to Depression wages. This doctor, this isn't for him. He's probably a millionaire now, charging three thousand dollars or more for an appendix operation when back then he probably got fifty for it. He come up the hard road, but he's made it. More power to him. I don't begrudge his becoming a doctor. I just begrudge his thoughts.

We used to be able to buy a weaner calf for a dollar a head. I don't know what they cost today, but I'll bet a weaner calf is more than a hundred twenty-five dollars. You can't get into the business anymore.

We are going to drive by a little valley out here that I could have had back in the thirties by simply moving on it and getting the squatter's rights. Andy Moore offered to lease me three hundred fifty head of cattle, and I could have gone into the cattle business. Well, on the surface that sounds good, and it was good, but it would have cost me, then, a minimum of three thousand dollars to hold out two years till I had a calf crop. Now, where in the world is a seventeen-year-old kid back then going to get three thousand dollars? It would be just like where could I get ten million dollars today. By the time I put a pump on the river and hired a man, bought me a string of saddle horses and everything to work with, I didn't have the money to do it. So working for thirty dollars a month you aren't going to come up with three thousand dollars. I didn't have the money, so I didn't become a cattleman.

Faun Chaffin told me that one time at the end of the year when he paid all of his expenses that had accumulated for the year at the ranch, that would be labor, food, feed bills, repairs, and taxes, he said he had four hundred eighty-five dollars left. He said, "Bill, I had so much money, I didn't know what to do with it." But when you think about it,

IN APPRECIATION TO
HARRY "BILL" RACY
FOR YOUR HARD WORK & DEDICATED
SERVICE WHILE COWBOYING ON THE
CHAFFIN RANCH · 1938 TO 1940
THE CHAFFIN FAMILY

A much-appreciated thank-you. Photo courtesy of Steve Forney and Bill Racy.

four hundred eighty-five dollars in a year from approximately four hundred head of cattle, his income was about a dollar a cow. Well, I worked for a dollar a day for a year, I made almost as much money as he did in working for him for thirty dollars a month. So he didn't have the money, so I didn't hold it against him. He didn't have the money—that was just the times. But they are gone forever, now. All of the folks are gone, most of them are all dead now.

Ned sent me a brick from the remains of the Chaffin Ranch house. The ranch house has been vandalized, and Ned picked the brick up when we visited the ranch in 1994. He had a bronze plate with an inscription engraved on it mounted on the brick. The inscribed words were to thank me for the loyal service I had given at the Chaffin Ranch in years past. To me that brick is worth its weight in gold. I worked all my life, almost five years in the military, over thirty years in heavy construction, other jobs like cowboying and picking fruit, and I never got so much as a thank-you from any other employer.

The ranch is gone now. Just a pile of rubble remains, but even the vandals can't destroy the remembrances of those years pushing stock through the most magnificent country in the world. Oh, there is still the old picket corral just east of where the main ranch house used to be. It backs up to a red rock shelf. I wonder if the ghosts of old Slats and Captain Kidd still kick up the dust in the corral?

5

Guy Robison

People who didn't live through the depression years of 1929–1938 may never be able to fully grasp the difficulties encountered in making a living in tiny rural towns in the western states.

Guy Robison, another cowman (they're common around Green River), also ran sheep, ferried rigs and stock and people across the Colorado River on the Hite Ferry, owned a store, became a trapper, ran a motel, and farmed. He did anything he could to earn a living and to provide for his wife and daughter. "To earn a living." What a respectable phrase, an important phrase to Guy and others like him who, without the benefit of higher education, had to learn to survive in those tough years. His wife, Nina, shared in that effort and now shares their home in Green River, where she works as a volunteer at the impressive John Wesley Powell Museum. Like most of the persons interviewed for these profiles, Guy and Nina are of Mormon stock. It is not unusual to learn that the parents or grandparents of many of those families were original settlers in Utah towns and villages. Some of them had been directed by Brigham Young to venture forth and establish communities. Their practical skills and determination to survive are traits that show up in Guy.

August 6, 1994
Green River, Utah

I was born in 1913 in Hanksville, but we moved to Green River in 1915. My dad's name was Joseph Alvin Robison. He was born in Chicago in 1872. His dad and several of his uncles moved to Fillmore, Utah, from Chicago in 1886. Fillmore is west of here, on Interstate I-70 near

Guy Robison, 1994.

Richfield. My grandfather, Alvin Locke Robison, moved to Loa in about 1890. He was appointed territorial judge in either 1890 or 1895 by the federal government. One of his main jobs was to prosecute the polyga-mists. Some called him Satan Robison.

Dad had been married twice. His first wife's name was Sarah Oyler. She died in 1907. He then married my mother, Cornelia Agnes Mae Andrews. She was known as Mae and was born in 1876 in Yankton, South Dakota. She had been married to George Arnot Wyllie before she married my father. Mr. Wyllie was born in Scotland in 1862. They had two sons, Stuart Arnot Wyllie born in Yankton in 1897, and Donald D. Wyllie was born the following year in Yankton. My mother died in 1926.

That was the end of our home and I was pretty much on my own after that. I attended school in Green River but only went from the first grade through the sixth grade, except I missed one grade when I had typhoid fever. That's the size of my schooling. People would have to know how the times were in those days to understand why I never finished school. I worked here and there for different fellows. When I was nine years old I got my first horse and my first calf and ever since, in all of these years, I have always had horses and cattle. When I was working somewhere else, like at the Hite Ferry, one or another of my half-brothers would tend my livestock along with theirs.

My father was here at our home in Green River, and he also had a ranch in Hanksville that he purchased in about 1912. Our home here just dissolved, and my two sisters went to live with an aunt. Dad had lived in Blue Valley, about fifteen miles west of Hanksville. He taught school there. You didn't have to have much education to teach school at that time. Anybody who was willing to teach school and do it for very little got the schoolteaching jobs.

They couldn't keep the dam repaired above Blue Valley and they had bad floods, so everybody had to move out. That's when Dad moved to Hanksville, but before he moved he married Sarah Oyler and they had eight children. She died giving birth. That left me with eight half-brothers and one sister and I came along last.

Dad had a small farm in Blue Valley, and a little bunch of cattle. At that time sheep were coming into the country pretty heavy in the winter. A little cattleman like Dad, whose roots were down in this country, had to stay on. When the feed was gone the sheep would leave, but the cowboy had to stay. A bit before the First World War, Dad and his brother Frank came up with the idea of going into the Angora goat business. They thought they could outlast the sheep with goats, and the price of mohair was pretty good. They each got a herd of Angora goats.

My first memories are of growing up here in Green River and going to school. The freight wagons were still running. There was an early uranium and vanadium boom here, down at Temple Mountain. It was all hauled by teams and wagons. There was a livery stable across the road from where we lived; I remember the big old mules and work teams when they were hauling ore. That ended about 1922.

Dad had a freight team. He had ended up with two herds of goats, about twenty-four hundred head, and freighted his own and other people's supplies, too. My first trip from Green River to Hanksville was with him on a freight wagon pulled by four of his mules. During the war he was making good money. Then he tried to expand, and in about 1925 he went bankrupt.

In 1926, after Mother died, things were pretty tough. The banks had taken over the goat herds and camps and all. He kept his farm in Hanksville; it was about forty acres. Pete Johnson owns it now. It's on both sides of the Fremont River.

My first trip into the Henry Mountains was in 1922. I got awful homesick. I was there with my half-brothers and the goats. I imagined I

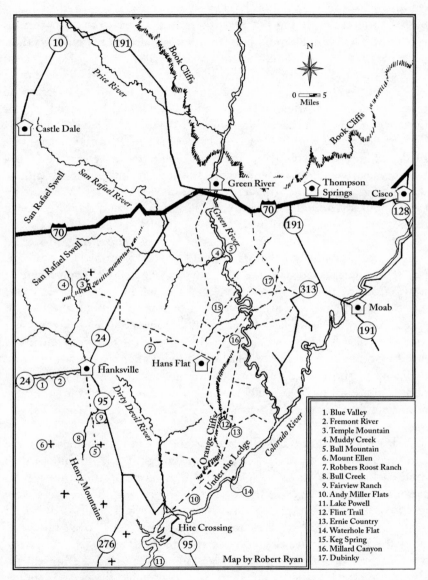

1. Blue Valley
2. Fremont River
3. Temple Mountain
4. Muddy Creek
5. Bull Mountain
6. Mount Ellen
7. Robbers Roost Ranch
8. Bull Creek
9. Fairview Ranch
10. Andy Miller Flats
11. Lake Powell
12. Flint Trail
13. Ernie Country
14. Waterhole Flat
15. Keg Spring
16. Millard Canyon
17. Dubinky

Map by Robert Ryan

Guy Robison's Canyonlands.

was accomplishing something, but I know now I was just in the way. I had a lot of fun and had a horse to ride and I liked that. We had two camps up in the mountains. I'd stay at one until I got tired of being bossed around by my big brothers, then I'd go over to the other camp where we had a hired hand. He treated me better than my brothers did.

Dad had gotten some literature in 1927 about raising livestock on an island off the coast of Washington and he wanted to go look it over, and I went with him. He had lost his business in Green River so he traded some stuff to Bert Silliman and got Bert's old Buick touring car in exchange and we headed out to Washington.

When we were in Washington, two of my half-brothers were with Dad and me. One stayed up there and went to work for the Forest Service. Dad wanted to stay up there, but my brother Joy and I said we were going to go home, so Dad decided to head home too. We were up there about a year and then returned to Hanksville, and then I got back to the old home in Green River.

It was a lonesome time. Both my sisters were living in Grand Junction, and no one was living in the old home. I bummed around here, and sometimes stayed with my sister-in-law. At that time you could go to work on the railroad if you had a guardian who would sign for you. I was fourteen then, and I went to work as a section hand on the Denver & Rio Grande Western Railroad for two dollars and eighty cents per nine hour day. A fellow named J. M. Brown was the foreman, a nice old boy. I worked there a week and I was so tired. When we started to work, they gave us short-handled shovels. I was always weak in the back, and I said to him one day, "Do you ever get hardened into this?" He said, "I've been here forty years and I never did." So I said to him, "You won't see me after this week."

I went back to Hanksville, back to the old ranch. I hung out there and finally got a temporary job with a sheep outfit. I had quite a tough time packing up a string of mules and moving camp until the regular camp man showed up. We moved twice while I was there. There were just two men to a camp, and the winter herd was about two thousand head. Of course, we had dogs, four or five or six. You moved the camp every three or four days to go on to better feed or water. The camp tender took care of the camp, did the cooking, and tended the horses. He also hunted the lost sheep. The herder, he just tended the herd. That was his job.

Coyotes were a problem for the sheepman. They killed lots of sheep. We trapped them and poisoned them. There were trappers in the

Guy Robison on Micky, 1928. Photo courtesy of Guy Robison.

country then, and they were welcomed to the sheep camps. They could get their horses' feed, their food, and everything else they needed as long as they were out there catching coyotes. Some of them made a good living; there were lots of coyotes. The state paid a bounty of six dollars for the ears or two feet. One had to be a front and the other a rear foot. They could also get as high as fifteen or sixteen dollars for a good winter pelt. You couldn't hardly sell the pelts of summer coyotes, only get six bucks. Two and a half dollars for a bobcat. There were quite a few fellows running a trap line across this desert and up and down the Dirty Devil River.

In 1922 an old friend of mine lived next door to us, Sam Sanders was his name. He came into this country from Wyoming, and had been raised in Steamboat Springs, Colorado. He had a little band of horses and wintered them on the east side of the Green River. We got to be good friends and liked each other. An outfit came in from Arizona in a 1920 or '22 Dodge touring car. They had a whole load of Navajo blankets. They made a deal with Sam Sanders and traded the blankets and a car for his horses. Sam was through with the horse business because it wasn't any good. The army had quit buying horses. You could buy a good saddle horse for twenty to twenty-five dollars just about anywhere. We peddled the blankets to anybody who wanted to buy one.

The Biddlecome Cattle Company started the Robbers Roost Ranch at Crow Seep. Joe Biddlecome died of tonsillitis. They didn't take the best care of him, and he died. Pearl Biddlecome, Joe and Millie's daughter, was married to Mel Marsing at that time. They had two little boys. Mel got a rope burn that caused blood poisoning that killed him. Pearl hired Sam Sanders to come out and run the outfit. He was a good, steady hand, and he hired me to help out. That's the first time I cowboyed for any person other than my dad or my brothers. This was in 1930, and I was still a pretty young man, just a kid, really, only seventeen years old.

I don't mind telling you that Pearl was two or three people. Sometimes she was the best person you ever heard tell of, and other times she was about the snakiest person you ever heard of. She'd get mad over nothing. I think she fired me fifteen times. Sam would explain to her how things were, and maybe two or three days later she was your best friend. I'd get awfully mad at her, but I still respected her. When I look back and see how it was for her at that time, I appreciate her. She wrote a lot of good stories under the name of Pearl Baker. They are fiction to a certain extent and history to a certain extent. They tell me history is a little smidgen of truth mixed with a lot of fiction, and I guess that is the truth.

I worked for her for quite a while, and then I quit and went to work for Andy Moore the next spring; this was in 1932. Andy's outfit was right next to the Biddlecomes' operation there on the desert. When it was roundup time the two outfits worked together. Those two experiences were my start at being a cowboy.

Back earlier, when I was just a kid, we still had our home in Green River before my mother died. One of her boys, a half-brother of mine, worked for a fellow named Pace. He took me to Hanksville and over to his Fairview Ranch. They were haying, and he had it in mind to take me out there to tromp hay. I did that for two weeks and wore out my britches. They bought me a new pair, and that was my pay for two weeks work. That was my first job on the Fairview Ranch.

After my father left Blue Valley and went to Hanksville, he bought a ranch at the head of a ditch just below the dam. He bought the ranch from, I think his name was, Alonzo Turner. He probably homesteaded it. Across the river was a little ranch owned by Pete Steele. Dad and my brother bought it and enlarged it considerably by clearing brush and leveling it, and made a pretty good ranch out of it. With the two ranches, one on each side of the Fremont River, they had about two hundred acres under cultivation. Dad sold the ranch on the south side of the river to Glenn Johnson, but two of my brothers kept the ranch on the north side and ran cattle from that ranch for several years.

I worked for several sheep outfits, mostly with Vern Pace. My half-brother Stuart Wyllie had a little cow outfit in Hanksville, and he wanted to leave. His kids were getting to an age where he wanted to get them in a better school than this one at Hanksville. I bought the place from him in 1938. I had saved up some money from my sheepherding days. Reo Hunt has that place now. A year later I married Nina and the following year we had our daughter, Sharon. When she got to be four years old, we had to make a decision. The school in Hanksville was just a grade school, and they were sending high school kids down there to teach. Actually, the school was very poor at that time, so we decided we had better get out with Sharon, and I sold out. Later we boarded her in Green River so she could attend a better school. She graduated from high school in 1957.

We moved to Green River, and I bought a little farm out in the country. While we were on that farm, I went to work in the W. F. Asimus hardware store. Clay Asimus wanted to sell the store, and I got together with Wayne Smith and together we had enough money to buy the store. Wayne is an old cowboy, and had been a cowboy all of his life. After we got in the store, he didn't like it, so I borrowed some money from Andy Moore and bought out Wayne.

In 1945 I had the store all to myself. I paid Wayne off and paid Andy Moore off. After nine years I got sick of the store business and when I got a chance to sell it, I sure did. Sold my farm off, too, and went back to Hanksville.

We stayed in Hanksville for a while, then we moved down to Hite on the Colorado River. I thought maybe I could do something with the boat business, a thing I didn't know anything about, but I was willing to take a look at it. While we were down there, the fellow who bought the ferry business from Arth Chaffin drowned. His name was Reed Maxfield and his wife was terribly upset, had kids, and wanted to get out of there. My wife and I made a deal with Mrs. Maxfield to run the ferry for about a year while she went off and looked around for some-place else to live. So in 1965 we had the experience of running a ferry and it was sort of fun.

At that time Hite was experiencing the closing of the uranium boom. The mill was shutting down, but still some traffic was crossing on the ferry from south to north. We averaged about six cars a day that needed ferrying across the river—some tourists and some river rats who were running the Colorado on their way to the Grand Canyon. We saw Georgie White and Jack Brennen there on one occasion. The river run-ners stored boats and supplies in big tents west of the ferry. Reuben and Beth Nielson kept sleeping and dining tents there and stored supplies while the uranium mill was operating at White Canyon. The post office was on the east side of the river. The ferry rates were a dollar per person, two fifty to haul an auto across, five dollars for trucks, but horses were free. Both my wife and Sharon enjoyed the time we spent there.

After the ferry-operating time we moved to Bicknell. Sharon was going to high school. Then we came back to Hanksville and bought the Fairview Ranch south of Hanksville near the Henry Mountains. We raised cattle and sheep. We built up a pretty good herd of sheep and sold them. And I built up two herds of cattle and sold them, and turned the ranch over to my daughter and her husband.

I kept Hereford bulls at first. In those days everyone was cross-breeding to get bigger size. I bred Angus and bought a bunch of Brahmans from Wayne Smith. They were wild sons-of-guns. They run everyone, they were mean. They have a better breed of them now, but they still are tough. Now they have a mixture of Durham, Hereford, and Charolais. They are getting big calves now, that weigh five hundred to six hundred pounds when we sell them. Of course, we have been feeding them quite a little. Compared to those who feed purely off the range and never get store feed, ours weigh fifty to a hundred pounds more.

Depending on the rain, we maybe average ten head per section. Snow is the most important thing. It melts down in the ground and is better for the grass. It is a tough proposition. If some fellow thinks he is going to come in and make a lot of money right quick, it isn't going to happen. You can make a living if you are careful. Some of these guys who had their outfits, or inherited them, or got them so they weren't in debt, if they were careful they did all right. High prices for water and feed can kill you. Back when I was at it, if you could get forty or fifty dollars for a yearling, that was a good price. Now they get five hundred dollars. You don't have to be much of a cowboy to make money. Still, it isn't what it's cracked up to be. They have to buy lots of feed, and they have to have trucks and a lot of stuff they didn't used to have or need. When I worked for Andy Moore we were on horseback and that was it. We lived out of a greasy sack. We had our bed roll, and you didn't come to town three or four times a week. You made it in town maybe once in two months. You didn't want to make it in; it was too damn far riding an old pony or driving a team. Andy had a team, but while I was there he bought a Model T touring car—really uptown stuff.

Andy wasn't in the cattle business for himself at first. He worked for a cattle outfit that ran steers in the winter. He had an uncle down in Texas, and they had a bad drought down there. This uncle shipped him a hundred fifty head of Hereford cattle. It was very cold when they got up here, and we fed them protein cake all winter.

This uncle, Billy Moore, went by the name of Billy Babb, too. I don't know his situation. He shipped Andy those hundred fifty head of cattle by train. That is when I went to work for Andy. We had those cattle on the San Rafael on that ranch the Hatts have now. [*The Hatt Ranch is located immediately north of the San Rafael River west of where it crosses Utah 24, south of I-70.*] There wasn't anybody on it, and I don't know who owned it at that time. This was in 1931 or 1932. That spring we moved them out on the desert and fed them protein cake all winter and spring. From then on Andy was a full-time cowman.

I think of the San Rafael Desert as being between the rivers, between the San Rafael River on the north and the Dirty Devil River on the south, and from the San Rafael Reef on the west to the Green River on the east. The Fremont and Dirty Devil Rivers kind of separate that country from the Roost country. Those canyons set the Roost country off by itself. I have been Under the Ledge several times, but never to run stock down there. The first time I went down the Flint Trail was when I worked for Pearl. Dave Rust had a guide service and would take college kids down there to look for artifacts. He had a string of eight mules, and lined up with colleges and took young kids out. I remember one of the kids was the son of the Scott Tissue business owner. He had little sample packages of scented toilet paper. We cowhands had quite a bit to say about that scented toilet paper. I had never seen that product before that date. Pearl wanted to go down there and talk to the boys. Ned Chaffin was there on this trip, I am sure it was 1930. Ned was the wrangler. They had everything in the world to eat and camp with. There were eight college kids and their professor. They found quite a bit of Indian stuff.

At that time, you couldn't go down the Flint Trail in an automobile. You had trouble getting a pack outfit down it because of jump-offs and ledges. Down there, Under the Ledge, at Ernie Country and Waterhole Flat, that used to be sheep country in the winter. But we don't get the snow anymore, and for sheep and cattle both that snow was important. Especially for sheep for water. Sheep can't water where cattle can water. A herd of sheep can't go into one of these little water holes, but cattle can string in there all day and water. There are too many sheep in a herd for water holes.

Nowadays there are only two small cattle outfits out of Hanksville that feed down there. The grass, if it isn't eaten off, it seeds out and keeps growing more and more. It used to be good every spring after winter, but the sheep business got awful good there for a while. All you had to do was have some sheep and some fellow to stay out there with them. Jobs were scarce, and it wasn't hard to get men to be herders. After the First World War, the Frenchmen came in here pretty thick. Some of them had money, and some of them had sheep herds and would send for some of their friends to be herders. They could take their pay in sheep, and then they had an outfit. There were a lot of them out here. Over at Keg Spring an outfit had ten herds of sheep out there, and they never moved camp. For years you could see where those camps were. They hauled corn in there for feed, and stayed there in the winter. That is blackbrush country, and good sheep country. The blackbrush is real good sheep feed.

This has been a real hot, dry year in 1994, and no one has said this publicly, but this grass has been growing and they won't let them feed it.

This dry grass is just as flammable as gasoline and that is half the problem with these fires this year.

Looking back and talking about the kids today and those kids long ago, my wife and I have been in a lot of things over the years. There was a CCC camp in Hanksville back when they were around. I borrowed money from a fellow and built a pool hall in 1938. I ran that while the CCC camp was there. Then we had a little store in Hanksville. Then we came up here to Green River and ran our farm and raised cattle, and I did the hardware store thing for nine years. My wife ran the post office in Hanksville during 1940 to 1943. Then she worked in the Green River post office. We ran that ferry at Hite. The Morrisons built the Poor Boy Motel in Hanksville in about 1968 and we ran that for them for a while. We also ran the cafe there, too. I built and sold three houses in Hanksville. We did anything we could to make a living.

My grandson, Donald Guy Lusko, runs the cattle now. I turned the Fairview Ranch over to my daughter and her husband, Donald Lusko, in 1978. He came in here during the uranium boom. They were living in Arizona, and Sharon wanted to come back here, so I deeded the ranch to them. He was from Detroit and didn't know beans from buckshot about ranching, but I registered a brand for him and stood right beside him and told him to put it on the cattle. He has had a hell of a time getting it going, but has done pretty well with it.

I've had trouble with the BLM ever since they started. Before it came along, you were free to go and do the best you could, and I'll have to admit the country was overgrazed. The BLM didn't start as it operates now. It started as a grazing service, and it was sponsored mostly by livestock men and then, hell, like all government things, they are not that any more. They want to be your boss, and they hire these guys, they are educated by schooling, but they—I just can't put words to it—some of the thoughts they put out. They took the attitude that the stockman and everybody else is the enemy. That's the way they treat you. The BLM has done some good; it made it so tough that migratory sheep herds can't come and go any more, and that is a good thing for the people who try to live in this country. If you saw a livestock man trying to live here and make his home here, he was stuck because the damn sheep outfit would come in when the feed was good, eat it off, and go on to somewhere else. But the livestock man, he had to stay. Well, that all stopped now.

Of course, the BLM has its goal in mind, and that is to get everything off the range, no public range. I don't know how it is going to turn out. It is not good, but they have done some good. The whole thing is, they just have the wrong people tending to it. It's a tough one; it's tough for them to carry out what they have in mind, what they are told to do. They have to hire some creeps or they wouldn't stay in there. They have hired some good men, but they quit. About six months is all they can stand it. Then they ship others in from somewhere, usually eastern cities. I don't know what the outcome is going to be. I'll have to admit they have done some good. We needed some kind of a control because you can see how it was. A fellow gets an outfit, maybe a little cow outfit, and is trying to make a living off of it and trying to use a little piece of range, public domain. Then some outfit comes in, feeds its stock out and moves on. The local rancher is stuck, that is all! He's got some expense now to keep it going, so he stays on. He has either got to sell out or buy a lot of feed, and that is the way things were back there before the BLM.

That is done with now, and there are some small outfits that are doing pretty good, but they still come at you with some ideas that are to your detriment. They insist they have done good, then they have got you where they can say, "Do this or get off." They dictate to us. You start off with a permit that gives you the right to run so many animals. Animal unit months is the term.

In Hanksville, when they first started, I was the first fellow they cut in Hanksville. I had seventy-five head of cattle, and I had a permit for them, and I had the required commensurate property. You pay so much per month for your cattle. Then they said, "You have commensurate property, and you have to take them off the public range for two months. So you pick the months you want to take them off the range." Well, we were taking them off anyway, more or less, to tend them and save some feed. A man picks the late spring months, that's the time to bring them in. That went on for a little while, and then they said, "We are going to make it three months, and it will be these three months." That got us into the summer a little, but I still got along with it pretty good. Anyway, they kept it up until they banned all summer grazing, and they allow just winter grazing now. And then they started cutting the number of cattle you could have. They cut my seventy-five head permit to sixty-three.

The first battle I had with them, their office was in Richfield, they had me written up that I'd have to come in off the range for thirty days and then I could go out again, and then I had to bring my stock in for sixteen days. No point to it other than harassment. I went up to Richfield where they had a fellow named Caudill in the BLM office there. I talked to him and said, "You can see this doesn't help the range, and it just makes a mess for me. I have to round up and come in, and it takes me as long to round up my cattle as it takes me to get them back out there."

He had to admit it didn't make any sense, but he said, "That's the way it is, and that's the way it's going to be."

I said, "Put yourself in my shoes and see how it fits."

He said, "I wouldn't give a ten-minute spot to sit in your shoes."

I got up and went out. There was a lawyer down the street and I went in to him and told him my problem. He listened and told me to sit there while he went out the door and got in his car. When he came back, he had it all written out on papers that instructed me that once my cattle were out, they did not have to be brought back in. He knew what they were doing, and he knew what to tell them. I didn't. I was just getting mad over the fact the BLM fellow should have been able to look at that and say, "Well, yeah, that's stupid." Because it was, so I got the lawyer. But I'm telling you, they were on me after that. Any little thing. If they saw a cow of mine out somewhere, boy they were right after me about it. I've had trouble with them, my kids have had trouble with them about their ditch.

We've got a bunch that don't know beans from buckshot. They're doing what they are told to do to accomplish an end, and they are making it damn miserable for people who are trying to live in the country. I don't know how long it can last. Babbitt is doing what someone is telling him to do. He has himself a good job there. There is no stockman that thinks much of him, I'll tell you that. The whole idea, and you've heard the story, "livestock free in '93." There is a group of people—sidewalk people, I call them—who for some reason or other don't want any livestock on the public domain. They'd rather have the owls and the fires.

Looking at today's cowboy and comparing with the old times, today you have trouble getting a dependable fellow to go out on the range. It's rough, it isn't easy, but maybe you don't need them. They don't make drives any more. Of course, you have to round up your cattle, but you truck them. You don't drive them. For a fellow running livestock, he has to have so much capital that it is almost impossible for a fellow to start out and get in the cattle business. He starts out so far behind, he may never catch up. A fellow that is in the cow business has got to be dang careful if he wants to stay in. If he happens to owe money, he has to figure carefully to keep ahead of things. He has to buy a lot of things. With this drought going on they are telling the ranchers on the summer range they have to leave early. They have nowhere to go. They can't go on the public domain because they won't let them on in the summer. If they haven't got some money to buy hay with, or haven't got any private land, it's going to cost them part of their herd. That's all there is to it—they are going to have to sell some cattle. That may push the price up because after that there will be fewer cattle, and there are more people all the time and they are eating beef.

There are damn few cowboys out on the range. There are lots of them that wear boots, but they have never been there. We have lots of people who straddle a horse, but they are not cowboys. Lots of fellows who run outfits are having trouble hiring good cowboys.

You know it is a tough life running stock out there in the desert. You are miles from a town, often a two-day ride on horseback, and no such thing as a telephone. Accidents happen even to the most experienced cowman, like the time Mel Marsing got that darn rope burn and complications from it killed him.

Just telling of incidents like that never reveal how tense it really was, and if one doesn't know the people involved or have experienced something like that, the telling seems pretty bland.

I remember the time when I was working at Dubinky for Arthur Ekker. Dubinky is in that country between the Green and Colorado rivers. Everybody knows it as Dubinky; it was named after Dubinky Anderson. His first name was Albert. He was an east-west cowboy who first came to Utah from the east and landed in Thompson town. I don't know how he got the name of Dubinky, but everybody around this part of the country knew him and liked him. I think he made moonshine at several places. He ran the middle San Rafael Ranch for a few years and raised mules. One of my brothers worked for him, and I stayed there for a few days in the spring of 1926.

I was working with Arthur Ekker and running a little trap line and had set some traps for coyotes. One day as I rode my trap line it was stormy and cloudy. There was about six inches of snow on the ground. Around eleven o'clock the sun broke through the clouds and was shining bright and clear. Having nothing to protect my eyes with, it only took about an hour until I was so blinded I could see only nothing for the tears and pain. I was worried because the horse I was riding, like most, was a little spooky. All I could do was to take a good hold of the saddle horn and give him his head, hoping he would head for camp, which was about five miles away. I had no sense of direction and just had to leave it to my horse.

I knew it would take about an hour so I tried counting to myself to guess how far we had come. The camp was right on the edge of Dubinky

Wash, which had a loose gravel bottom. There was a drop-off into the wash. When the pony went over that I knew I was home safe. The horse walked up to the corral and stopped and I hollered at Art and he came and helped me off and led me to the dugout where it was dark. I stayed in the dark for several days with Art leading me out and bringing me food and water. It was an experience I wouldn't want to have again.

Here is an incident told to me by my father: My uncle Frank was missing four of his front teeth and they were replaced by a dental bridge. This happened early in the 1900s. Dad and his brother were building fence in Fillmore, Utah. They were both wearing pistols, and were practicing fast draw as they worked. They had removed the bullets from the pistols and would draw on one another, snapping the hammer each time. After a while they got busy with their work, and Dad reloaded his gun. Some time had passed and all of a sudden Frank yelled, "Draw," and pulled his gun on Dad, who had forgotten about reloading his gun, and he pulled and fired. The bullet hit Frank in the mouth. The bullets were old-time black powder. It knocked Frank's teeth out and lodged in the roof of his mouth, dropping him down and out cold. Dad supposed he had killed him, and ran home to tell his folks, who ran back with him only to meet Frank coming, bleeding all over the place. Their mother got him home, and dug the bullet out of the roof of his mouth and stopped the bleeding. So much for that.

One time I was riding a half-broke colt. My brother, nicknamed Cactus, was with me. We had gone to town to get mail and groceries. At the store I started to get on my horse and carelessly let my spur rake his hips. He began to buck and threw me over the saddle horn to the ground. It knocked the wind out of me but I was still holding the reins. I stood up, trying to get my breath, and Cactus said, "You get back on."

I said, "In a minute; I'm hurting some."

He raised his quirt and said, "Brother, if you don't get on right now, this quirt will hurt you lots worse!" I knew he meant it, so I got right back on and, needless to say, carefully, so my spur didn't touch the horse.

There was one time that I remember very plain while I was working with Art Ekker at Dubinky. He had a bronco running out with some other horses. It had been broke to lead, but was pretty wild. Art wanted to get him in and finish him to ride while I was there to help some. Anyway, we had a hard, fast ride, got the horse corralled and put a halter on him. We also caught a little mare out of the bunch that Art wanted to keep up. He decided he'd rode his horse pretty hard, so he put his saddle on the little mare. She hadn't been rode for about a year. He tied his rope to the bronco and the other end to the tired horse he'd been riding, and started out the gate. The bronc ran past him and his old horse set back; the little mare started to buck, the rope broke loose from the old horse and flipped in some manner and caught in Art's spur and boot, jerking him off the little mare. Away the bronco went with Art dragging behind. I spurred my horse to run past the bronco to stop the runaway, but my horse refused and spooked at Art dragging there and would not pass. About then Art's spur strap broke and turned him loose. Art was scratched up pretty good and shook up a lot, and I was too. This all happened in less time than it takes me to talk about it. We never did get the bronco in again. Needless to say, Art got back on his old, tired horse, and was real quiet for a while. Over my lifetime I have been in or witnessed a number of close calls handling horses and cattle, but I've been very lucky and never been seriously hurt.

If you run livestock, cattle or sheep, the very first thing you have to do is have a home for the livestock. I mean a year-around home, a place where they can winter or summer, and you can tend them. You can't just start in and get some cattle and be in the cow business. That is not the way it is any more. What the future is going to be, I have no idea. If the powers that be are going to run everybody off, then there will be just little farms.

Here is a message for Ned Chaffin. I know he is going to read this. You can come and pick a fight with me over this. I was camped at the Gordons when you and Clell came down. We camped there that night, and decided we would go down Millard Canyon hunting donkeys the next day. Do you remember when you unpacked, you spilled a half a gallon of honey in your pack bag? You grabbed some brush and wiped it out the best you could, but the next morning you just folded up your blankets and quilts and shoved them right square in that bag, and it had honey all around the edges. I remember when you pulled them out down Millard Canyon they were pretty damn sticky. Can you remember that?

It is awful hard for a fellow who has lived here to see it exactly through the eyes of somebody else, but I've tried to. I couldn't stand to live in a tight city, no way in the world. I just would not do it. I couldn't live and I wouldn't try, but I can see why a man from the city would want awful bad to get out here and enjoy the space and the scenery. And it is beautiful. There is no question about it, but when you live in amongst it, it is not quite so beautiful to you until you have time to sit back and see it from a different perspective. We see this country, and we see the shape and the colors; it reminds me of a poem.

There is nobody that doesn't appreciate this country, except when you work in it you fight the elements—the wind and the cold and the heat. That's on your mind all the time, so it takes a little of the beauty away. When you have time to set loose without any worries about it and look at it, it looks just as beautiful to one fellow as it does to another. I don't believe the human race is going to spoil this country. I don't see how they can. I don't see how anybody can protect it and save it. You can't spoil this country. It's gone through earthquakes and floods and droughts and severe cold, and it's still here—in spite of sheep, buffalo, and the EPA.

6

Nina Angela Johnson Robison

Nina Angela Johnson Robison has lived a life as diversified as that of her husband, Guy. During the early years in the life of a successful ranch, a monetary subsidy from an external source is frequently required. Throughout her marriage, Nina took on outside work to help pay off the ranch mortgage. She juggled her life, and when times were tough and the price of cattle hit rock bottom, she was the household's primary breadwinner. On the Fairview Ranch she was a mother, kept the house and ranch, and worked as a cowhand. When necessary, she worked for others as a postal clerk and a retail clerk, managed a motel, taught school, and was an office nurse, cook, and "billet-mess" cashier at the Green River Missile Base.

Her ancestors on both sides of the family were early converts to the Mormon religion. One of her grandmothers arrived in Salt Lake City after walking beside a wagon practically all the way from Vermont. Nina too has inherited some of those determined pioneer traits. She and Guy have pulled together for nearly fifty-eight years, during rough economic times and even rougher times when they lost loved ones.

June 21, 1996
Green River, Utah

I was born in 1917 in Cannonville, Utah, and am the ninth child in a family of eleven children. At an early age, I suspected that my parents, Sixtus Ellis and Lovisa Cox Johnson, named me Nina to help them keep an accurate count of their children.

Nina Robison dressed for a deer hunt, 1968. Photo courtesy of
Nina Robison.

My paternal grandfather was Seth G. Johnson. He was one of the early pioneer plural marriage fellows. His father and mother had emigrated from England in 1800 and settled in New England. They came west after the Mormon expulsion from Missouri and Illinois. My father was one of twenty-five children from Seth's two wives. The family was sent to settle in Iron County, and various family members platted and settled the town of Parowan, and then they moved to Toquerville, Tropic, and Cannonville and other small towns along the Virgin and Sevier Rivers. My grandmother emigrated from England. Her name was Lydia Ann Smith, and she was Seth Johnson's first wife. Later he married Martha Jane Stratton, and the two wives and all of the children intermingled and got along very well. That was contrary to a lot of things that you hear. My grandmother was a midwife and did many deliveries. Granddad was a pharmacist, not a registered or licensed pharmacist, but he practiced pharmacy. He got a lot of his knowledge of pharmacy from Indians who lived there. He could speak Paiute, Goshute, and Ute. Those tribes were all part of the Shoshoni Nation.

My mother's people, the Losees and Coxes, were Dutch and English. The Losees settled in Vermont and came west in 1849 when my grandmother, Eliza Jane Losee, was five years old. She did a lot of walking during the next five years as they trekked on their way west from Vermont, to Missouri, to Nauvoo, Illinois, then on a wagon train across Iowa until they reached Utah. After the family arrived in Salt Lake City they were sent to settle in southern Utah by Brigham Young. There she met and married my grandfather, Orville Sutherland Cox. My mother was his youngest child from the youngest of his three wives.

Whether or not plural wives got along well depended upon where they lived and the influences around them. At one time the LDS church adhered to the doctrine of the "United Order." It only was in existence for about ten years and was based upon the theory ". . . that we will all look out for one another and live the law that they did in Christ's time whereby everybody shared the same." There were no rich, no poor. My mother was seven years old when her family entered the Order, and it happened in the town of Orderville. That's how the town got named. She remembered some of it. It failed because they couldn't live the law, couldn't obey the rules. There were people who came into the Order who had nothing to contribute, but they drew off like it was a free lunch and were resented and ostracized.

As was true of so many of the pioneer towns in southern Utah, Cannonville subsisted on livestock and farming operations along with other small family-oriented occupations. Cowboys rode for their own brands, which means they were loyal to the brand they worked for just as though it was their own outfit, and you don't steal from the outfit that hired you. The Butch Cassidy syndrome had hit the bigger spreads, and rustling was common.

Our family ranch was known as the Willis Creek Ranch. It was eight or nine miles south of Cannonville. We wintered and schooled in Cannonville and summered at the ranch raising food for ourselves, and hay in the pastures for the livestock.

The First World War had come to a boil and the war had brought prices up, especially in cotton and wool. Cotton appealed to my father because he had lost his shirt when a bad blizzard hit the valley and his entire herd of sheep froze to death just after shearing. He had put a lot into that sheep herd of about a thousand head. This happened before I was born. The Indians, at that time, were in tough straits, especially in the wintertime. Most everyone heeded Brigham Young's advice to "Feed 'em, not fight 'em." It is reasonable to suppose that the Indians would have learned of the sheep disaster and traded for pelts and meat that they could have used. They didn't have any money to buy anything with, and trading was their way of doing business. Otherwise it was a total loss. So Dad invested in cattle which he later sold with the ranch for ten thousand dollars, which was quite a lot of money then. I have no idea how many head of cattle he had. The breaks and valleys of Bryce Valley held many wild cattle, escapees from local and passing herds. They were free for anyone tough enough to locate them, rope, and gather them. My father did some of this with the help of a special dog he called Sooner. He added them to the cattle herd he had for the next ten years before the First World War. It was then that he sold out and went to Arizona, to raise cotton.

In 1920 we moved to a small town near Mesa, Arizona, where the biggest boys in the family joined the Mexican pickers in the cotton fields. I remember seeing the cotton picking, but never picked any myself. Our baby brother Garth died of nephritis. He was just under a year old and is buried in Chandler, but I got a new baby sister while we were there, Delpha Almira. I was five years old and remember playing and learning a little bit of Spanish from the Mexican playmates. I also remember living in construction camps while our menfolk worked teams and scrapers on the roads.

The war ended and so did any profit in raising cotton, so the family trekked back to Utah. We traveled with a horse and wagon team, and crossed the Colorado River at Lee's Ferry and on to the coal mines of

Carbon and Emery County. We settled in Mohrland in Emery County. It was a little coal-mining town and is now a ghost town. The town was named after a Mr. Mohr, an English cattleman. There were seven of us then. Dad and Mother had lost two girls, Thelma and Velta, at one and two and a half years of age. They were their first children. Thelma died of diphtheria when she was eighteen months old, and Velta died after eating some poisonous nightshade berries.

While in Mohrland Dad acquired some dairy cows, so we milked cows and sold milk to the miners' families. Dad and my brother Ellis got jobs in coal mines. They lied about Ellis's age because he wasn't old enough to be hired.

We expanded the dairy herd later and moved to Price. Dad bought the Price Carbon Dairy. We delivered milk in bottles, and some bottles were washed by seven-year-old me. I had to use an electric bottle brush that was sticking out of the edge of a tin tub sink. I remember it well because the friction made static electricity and it just sizzled me. This was in 1923 or 1924. My sister Merintha had married Glenn Johnson while we were in Mohrland, and they followed us to Price. Glenn delivered the milk that we produced. While in Price, I went to third grade in a little red schoolhouse.

Later we moved to a farm in Wellington so we could raise more feed for the dairy cattle. When I was ten years old we moved to Victor, which was another potential ghost town. In fact, it died two years after we left there. I went to school there in another one-room schoolhouse with about twenty other students, all grades. We were there two years, and then Dad heard about the Henry Mountains where there was free grazing for cattle. Of course, this was before any grazing fees came into being. He wanted to get back into range cattle rather than dairy herds, so we took the dairy herd and headed for the Henrys from Victor. Victor was near Cleveland and, after five days of trailing our cattle on the desert, we got to Hanksville via Green River and the San Rafael Desert. We had an old Model T truck that I rode in the back of with my little sister Delpha and a pile of camping and household gear.

Hanksville in 1927 to the present time was home to us and a couple of hundred other people from time to time. Once Hanksville got to be over five hundred people. That was during the uranium boom, but there were always ranches there from the very beginning when Ebenezer Hanks founded the town around 1880.

My father slowly converted his dairy stock, from Jersey and Holstein cows into Hereford and Durhams. He was pressured by the beef ranchers about our Jersey and Holstein bulls. We always depended on livestock as the basic source of our livelihood. It was supplemented from time to time by other ventures. For instance, the Henry Mountain legend of the lost Josephine Gold Mine and other old Spanish mine stories always intrigued Dad. Those stories beckoned him, so he did some prospecting. The story about the Josephine was that it was a lost Spanish gold and silver mine that was supposed to have been rediscovered in the 1880s by two prospectors. The mine was rumored to have been cursed by Indians who provided slave labor to the Spaniards who operated the mine. The curse said that anyone who tried to work the mine would become very sick. One of the prospectors who rediscovered the mine died, and the other was scared out. That's the story.

I spent three years at the Hanksville Elementary School, a year at Green River High, and two more at Wayne High in Bicknell. That finished my formal education except for a few extension courses from Utah State University. I accomplished that high school education in three years because I was interested in graduating and was quite a bit older (I was twenty) than the other students. I seemed like a grandma to some of the younger students, so they made me student body president in my last year.

I had enough credits to do substitute teaching, which in those days most graduates did some of. I boarded with Dr. E. C. Brinkerhoff in Bicknell while I was in high school. That stimulated my interest in medicine. As time went on that gave me the opportunity to work as an office nurse in Green River for Dr. H. T. Barton. Later I helped with the establishment of the rural medical clinic in Hanksville under the auspices of the Flying Doctors, Dr. Eugene Davie and Dr. Keith Hooker.

Guy and I were married in May of 1939. For many years between 1937 and 1973 I worked at whatever job was available: at the post office as a clerk, in stores as a saleslady, and at the town's information booth.

I grew up with cows, pigs, sheep, and chickens, but didn't become involved other than to help herd and feed the animals, and plant and harvest, and cook and eat what we raised or traded for. The mechanics of ranching, though, fell to the boys. I wasn't wise enough to avoid learning how to milk cows or separate cream or make butter or bake bread. My mother and I kept our noses to the grindstone cooking and keeping the laundry done up with a scrubbing board for the whole family. Finally, in 1932, when cattle prices came up, Dad bought us a gasoline-powered Maytag washer. It was the first one in Hanksville and it was wonderful. We had that for a long, long time. In fact, after Guy and I moved to the Henrys onto the Fairview Ranch in 1957, we bought another Maytag because they were still the very best. Anyway, that washing machine was the most wonderful invention I had ever seen. No more skinned knuckles on a metal scrubboard, and hours of soaking, boiling, rinsing, handling of stiff, sweaty, dirty socks, shirts, and Levis.

I never shot a gun for fun. Of course, I knew how to use one. I shot predators when they came around the ranch. There were too many coyotes and they were too daring and destructive on the lambs and calves.

Once I was attacked by a feral cat and I shot the daylights out of him. He was there on the ranch when we first moved there. He occupied the old shearing shed that served all of the sheepmen in the area. That big old yellow cat was there, and I used to go out and feed him. One time, after I had fed him, I turned my back and was going back to the house when he lit between my shoulder blades and dug in. I was absolutely stunned, but I got him off and went and got Guy's .30-30 because I couldn't find his .22. I came back and disintegrated the cat with one shot. I wasn't too bad a shot.

There were bears, but they stayed down by the river and didn't come anywhere near us, and once in a while we heard a wolf or two, but they stayed out in the desert and there were not enough of them to really be a problem.

Guy taught me about cattle and sheep raising. My parents and my brothers took care of all of that stuff when I was growing up, so I never got involved. As a matter of fact, I never learned a thing about ranching until I married Guy. He taught me about cattle and brands, and what we have to do to get along on a ranch.

When we bought the ranch, Sharon was in high school, so Guy and I ran it by ourselves. I learned a lot then, but somebody had to work off the ranch to make some money to make payments when we didn't have enough stuff, crops or stock, to sell. That's when we started working for other people—off-season work—in motels, or as store clerks, substitute teaching, or working at the missile base in Green River, whatever we could get. We raised one daughter, Sharon. We lost two other children, a boy and a girl.

I had gone to Green River High School for my freshman year and the other two years in Bicknell at Wayne High. I didn't start high school here at Green River until I was seventeen. My parents could not afford to send me to school. Hanksville was sixty-five dirt miles from Bicknell and fifty dirt miles from Green River. They just couldn't do it. So I boarded out in Green River and Bicknell so I could attend school. I worked for my board.

In Hanksville there were three, probably four, big dances a year. During spring sheep shearing we had the Shearer's Ball, and on the Fourth of July we had a big celebration and dance. And on New Year's Eve we usually had a dance. Then somebody would come along like C. B. Hunt, who was known as Mr. Henry Mountains; he was doing survey work in the mountains in 1934 and 1935. He would bring his survey crew of men into town, about ten of them, and all of us gals loved it. I wasn't a bad dancer; I was tall, but I liked to dance. There was a fiddle, guitar, banjo, and a harmonica. Later the LDS church ward bought a player piano with about fifteen rolls of music. They were all oldies that were good music.

I loved riding horses and got to be a pretty good rider. The boys all had to have the saddles so I got to ride bareback. One incident while I was working for the postmistress in Hanksville in 1935: I was seventeen at the time, and the postmistress also ran the general store. Somebody wanted a lot of eggs, so she sent me down to her brother's ranch that was about three miles out of Hanksville to get the eggs. Somebody loaned me a horse, no saddle, so I rode it bareback and got the bucket of eggs and got them back to the store without breaking one of them.

At the Hite Ferry we lived in a cabin and Guy operated the ferry. Beth and Reuben Nielson farmed and ran a boarding and eating business in tent houses, but they had moved to Blanding and the tents were in storage when we arrived. We got the tents out of storage and used them for boarding people.

The boats and gear that were there belonged to river runners. Georgie White, Norman Nevills, Jack Brennen, Bus Hatch, and Bert Loper stored their boats there. We didn't think anything about these old river people. We thought it was just somebody's idea of having a good time. We cooked for the people who came by and we didn't realize they were really making up part of the history of the early river running. They were the pioneers who lay the groundwork for all of the river running industry of today.

This was the time when Reed Maxfield had fallen off the ferry and drowned in 1961. I flew down the river with Bill Wells, the Flying Bishop. He owned the only plane in Hanksville at that time. He was the LDS bishop of Hanksville's ward and had been a navy flier. I went with him to see if we could spot Reed's body floating because they were building the Glen Canyon dam. The body was found two weeks later at the dam site. When he died, they had to find somebody to run the ferry and, because we had lived at Hite and were acquainted with the Maxfields, we were chosen to operate it.

Hite was located at a wide spot in the canyon where the old Dandy Crossing of the Colorado River was; it was very near the confluence of the Colorado and Trachyte Creek. The climate there was semitropical, and there were fruit and nut trees galore. We had figs, pomegranates, almonds, and walnut trees as well as peach, apple, pear, plum trees, and grapes.

Cass Hite had built the first ferry. He used a boat as a ferry for everything but livestock. The livestock had to ford the river at Dandy Crossing. Arthur Chaffin had the crossing after Cass Hite had died. Arthur (Arth) ferried for several years and sold the business to Reed Maxfield.

We went down there to live because Guy had met an old Oklahoma cow puncher named Clarence Bray at the Chaffin Ranch. They had an idea they could go down there and catch some wild horses and cattle, or do some wonderful thing that would make them some money. The uranium boom had passed by and the mill at Hite was all done. There was quite a lot of stuff left there. Guy and Clarence didn't get a lot done, except we got acquainted with that great old cow puncher.

After the lake filled up we ran the Hite Marina at the new crossing for a summer and fall. At that time Sharon was married and was living in Huntsville, Alabama, where her husband, Don, taught at the Redstone Arsenal.

Guy and I moved around a lot and did a lot of different things, but we always talked things over before moving or taking on new things or occupations. I always felt I was involved in making those kinds of decisions, and was glad about that. It was not so with my mother. She didn't have much say-so in the decision making because the times were so much different, and when you had that many kids you were making decisions about home all of the time.

While on the ranch I never could have run it without Guy, but I don't want him to know that because I wanted him to think I could have done it. If I had a hired hand or two, or a cowhand like Clarence Bray, I could have run it. I didn't think about leading any other life because I liked what I was doing and I liked my life. Guy is a good teacher; he taught me about brands and tracking, although my dad did too. Our cattle ran on the open range, no fences, so Guy taught me how to tell how old a track was, what direction it was going, and whether the critter was hurrying or just leisurely moving along. I can read track: buffalo, deer, elk, others; I can tell which animal left his prints and how long ago.

I find it hard now to consider myself without considering Guy. He sort of was, and continues to be, my best friend and, besides that, I still kind of like the old fellow. I could see the potential of that ranch just as well as he did. What we needed was the cooperation of the weather so we could have good wet years and raise lots of feed, and naturally we were always pressured by the Bureau of Land Management because we had a grazing license permit. We bought a grazing permit from someone once and it included Mount Ellen in the Henrys and on south Caineville Mesa. That one had been a sheep permit. You couldn't use those permits for cattle, so when we sold out we were able to sell it to the Division of Wildlife Resources. There have been times when we were sorry we did sell it because they just retired it from any grazing.

I never did feel trapped with my life because one of us almost always had to work off the ranch, and I enjoyed that and got paid for it. Guy worked as an engineer's assistant when they were building Utah Highway 24 and moved it out of Capitol Gorge and rerouted it to its present location. I worked here in Green River off and on, and when the missile base was here we both took turns working there—one at a time, while the other one of us was at the ranch. You learn a lot. When your back is to the wall, you learn to cope by yourselves.

I never did like a big city, and Guy couldn't stand one either. Green River is big enough. The difference in living in town is that you have more worries than you do on the ranch. They are different kinds of worries. Here you have to worry about other people too. On the ranch it's just other people who are in the same boat you are in. They have livestock too, and their land adjoins yours, and you learn to cooperate. You can hardly make it without having a group of you doing work together. You gather your cattle together, you brand together, you tell the other guy that he has a cow with a prolapse, or he has a cow over here in trouble.

Our grandson, D. G. Guy Lusko, and his wife, Saleta, operate the Fairview Ranch now. Even though we sold the grazing permit he has enough land; if he can fence the land, he can run his fifty head of cattle. At times we ran up to 150 head, but never more than that. Now that he doesn't have a permit, he can only graze on his own property. He, the Fairview Ranch, has the water rights on Bull Creek. They have the prior rights and will always have those "granddaddy" rights. Sometimes Bull Creek doesn't have much water to distribute. Fairview is close to one thousand acres, but it's desert land and has to be taken care of either by the good Lord above who lets it rain, or you have to do something to keep the cattle going.

We have a well drilled there that is beautifully developed. It has a windmill and a big storage tank so they can water their livestock when they need to. There are also seeps and springs, all with good water in normal years. We also lease a school section. We have had it for twenty years or more and it is kept current.

The weather and the climate are things that rule for ranchers. Water is so important, and though winter storms can be dangerous, they are important when they place a blanket of snow on the pastures.

In 1955, before we bought the Fairview Ranch, we leased the old Chaffin Ranch. In the middle of March of that year we were trailing about sixty head of cattle out of Green River south on the road to Horse Reservoir on the way to the Chaffin Ranch. We held the herd at the reservoir and camped there one night. The next day we set out past Tank Wash to go to Dry Lakes when a March blizzard blew in. The two Hatch boys, Carl and Allen, their cousin Laddie King, our Sharon, and her pal Karma Halverson were our crew punchers. Guy was the trail boss. The kids were all about fourteen, and I was the chief cook and drove the truck. When the storm hit, the boys wanted to get on home to warm fires, so we sent them back to town with all of our extra wraps, including a tarp and a blanket. After two or three additional chilly miles, Sharon and Karma elected to ride in the truck with me. Guy took their horses and hooted the herd for more speed over the cut-off from Dry Lakes and we headed for the ranch and a warm up.

The old ranch house was shy a window and the drafty old fireplace was the only thing left for heating. Any wood to be found was damp and we burned all the paper we had trying to dry the wood. So we tried burning an old saddle, which was the biggest mistake of all. It smelled worse than anything and only smoldered over the ancient leather and the rawhide tree. It was awful!

When Guy arrived with the herd he was cold and wet and here we were with that smokey, smelly old fire. Well, Guy gave us a lesson on how, what, and where to get a fire going. It took his knowledge, an old chair, and some of the wooden and pasteboard boxes we used for holding supplies. That night we were thankful for sleeping bags and dry clothes.

We spent the summer and fall at the Chaffin Ranch, installing a pump on the San Rafael River to irrigate corn we had planted and spreading the water anywhere there was a possibility of growing feed for the cows. Clarence Bray came down and helped. He also broke a few horses for other ranchers, and we hardscrabbled a crop of sorts. Sharon and I explored the old Dry Lakes bed and found some pieces of brain coral and a stingray tooth. We also found nice meteorite fragments and some good agate. It was a fun summer for us.

Overall, looking back, I think one of the things I liked best was when Guy needed me to help ride and herd. I would have to ride to a certain area to see what the cattle were doing while he was off in some other area checking that bunch out. Even though it was miserable and full of gnats and your horse was homesick and wanted to go home, I was still out by myself on the range doing something I loved to do. I loved being by myself, and felt useful. I had this feeling that nobody but God knew where I was right then.

For two years I served as a guide for Alice B. Hunt. She is C. B. Hunt's wife; he is a well-known geologist who was conducting a survey of the Henry Mountains. Alice is an archeologist, and they would bring his students from John Hopkins University to the ranch. The ranch had all kinds of Indian artifacts and ruins on it, and the students were working on their theses. She headed the archeological study for the Henry Mountains under Dr. Jesse Jennings, who was a University of Utah professor of archeology. For those two years I just loved it. Every time they gave me my check I'd feel like it was a bonus because I enjoyed showing them the various Indian sites along Bull Creek from the foothills down to the border of the desert.

I didn't mind the ranch work because you could stop, but I disliked the feeling and the pressure of being in debt and the pressure of somebody telling you how best to run your ranch business. That was frustrating. That was the Department of the Interior with its rules and regulations that couldn't apply to you profitably. You had to object to them right along. We were not alone in that. This was when the Sagebrush Rebellion came into being; it came out of Nevada and we were enthusiastic about it, hoping maybe we could get something done about those foolish rules. The Sagebrush Rebellion's motto is "Much good can be done if one doesn't care who gets the credit."

There are little aggravations like the gnats and the mosquitos, the heat and the cold, and the wind and the dust. Those are all natural things that you went into knowing you had to endure them and there wasn't anything you could do about them.

The Fairview Ranch has a wonderful atmosphere about it—a friendly atmosphere—I guess because everybody who has been there has been peaceful and friendly. I could stroll out at night and not feel any danger around me unless I was dumb enough to fall into a ravine. One time Guy had a horse named Cultus. He was a little bit "original," which meant that he was gelded improperly so he felt he was the king of the roost. I went out on foot one time to bring the horses in from the spring. They were outside of the fence and I headed over that way. There were maybe ten head of horses and several of them were mares. When Cultus saw me, he whistled and laid his ears back and came after me. I had to run. I guess it was a matter of rods till I got to the fence. I knew where I could get under the fence and dove under it. He came right up to that spot. That was a fright! I told Guy about it, but he didn't think the horse was serious, and he thought maybe it was the way I was dressed because I had ridden that horse in the past with no consequences. That was scary, but I often stayed on the ranch for three or four days by myself and never worried, but one time we heard on the radio about a dangerous fugitive who had escaped and they thought he might be heading down toward our direction. I was wishing that Guy was home. About that time a man drove up in an old, beat-up vehicle, and he didn't look wholesome, so I met him outside of the gate. I didn't let him come up to the house. He wanted to be invited into the house, and got his coffee pot out of the car and drank up what was left. He drank it right out of the spout. He said that was the last he had, and hinted that maybe I should give him some fresh coffee. I told him I didn't have any coffee made with which to give him a refill. Anyway, I kept him out there, and I froze him out and he left. I didn't like that. I don't know who he was. I didn't think he was that fugitive, but that bothered me some.

The other day we were both sitting on the couch and I leaned my head over on Guy's shoulder and said, "I sure am old and done for."

He reached his arm over to give me a hug and about that time he must have pulled a muscle and hurt himself, and he said, "Ouch! I'm the one who is really old!" Then I got a crick in my neck. We just sat there and laughed. We can't even cuddle anymore.

But I wouldn't change it. Not a thing. I'll stand by my Guy and the life we have lived. Living on a ranch or in a small town, there is no way this life can be beaten.

7

Lowry Seely, Gwen Seely, and Hugh Seely

Brothers Lowry and Hugh Seely live in Craig, Colorado, and remain active in the cattle and sheep business. Gwen, Lowry's wife, frets when he defies his age (they were married in 1937) and enters roping contests as he did this past summer. He won some ribbons, too; he also got a banged-up shoulder, again. It required surgery this time, but he is back roping calves, working as part of a two-man team with his "heeler," striving to shave seconds off the clock.

Though both of the brothers have been on the San Rafael Desert with stock, it was their father, their grandfather, and their grandfather's cousin Karl who ran sheep Under the Ledge and up on the hills above the leading edge of the Book Cliffs.

Their interview addresses problems with coyotes more so than the other interviews because the Seelys were more sheepmen than cattlemen. Coyotes, being smart critters, prefer killing docile sheep to taking on nine-hundred-pound, overly aggressive cows. The interview also speaks of some of the trouble the Seelys have had with the Bureau of Land Management (BLM), not an uncommon theme with ranchers.

December 1, 1994
Craig, Colorado

Lowry Seely: My grandfather and grandmother raised their family in Mount Pleasant, Utah. This was before 1900, probably around 1880. Granddad, Orange Seely, was named after the Duke of Orange. After he

161

From left to right: Hugh Seely, Gwen and Lowry Seely.

had converted to the Mormon Church he had been directed by Brigham Young to gather his family and other settlers and go to Emery County and start a settlement. The settlement just naturally got named Orangeville. My father, David Randolph Seely, and mother, Elva Singleton Seely, met in Ferron where her father ran the Singleton Hardware and Grocery store. Our mother grew up there managing that store for him as a young girl. She had many experiences—a saloon was right next door to the store. She would tell of times when some members of the Robbers Roost Gang would come in the store after drinking in the saloon. I may as well throw this story in now. Mother told us that one time her father, Sam Singleton, was in the store and she was in the back office of the store doing bookwork when Butch Cassidy walked in the store. He had an old, sloppy, worn-out hat that he took off, took a new hat off Grandfather Singleton's head, and set his old hat on Granddad's head and told him thanks. My mother was embarrassed that he didn't contest Butch about the taking of his hat.

Grandfather said, "I'm only glad that's all he wanted." Butch had a lot of friends and I always understood that if he stole anything he gave it to the poor.

Hugh Seely: I know a man by the name of Jim McPherson who knew Butch quite well. The stories he tells are that Butch was a robber and a thief, but he didn't steal from people of his class, poor people. There is one story, it's written in a book, about him and two other guys. I don't know who the other people were. It happened in Wyoming where they rode in, and they were hungry. This older couple lived way out in the country and she had some real nice Rhode Island Red chickens. They shot three of these chickens and took them in and asked her if she would cook them. And she said, "Sure," and Butch supposedly gave her ten dollars for each chicken. During the meal while they were eating the chickens he noticed something was wrong, like something was bothering her and her husband.

He finally asked them and she said, "Yes, something is bothering us. We owe seven hundred dollars and it is due today and the banker is going to come and collect it. We don't have the money and we're going to lose our place." Well, Butch Cassidy, according to the story, gave her the seven hundred dollars and left. He saw the banker come in and saw the banker go out, and later relieved him of the seven hundred dollars and went on his way. The people had their place paid for.

Lowry: I was born in Castle Dale. Our folks were married in 1909. We had a sister who died when she was one year old and there are four of us living. Dad was a livestock man right from the beginning. He went to work for his uncle, John Seely, at a very young age. In his early days he was down in the Sinbad country on the San Rafael Desert working with Chris Peterson taking care of John Seely's cattle.

Hugh: Then later he ran his own cattle and took care of other people's cattle too. I was down there on the San Rafael, I was about ten or twelve years old, and there were some people there by the name of Nugie, Joe Nugie. They were Frenchmen. On this ranch they had a little commissary where they sold flour to sheepherders, and coffee and some whiskey. There were two other people near there, this was about 1922 or 1923, and we went down to see Tom Cottrell. He was living where the San Rafael River empties into the Green River. We were looking for cattle and stayed there all night. This was in the spring of the year and they were getting ready to leave with all those cattle. They were just scouring the countryside to gather the cattle and take them up to Castle Dale and on in the forest to graze for the summertime. They had to ride the San Rafael River every day in the spring because of cattle getting into quicksand. On the days the river was real high Dad wouldn't let me cross, but I've crossed the river when I was ten or twelve years old and

Pictograph in the Sinbad area, San Rafael Swell.

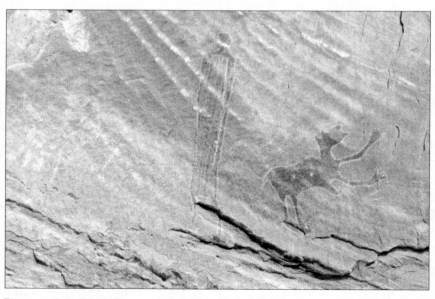

Pictograph in Black Dragon Wash, San Rafael Swell.

my horse would be walking on the bottom and the water would be hitting me around my hips.

Lowry: Nowadays there's no water in the river to speak of. Ferron Creek, Cottonwood Creek, and Huntington Creek, when they all came together in the spring of the year, there was lots of water, but they constructed dams on each of the rivers and today the water is tapped off for the use of the Utah Power and Light Company and for irrigation. The ranch hands would swim back and forth across the San Rafael checking to see if there were cattle there. If they didn't get those cattle out of the quicksand, at night the coyotes would come and eat the meat out of their hind legs even while the cattle were still alive. The Gillis family had a ranch there at that time. They had some log cabins there, and put up some hay. We camped at their place off and on.

Hugh: I rode out around what is called the tanks and all over the desert. The tanks were large sandstone rocks with huge depressions in them. The depressions captured rain water and were used for watering stock, and we drank from them too. These tanks I refer to were north of the San Rafael River.

At that particular time a man by the name of Neal McMillan had run lots of cattle there, and there were two different banks claiming those cattle and gathering them. One day one outfit had them going one way and the next day the other outfit had them going the other way. He didn't have money enough to pay off, and he had lots of cattle, so that's what the banks went after.

Lowry: My wife, Gwen, was born in Preston, Idaho. We met at Utah State University in Logan. We got married in my senior year, and after I finished school, we moved to the ranch that summer to help Dad with the livestock and the ranch work. That year was 1938 and Dad's ranch was about thirty-five to forty miles south of Craig. Legally, the ranch was identified as the D. R. Seely & Sons, Inc., but sections of the ranch were referred to by the name of the homesteaders: the Phibbs place, Gray place, Geddes place, Ellis place, and the Godlove place.

Dad moved from Emery County, Utah, and had gone to the Book Cliffs north of Green River. Later, in the thirties when the BLM was established, the government bought all of the private land up in that area of the Book Cliffs and returned that land to the Ute Indians. They used it to set up or add to their reservation. The Indians bought 460,000 acres. It was appraised by Frank Moore, and Hugh helped with the appraisal.

Hugh: We got out here when the guy who owned the Crawford place went broke. The mortgage was held by the Carbon Emery Bank.

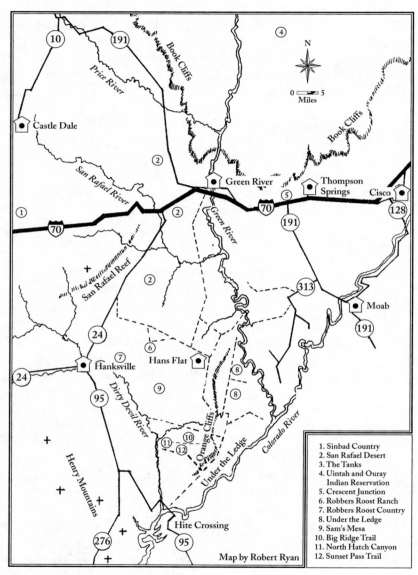

The Seelys' Canyonlands.

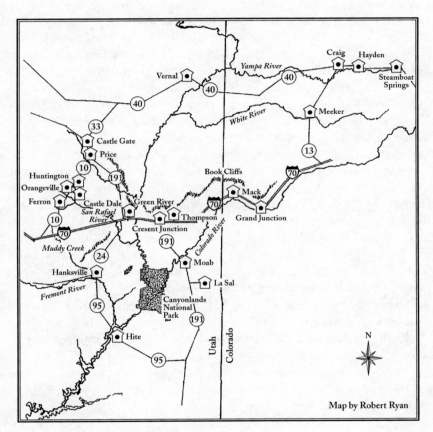

Region of Seely ranching activity.

A deal was made for it that winter, and in the spring of 1934 we came up here.

Lowry: We still call it the Crawford place. It is where our dad and his partner, Mr. Crawford, lived in the summers until 1939. They were married to sisters. Then in 1939 they split up and Mr. Crawford got the place down there and Dad took what we call the Phibbs place. Our dad was running both sheep and cattle Under the Ledge in Emery County. He knew all the Chaffins and Biddlecomes. Hugh knew Millie Biddlecome and Hazel, but at a much later date. In 1922 Dad left the Robbers Roost country and the Under the Ledge area and moved up to the Book Cliffs. In 1939 he was in a partnership arrangement with Mr. Crawford and he took Hugh and me in as partners in his half of the operation. We had worked at it for some time. The move to the Book Cliffs was a big one. This was part of the Bounds Livestock Company. There were a lot of people in Emery County who put their livestock in this company to save it. It was Dave Seely's skill, expertise, hard work, and good management that made it financially sound. Our grandfather, Sam Singleton, and Chris Peterson put a lot into the company. Everybody they could get put their livestock into it and they made Dad the general manager. At that time they had around eight thousand head of sheep and two thousand head of cattle. Prior to 1922 my father ran his livestock in the eastern part of Emery County, which includes Sinbad, the San Rafael Desert, Robbers Roost, and Under the Ledge that was down in the canyons of the Colorado River.

During the Depression of 1929 the big stockholders of the Bounds Livestock Company reached a point where they could sell off their livestock and pay off the debt; so my father and Edmund Crawford bought some of the sheep and continued to run in that area.

Hugh: When they kept sheep on the range in those days they were out there all year long. All twelve months, and sheepmen in that country didn't plan on feeding anything. They went to the high country in the summer and the low country in the winter. In those days you didn't have big trucks to haul feed; you walked the sheep. Instead of hauling feed they would take mules or horses and break trails and scatter the sheep all over the country. They would have to move a little bunch here and a little bunch there, but that is the way they wintered them, even in deep snow. Ordinarily when I was there with Lowry, it was during the years when we had good winters—no snows, or rather no really deep snows, but just about the right amount of snow. About a foot, with that you could melt plenty of water for the horses and there was plenty for the camp, and the sheep eat snow. That is how they get their water. If there is plenty of feed and water, you don't need to stay with the sheep all of the time. We turned the horses loose, grained them at night, put blankets on them and let them go footloose. Some nights they'd go five or six miles, but about daylight they'd come back. You had better be there to grain them because if they stood around too long they'd leave. Hard telling where they would go.

Gwen Seely: We had only one French Basque. Then we used young and old western men who grew up learning how to care for livestock. As the wage scale rose, the Mexican herders took over. Nowadays a sheepherder is an endangered species. A good shepherd is one who loves the open country and tending his flock. He starts at the break of day with a cup of coffee, taking pride in being out in the early morning, watching the sheep as the sun rises over the horizon, enjoying God's creation. He tries to protect them from coyotes, lions, and bears and sees that they start out in one direction together, and brings up the stragglers. Then he goes back to camp to prepare his breakfast. He always looks for lost sheep. He takes pride in his companions, the horse and the dog, and he trains the dog to herd and to protect, too.

It is a natural instinct of sheep to move together for higher elevations. The camp was always on top of high ridges where the sheep would sleep, and the herder would stay close to the flock late in the evening and early in the morning because that was when the coyotes or lions or bear, and wolves and bobcats attack. Camping high on the ridges would require packing water for camp and taking the horses to water midday while the sheep were on water.

When two men are in camp, one herder and one camp mover, the herder is in charge. The other is a helper, a "chore boy"; he helps with the sheep, cooks, does the dishes, and cares for the horses. He is always looking for lost sheep and bringing them back to the flock.

Lowry: The west Book Cliff Mountains were a crossing point on the route from the Robbers Roost hideout up to Brown's Park, which was another hideout that was used by Butch Cassidy and various members of the Wild Bunch. My father, after moving his livestock from the San Rafael Desert or Sinbad or the Under the Ledge country and the Robbers Roost areas, went north to the Book Cliffs. While he was in the Robbers Roost country he had become well acquainted with members of the Wild Bunch. He was known to have the best cavvy of saddle horses in the whole area. [*A cavvy is the equivalent of a remuda of working mounts.*] He told me of the time when the hold-up and robbery of the

Petroglyph, Book Cliffs.

Petroglyph, Book Cliffs. Depicted: a serpent with five human forms in its stomach and about to swallow two others.

Castle Gate Mining Company payroll by Butch and his gang took place. Dad was staying at a ranch west of Green River City on the San Rafael where he was keeping and feeding his horses. The sheriff's posse came by and told Dad they needed to take his horses so they could try to catch the robbers. My father said, "You are not taking my horses on that kind of a chase!"

The sheriff answered, "You don't have any choice. We are taking them whether you want us to or not." During that chase a deputy by the name of Tuttle was wounded and died.

A few days later when Dad returned to the corral where he kept his horses there was a note on the gate which read, "Dave, we didn't think you would furnish horses for the posse to run us down. We will return and steal every horse you own."

For thirty days Dad had his bedroll in the center of the corral and slept with his .30-30 rifle under his head to guard those cherished horses. One night a good friend came by, and as was the custom, opened the gate to turn his horse loose in the corral. Dad startled him by shouting, "Who's there?" He already had his gun out and a bead on the guy before he could answer.

Matt Warner was one of the Wild Bunch, and after he had served his time in prison, he became sheriff of Carbon County. When Dad and I would go through Price we often stopped and visited with him.

Gwen: One hard winter on the winter range in eastern Utah—it was the winter of 1948–1949—we had a very bad snowstorm. Then it rained, just a little bit, but the next morning there was a sheet of ice on top of the snow. It stayed cold, got down to thirty-five degrees below zero. The men were trying to feed the sheep because they had gotten such sore mouths from trying to graze through the ice crust. Their mouths had gotten cut up and they couldn't eat. The men were using horses to try to get hay to the sheep and the icy crust was scraping the horses' legs, so the fellows made leather leggings to fit the horses' legs and that protected them.

Lowry: A typical herd of sheep was two thousand to twenty-five hundred and it took one herder and a camp mover to tend them. The camp mover's job was to melt water for the horse, get firewood and water for the camp, and cook for the herder. The sheepherder was the boss. They always had dogs, but more for company than anything. Some dogs were really good, but not everyone can train a dog. Most of the dogs you find with a sheepherder are for company. In the country around the San Rafael Desert you can graze five head of sheep to the acre. I would guess down in New Zealand it is probably about twenty head of sheep to the acre because of the difference in the amount of rainfall and the rotation of pastures.

Gwen: Charlie Redd said it takes ten acres in New Zealand to run the same number it takes ten thousand acres in the San Rafael Desert country. He went down to New Zealand and ran twenty thousand sheep and about the same number of cattle on ten thousand acres. He and two other fellows were in business over there. My daughter Sunny and her husband, Hardy, a son of Charlie's, were over there at that time.

Recently Hardy invited students and teachers from private schools, one from Hawaii and two from the eastern slope of Colorado, to their ranch for a seminar. An attorney, a newspaper editor, a rancher, and a BLM man participated in an educational program at his ranch in La Sal as speakers, one each night. Besides touring the ranch and learning what it takes to run a cattle operation, they had a discussion or lecture each evening, and the following morning they would go out on a field trip to observe what they had been talking about. They got to see the sawmill, and the oil wells pumping. The environmentalists were just screaming against having an oil well on that 100,000 acres. The drillers won; the aesthetic interest in that vast country is unharmed because you can hardly find or see it. It provides the jobs, the fuels, and the industries our culture needs. I asked an environmentalist why people would rather have forests burn up than be harvested for homes and so forth and then replanted and cleaned up. He didn't really answer. He could have been a little confused because he had to open up his mind and think. I think he just was not prepared to see how the youngsters reacted.

Most of the young people said they thought "they" (I guess they were referring to extreme environmentalists) had exaggerated everything, and the truth was not the way they told it. They were impressed with the way particular occupations were conducted and they understood the whole picture of the land and country better. They had to write reports each day. They were intelligent, thinking youngsters.

Lowry: That is a good way for young people to learn. They get right out there and see how one handles the cows and what goes on at a ranch.

Gwen: Most of the youngsters who were guests there had discussions about what their attitudes had been and what they had learned. This meeting was based upon an educational theme, a field trip, to acquaint them with a firsthand look, not only at the operation of a ranch, but other uses of our land. They were high-school-age youngsters, about thirty of them including their teachers. The professionals were local people from Monticello, Moab, and La Sal.

Hugh: Well, you know that the general opinion of most of the people in the United States is that sheep are the worst animal in the world on rangeland. They probably are the best domesticated animal if you treat them right. They won't overgraze the bottoms, they pull up on the side hills, and if you want the grass to grow thicker, if you treat the country right with sheep on it, it will do just that—simply because they eat the weeds in preference to grass really, and they like to browse on bushes. They compete with everything that causes the grass not to get thick.

Lowry: They eat larkspur; it is poisonous to cattle, but not till later in the season. You can take sheep through larkspur country and they'll tromp some of it down and they'll eat some of it. It makes the grazing much better for cattle. Locoweed is another brush that is poisonous to cattle, but it is found mostly in desert country. There is some near Thompson, Utah, and on down to Hanksville over there near the Robbers Roost country, but there isn't any here around Craig. Cattle and sheep and horses, too, if there is a shortage of feed, they will feed on locoweed. In the springtime when it is green, I think that is when they are inclined to eat it. It is kind of addictive, so they tell me. I've never been in any country where we had trouble with it though. Greasewood is another one. Sheep will eat the leaves off of the bush. If they aren't used to it, and they can get used to it, they can get killed by it. It is when they are on it for the first time that it will kill them.

Coyotes are vicious on the sheep. We have neighbors that still run sheep. The Tuttles run five or six thousand head, and they were short a thousand lambs from the time they docked them.

Hugh: Out of five thousand sheep they probably docked maybe six thousand lambs. The breeding season in this country is from around the first of December until the tenth of January. That is the only time the rams are around the ewes. So when we talk about a herd of five thousand sheep we are talking about very few rams. It would take maybe thirty rams to serve a thousand ewes. In the spring when the lambs are born they dock them. That is, they cut their tails off, castrate them, brand them, and earmark them. If you had a thousand head of sheep then, with an ordinary percentage, you would have about twelve hundred lambs in the spring. On that basis if you had five herds you would be short about two hundred lambs out of each herd from coyotes getting them.

Lowry: The majority of the loss is from coyotes, but mountain lions account for some.

Gwen: David Seely lost half of his lamb crop to mountain lions. He is our son and runs his sheep in Moffat County. The sheep were close to the ranch house too. Hugh said the herder who runs sheep for Wyatt said they were short about six hundred lambs. Tom Theos was short about four hundred and Nick Theos about six hundred. Around here there are probably a total of two thousand lambs that were lost to predators this year, and at seventy dollars a head that adds up to a lot of money.

The herds are spread out and most people don't understand that coyotes are quick and sly and their color blends with the country so that they are difficult to see. More herders would not solve the loss problem because of the expense of extra camps and horses. Few herders can get along with another one that close. Dogs, and occasionally llamas, are used. Government control people can't control federal land; lions and bears are protected and poison is outlawed. At denning time coyotes pack carcasses to the den. Then they kill to teach the young ones how to kill, and they kill for the sheer joy of it. A lion will cover a carcass and come back and finish it. A bear will let it rot, then finish it. Coyotes eat their prey alive and kill more.

Lowry: My feeling about reintroducing wolves is that we are asking for trouble. You know we have gotten along good for years without them.

We still have pictures of them, everybody knows what they look like. If people need to hear a howl to try to make you think of the wolves, why, anybody can get a recording. The thing about those wolves is they are just as hard on cattle as they are on sheep and deer.

Hugh: They will kill the fawn deer, the calf elk, they're going to eat the eggs of sage chickens which the coyote is already doing, and of the grouse. And they will eat the little antelope and the big antelope. The coyote in the right kind of weather can kill, well, two or three coyotes can kill an elk. The elk will break through the deep snow and the coyotes are running on top and eventually they will run them down and they will eat them alive. I have definite opinions about predators, and one time, when I was president of the Wool Growers Association, I made the Sports Illustrated and Reader's Digest magazines. Of course the articles were about what I thought about coyotes.

Lowry: The BLM doesn't know anything about livestock. Their employees come from back east, mostly, and they are good enough people, but they don't know what they are talking about and they don't know what they are trying to do. Most of the work they do today is paperwork in the office. All they do is throw it away or it collects dust. They have too many people.

Gwen: That's what gripes me. We used to run all of the BLM in this county with one man in the office and a secretary and a field man. Now we have two buildings clear full of BLM employees. And they used to run the Meeker district from here. They enlarged the first building, then they built a second building and they are all full. For the same acreage!

Lowry: The BLM built and occupies this one building, but the other building is mostly environmentalists. I don't know what they do, really.

Gwen: Just sit around thinking up more restrictions.

Hugh: I think the best time for the United States has already gone by. I don't feel sorry for myself because I've lived my time, but I do feel sorry for my grandkids because a lot of things I've seen have gone by the wayside.

Lowry: We truck our sheep to Denver for the market. A lot of them are purchased right here in Craig. All the lambs today go to a feed-lot. Years ago we used to sell eighty- to hundred-pound lambs and they were the prime lambs, and they would go right to slaughter. They would leave here one day and be killed the next day. But today's market—I don't know if it's because of the cheap feed, and lambs have been cheap, they can put the feed on them and take the lambs up to 125 pounds before they slaughter them. Even up to 135 and 140 pounds. They are beyond the point of lambs. That's what made this western Colorado lamb so popular. It was the fat lambs. They were milk-fattened lambs, with no additives, no nothing. Carcass lambs now, when they get up to 135 or 140 pounds, why they are what we call wethers.

Hugh: They have a lot of waste, a lot of fat on them. Most people don't like mutton tallow. I, for one, sure don't. You just have to cut it off and throw it away. We think the sheep industry, as we have known it, is a thing of the past. There is nobody to herd the sheep. Labor, predators, the BLM, the Forest Service, and the market, about in that order, all work to our detriment today. Most of the lambs on the eastern slope of the Colorado Rockies are still owned by the man that owned them originally. There is only one packing house over there; well, really there are two, but one only kills about twelve hundred lambs a day. It used to be Monfort, now it's owned by ConAgra. They kill about twenty-six hundred lambs a day, but they like you to put those lambs in the feedlot. You pay the feed bill, they will feed them, then they will take them, kill them, and then pay you.

The tenderest lamb, if it was for myself, I'd go buy a live lamb from my neighbor or from my son and I'd kill it myself. That would be the best lamb you could eat. Most of the lamb they sell in grocery stores and meat markets doesn't compare in any way with what I'm talking about.

Lowry: If you notice on lamb chops, the fat around the fleshy part of the chop gets larger as the meat part gets smaller. That's why the eighty- or hundred-pound lamb that used to go out of here, they loaded it here and trucked it to Denver. It would be on the market the next morning and be killed that day. Well, there is nothing to equal that lamb. It's so much better than what we have today that goes through the feed lot.

Hugh: The first time I ever went into Denver with lambs was back in 1929 or 1930. I rode the caboose from Thompson to Denver. That particular day there were ninety-five thousand lambs on the market in Denver. If you had ninety-five thousand lambs on the market in Denver today, you couldn't get rid of them in a year's time. By three o'clock in the afternoon those lambs were all sold and being loaded to go to a feeder or a slaughterer. A lot of the lambs went to Chicago. They had commission houses and those guys would buy these lambs for other people and load them and send them on. That day lambs brought a top four forty a hundred. So a hundred-pound lamb brought four dollars and forty cents, but you had the freight to take off that, and you had the commission and the feed to pay for. Actually, you only got two fifty, maybe not even that much. The only reason I was able to go to Denver is that they had a two-bit slot machine in Thompson. Some people by the name of Taylor owned the hotel and store and a bootlegging whiskey business, and they had a slot machine in there. My dad's partner put two bits in there and won thirty dollars. So I got to go along on the trip to Denver.

Lowry: There are a lot of folks today who don't like lamb. The reason is they have never eaten any, for one thing, and another thing is that they have never had good lamb to start with.

I was out there to Sam's Mesa about six or seven years ago. We were down in this canyon; we went out from Robbers Roost on the road the uranium people had built out onto Sam's Mesa. We drove out there as far as we could go with horse trailers and set up camp. The next day we rode across Sam's Mesa and looked across that whole sand dune area. Glenn Berry, a friend, had filed some uranium claims in there and because of my dad's early days around the Roost he offered to go down there with me. This was about 1988. It was quite a thing. Glenn had quite a story about it. They went out in there prospecting and ran out of their water supply, and somebody had told him about this spring in Hatch Canyon. He climbed up on the highest place he could see, and finally he saw a cow trailing in there, and she dropped off of that hill and went down there, and he found the water. We went across that sand dune, the air seemed like it was fairly still, but when we came back out of that canyon you couldn't see our horse tracks across that sand. Karl Seely and Pat Winters said Hatch Spring was where they watered their sheep when they were going and coming from Under the Ledge. That spring was under a shelf and you could probably put this house under that shelf. That spring boiled out of there, there were probably three or four feet per second of water that came out of that spring. It was pure, sweet spring water.

Hugh: Under ordinary conditions horses and cattle prefer grass to sagebrush, and they will eat a certain amount even if there is plenty of grass. But under severe conditions where they have to eat sagebrush alone, it will kill both horses and cows, and elk too.

Yesterday I went up to the ranch; my son is keeping about thirty head of heifer calves there. There's a board fence about four and a half feet high and there was at least sixty head of elk in there feeding with those calves. It was within a few feet of the house. They saw me coming in my truck and they ran over and jumped the fence, and the elk went walking by me just as nonchalant and calm. They are more gentle than the cows. Those elk have never been anyplace else. They were born there, they stay there in the summer, and they never have been anyplace else.

Lowry: I have about a hundred acres here and I still have about two thousand acres of pasture land. I have sold most of mine, about nineteen thousand acres.

Hugh: I have about seventeen thousand acres, but it is broken up in three different counties. We all love it up here. It is a wonderful setting for our way of life. The Yampa River Valley is beautiful with a great climate and scenery, and it is really ideal ranching country. It's a wonderful place to bring up kids.

8

Gwen Seely

Gwen Seely is statuesque and graceful, a handsome woman indeed. She is a well-educated and determined woman of the West. She must have seemed out of place during her younger days when she and husband Lowry made do in the remote log cabin that was all they had back then. Although she learned early on that a smelly kerosene lamp was a lousy substitute for her teenage vision of dinners by candlelight, she built the foundation for a solid family life and a marriage that soon will reach its sixtieth year.

Drama classes and bridge lessons did her little good when Lowry chose ranching and started a spread from scratch, and far out from town to boot. She learned though. She learned that cooking, helping to move cattle and sheep from one pasture to another, raising the kids, nursing a bunged-up husband, canning, bottle-feeding newborn lambs—all these things and a myriad of others are required of a ranch wife. She since has maintained a compassion for those newborn lambs and calves. Now she looks with pride both at the three children Lowry and she reared and at a well organized and managed ranch home in Craig, Colorado, where she doesn't have to put up with having cold feet any longer. Once in a while nowadays she actually can find time for a hand or two of bridge.

June 28, 1996
Craig, Colorado

I had a very secure childhood. We didn't have a lot of money, but I don't think we were poor. No one had a lot of money in those days. In fact, we were considered quite well off. I was born in Preston, Idaho. My mother

Gwen Seely, 1996.

was Scots and my father was Danish. My great grandfather's name was Nielson, and he was a miller in Denmark. He was taken prisoner during one of the wars with Germany. There were two German soldiers coming toward him. He shot one, but could not reload in time, so the second soldier captured him. While in prison, he invented a puzzle that so intrigued the prison guards that they released him. When he went in the army, he left his money with his sweetheart, my great-grandmother-to-be. All the young fellows told him that he wouldn't have a girl or his money when he got back because that made her all the more attractive. After he got back, he married her and they were converted by Mormon missionaries. The money he had entrusted to her was the money they used to travel to the United States. Brigham Young sent them to settle just outside of Ogden. They were some of the original pioneers there. My Grandmother Geddes we called Grandmother Eccles after her second marriage. Grandfather Geddes was on a mission to Scotland. They used to have street meetings in the olden days, and they would sing to attract a crowd. Grandmother had a beautiful voice. They asked her to sing at the start of the meetings.

Finally, they enticed her to attend one of the church meetings. It was at a rented hall with rough benches, and she sat there and thought to herself, "I could never belong to a church like this." She had come from rather an aristocratic background. They had their own beautiful church, and the family owned their own pews. But during the meetings, she said she felt this burning in her chest, and she knew every word they were speaking was true, and she joined the church.

She was not one of the early pioneers. She came on the railroad to Utah right after the Union Pacific came in 1869. She was a popular guest because of her talents. She would sing and entertain people. One time there was so much activity going on that she asked, "What is happening? What are they preparing for?" It was the wheat threshers! In those days all the neighbors would get together and make a crew of at least twelve men to do the threshing. She found out what the women had been preparing. It was all the food to feed those twelve men. She up and packed her suitcase and went back to Salt Lake. Her family had servants in the home, and she hadn't done any of that kind of labor. She had no interest in participating in any effort to prepare food for a dozen men—strangers at that! Her skill was handling silk, so she had to keep her hands perfectly soft so they wouldn't snag the silk. The Mormons brought silkworms to Utah to start a new industry that was centered in the Dixie area of the state, adjacent to the border of Arizona. Brigham Young had asked her if she would weave the silk. She said she would if she could have a length of silk for herself.

On my mother's side my grandmother's name was Margaret Cullen Ferguson. On my father's side my grandfather was Hyrum Carl Nielson. My father was Hyrum Carl Nielson and my mother's name was Williamena Martha Geddes.

Lowry and I met at Utah State University. I had known his brother Hugh through my brother H. C. Lowry said I'd walk by and wave at Hugh and wouldn't even look at him, and he was the brother who was trying to get my attention. Lowry and I became close friends and while we were still in college we married during the 1937 Christmas vacation. Instead of a honeymoon, we furnished our apartment.

Lowry had gotten a job with the Forest Service. His job had to do with identifying and inventorying plants and grasses in southern Utah. The first winter we were out of school, he helped his mother in her store in Ferron, and he also taught school as a substitute teacher. He decided he wanted ranching, and thought he could still help his folks while working in the store. His degree was in animal husbandry and he minored in range management and agronomy.

I majored in English and speech in college. I didn't think I ever would go and live on a ranch. I really didn't know. I totally enjoyed college. I belonged to the Spur organization, which was a national pep organization. I also belonged to the Alpha Chi Omega sorority and did a lot of dating. A lot of fun. I loved learning, and I still seize every opportunity available to attend classes. Sometimes professors from BYU come in town and offer classes. I took the Dale Carnegie course, and I got a certificate in interior decorating. The Relief Society organization is an educational one. We not only had classes, but we studied the Constitution of the United States for five years. I still love drama, real life or portraying it on the stage or in the movies. I participated in a lot of plays, and then as I got older and while here in Craig, I had a job in the church with a young people's organization. I directed many plays and also designed quite a few floats for the parades. Those kinds of things were enjoyable. Some of the floats won first place.

I came with Lowry to the ranch that was up on the South Fork road, thirty-five miles southeast of here. During World War II we stayed up there to care for the cattle; every hired man we had went into the service. We got snowed in. They didn't keep the roads open in those days. I felt when I moved out to that ranch that the pioneers had nothing over on me, except the Indian wars. I hauled water from the river. We put evaporated milk in the bucket, sprinkled some on top of the water to settle the silt out. At first I had trouble drinking it, but managed to choke it down. After getting the water to the house, we heated it for our baths. I cooked on a coal stove. We did everything from scratch, even made soap from mutton grease and lye. There was no dry yeast in those days, so we made yeast. We started with potato water and sugar and kept it going. That was how you had to do it to make a good batch of bread. Now, anybody can make good bread with the yeast we have. We depended a lot in those days on the yeast, unless we made sourdough. I helped with the wood chopping and hauling it to the kitchen, hauled the ashes. Then on days when the air was heavy the stove wouldn't draw and you couldn't get it to burn.

Lowry always got up first and would start the fire. One day I was kind of desperate, and I had seen him put some coal oil on the fire, so I got the can of coal oil and poured it on the coal and it exploded. Blew the iron plates off the stove, damaged my hair and my eyelashes, burned my lips. Lowry told me afterwards, "Never put coal oil on hot coals." It has to be aflame. I learned the hard way.

Around the ranch I did most of the gardening, and I rode with Lowry. He couldn't send me off by myself because I don't have the sense of direction and I was always afraid of getting lost. Then I had the babies, but the riding I'm talking about, the riding he did, was up and down mountains, it was awfully hard riding. It was for long distances and hours, so I didn't do a lot of it.

I didn't get to ride like I would have liked to. Lowry had given me a beautiful horse that was hard riding and very high spirited, and later on in our marriage he gave me the mare, Stormy. She was the easiest riding horse on the ranch and, with a new saddle which was comfortable, I could ride all day. Otherwise, at the end of a day I was just suffering with misery—my knees, mostly. It makes a lot of difference if you have a saddle that fits.

There is a little more to being a ranch wife than I have mentioned. Other than cooking and feeding everyone who visited our home, including ranch and field hands, there were all of the usual homemaking responsibilities. I helped trail sheep and sometimes helped with the docking and marking of the sheep. I helped catch the lambs or branded them with paint, or doctored them with the creosote dip. Riding horseback and helping gather the cattle and driving them to different pastures was routine. I often was the "flagger," moving from winter to summer ranges and back, and all of the time preparing and delivering the food to the drovers. Lowry always saddled and unsaddled the horse for me so I could have time to prepare the meals. If I helped when branding cattle, it was mostly to push the calves up the chute, or administer the vaccines; or, when branding on the range (after delivering the meals), I was the one on horseback holding the herd while the ropers and branders worked the herds.

There were times when I was needed in the fields. I either raked or baled the hay, usually baled it. Often I had two of the children on the tractor with me. This would be illegal now and interpreted by some as a form of child abuse. When possible, if housewife duties allowed, I would ride with Lowry to the high country to take supplies and move the sheep camps to new locations. Every year there are little orphaned lambs that have to be cared for. I used to bottle feed them. Three times a day! One time we had sixty orphaned little ones.

Many things can go awry that result in orphaned lambs. Sometimes the ewes die during birthing. Or they will reject a twin, and when there are triplets, they can't feed three. They don't produce enough milk for three. Ewes have been known to go off feeding or grazing and seem to forget that they have lambs, or they just desert them. During range lambing, the herders will tie a ewe to a sagebrush to hold her with the lamb until the lamb is strong enough to follow and they become accustomed to each other. Unfavorable conditions—such as a shortage of feed or water, or a lack of good herders, or maybe you have to move them off Bureau of Land Management land in the midst of the lambing period and the mothers never get together with their lambs—any of those things can produce orphans.

Some ewes are overly motherly, and want a lamb so badly she will go around gathering up all the little ones she can coax away from their real mothers. Sometimes a lamb, usually a twin, will be too weak, or deformed, or handicapped in some way and has to be hand raised. We had one that had no front legs and another with no hip joints. It died after two weeks. We had another that was a twin that we called "Kinkers." She had a crooked tail and crooked legs and the mother ewe absolutely refused to claim it. We tried everything we could think of, but the mother would not let Kinkers nurse. We cared for her, hand-raised her, and she lived to have a lamb herself.

Many of the orphans, called bum lambs, never forget you and will leave the herd to run and greet you and do things to gain your attention. When they are weaned, they usually are put back in the herd to pasture feed and fend for themselves.

While feeding the lambs, each one gets a name and is recognized by its own personality and appearance and characteristics. When you lose one, it really hurts and saddens you. Sometimes it is from overfeeding, but when they are attacked by the murdering coyotes, there is anger as well. I have seen them blinded and had their legs broken, and the coyotes will start to eat them while they are still alive. A row of eagles will sit on thefence watching for a newborn, and dive and peck out the eyes first of a lamb or a calf. It is a heart-rending experience, for those little lambs are so beautiful, innocent, and playful. Our children, when they were little, used to cry over the loss.

It sickens my faith in the reasonableness of people to want to turn wolves, lions, and bears loose on us. One lion killed six of our son David's lambs in one day, and another lion tore the hide down both sides of our beautiful, hard-working horse. One single bear can kill, scatter, and throw about thirty sheep in one attack! There is no ecology in that! If the Sierra Club members love their wolves, lions, etc. so much, they should have to fence them, herd them, keep them from disease, feed them, and care for them as we do our livestock!

Aside from that, I enjoyed the outdoor work in the wonderful fresh air, and the views and sweet nostalgic smells. I also enjoyed gardening and raising vegetables. I drove a truck a lot, chasing after machine parts and delivering them to a site where they were needed, and I often delivered the meals to the field workers by truck.

Out on the ranch I was by myself. We were isolated; we had no mail delivery because the roads were too muddy. One day we were traveling down the canyon in our car and dropped deep in a mud hole in a shady lane section of the road. I suggested we find some sticks, branches, and limbs and use them to stuff the holes and mud so we could get the car out of the mire. Lowry said it wouldn't work and left to walk the two or three miles to his uncle's place to get a team of horses. I got tired of sitting in the car waiting and decided it could do no harm to start filling the mud hole, and it might even help. So I hauled everything I could lift and drag over and crammed it in the hole. It began to look pretty good, so I started the car up and carefully drove out. I met Lowry a half mile down the road. He had his harnessed team and a shocked expression on his face.

From the ranch site we had to go about fifteen miles just to pick up the mail, and in the wintertime it was either on horseback or with a horse-drawn sled. Lowry had fixed up a small bobsled for the children and me. I'd wrap them up in homemade woolen quilts so they'd be warm and comfortable.

One time Hugh brought a little fawn into the ranch. Its mother had gotten caught up in a fence and died. They raised it as a pet and it followed the children around. When they came out to play, the fawn would show up. When we'd go to town, he wanted to go too. He'd follow us all the way down to where we had the car stored, and I'd ask the neighbor if we could lock him up at her place till we got back.

Neither one of us had any money in our pockets when we first started out. But we didn't spend any, either. We had a cow, and we had the staples. We had a big garden and I did a lot of canning, and I made the children's clothes. My father and mother gave me new draperies, clothes, and other things that I wanted. We bought very few things and we got along.

When we were first out of college, that summer we lived at the Crawford Place. They had a housekeeper. I wanted a home of my own; Grandpa Davies had just bought the Phipps place, and I wanted to go up and fix that log cabin up. That was quite an experience because an old bachelor had lived there for quite a few years. My sister-in-law Marjorie was there helping me, and when she opened the dark green blinds on a window she let out a scream. "Bedbugs!" Well, we had an eternal bonfire going in the yard where we had been burning trash. She picked up the mattress and heaved it on the bonfire. Everything else was carried or drug to the river to be scrubbed. I didn't know what a bedbug looked like until then. We even had to scrub the cabin's inside walls down. They were made out of rough-hewn logs, and before long our hands and knuckles were red and all torn up from getting scratched and scraped on the logs. We didn't have any rubber gloves, and after all of the scrubbing and burning, we still had to have the place fumigated.

My father and mother had come to visit, and when my father saw what I looked like, he said something to the effect, "That is not what I sent my daughter to college for." He was ready to drag me back to Idaho, but Mother wisely insisted that they should not interfere.

Oh, I learned a lot out there. Another time I was riding with Lowry, and I thought the horse wanted to drink, so we rode out into a little beaver pond. I thought he was sinking in quicksand, but Lowry told me later all he was doing was lying down in the water. I was in a panic, but I guess horses do that. Lowry helped me get out.

When it came to decision making time, I always put in my two-cents worth. Lowry always made the final decision. Anyone who knows me, knows I always have my say. If Lowry weren't here, and even if I had reliable ranch hands, I wouldn't try to run the ranch. I would sell. I admire, but I don't envy, the widows who have tried to keep the ranch. It's just not something I would enjoy doing. I wouldn't have confidence; as much as I have worked with Lowry and with the cattle, I still wouldn't know when to change pastures or be able to identify a sick cow and know how to doctor it. Lowry is a wonderful animal doctor. Administratively, I kept the books for the ranch and paid all of the bills. He spent the money, and I made sure we paid the bills.

When younger, I thought I'd be dressing for dinner at night with candlelight. There have been times when I felt like I could hardly stand the way we lived, like the time the cabin at the ranch burned down. That was in the winter of 1947, and we were thirty-five miles from town. There was no chance of getting any fire fighting equipment; we lost all of our furniture and had no insurance. A darling antique organ and a full set of wicker furniture, everything went up in flames. The children were small, David was six and Sunny was eight, and they were in school in Craig.

After the fire, for one whole summer we were jammed into a store-house where we kept all of the ranch supplies and the motor to generate the electricity. It was awful. I hated it. I would wonder how much longer

I could stand it. But, as the Bible says, ". . . and it came to pass . . ." And the wind—the only kind of weather I really didn't like is the wind. I do like a soft, cool breeze, but wind—I hate wind.

Lowry dragged down a little cabin that seismographers left on one of the ranches we had accumulated, and fixed us up a better bedroom in it, so we had a little more decent way of living.

The most frustrating thing in my life was, at first, the struggle for a home. At the ranch we all lived together—the sheepherders, the hired men, Margaret and Hugh, all those men guests, all of us together. We all used the same kitchen. We did have separate bedrooms, of course. Through working so closely together, we learned to love each other.

We finally bought this place here in Craig when Sonya started elementary school because there was no school near the D. R. Seely & Sons Ranch. Later, in 1958, Lowry and I bought the Sweeney Wellsweep Ranches that are located in Lay and Hamilton. At Lay the Yampa River runs through the ranch and at Hamilton the Williams Fork River goes through that one. But the old Murphy place, it was such an old house, it was full of frustrations. Lowry would not get me a new linoleum because the foundation was not sound, and the boards were showing up through the linoleum, and none of the doors would shut properly. I had freezing and cold feet all my life until I got into this house. Lowry can remember my cold feet because I always put them on him. He was always warm.

My children and helping to keep Lowry alive and taking care of him, those are the things I am most proud of. David is ranching at Hamilton and here near Craig. My younger son, Geddes, has worked for the City Market store for twenty-one years. Geddes has a handicap which is always a heartache. His handicap is poor muscular coordination and that affects his speech, and that has made him shy. He is a sweet, darling fellow who liked his life ordered. He liked to know what he was doing and when, but life was so different on the ranch that he had a hard time coping with it. Lots of people are that way. On a ranch things change; a ditch breaks, or the weather, or cattle get out. Things were always happening, upsetting him. He could not handle all of those changes.

My daughter Sonya, nicknamed Sunny, is married to Hardy Redd, a cattle rancher and politician. They live in La Sal, Utah, where she operates a mountain guest ranch as a bed and breakfast on their cattle ranch. When she was a child, she was such a happy child my mother called her "my little ray of sunshine." Hence her popular name, Sunny. She was a wonderful student and finished high school in three years, with four more credits than needed. She was very active in college, a student senator, and many other things. In Monticello, near La Sal, she has chaired the School Board and she and Hardy have traveled extensively. She remains active, running the B & B, and has served on the Utah Arts and Humanities Council and the Utah Historical Society.

When Lowry was just a child, he roped wild horses. He had roped and broke this little horse they called Hop-Along-Happy. A whole group of cowboys were gathering cattle to ship on the railroad at Thompson, and this one big cowboy kept kidding Lowry and teasing him about his little horse, saying, "That horse doesn't amount to anything. Couldn't you mount a better horse than that?" The big cowboy continued to tease Lowry and make fun of him and his little horse.

Finally Lowry retorted, "Bet my horse can outrun yours."

The cowboy said, "Oh yeah? I'll bet my horse against yours in a race."

Well, Lowry got prodded by the other cowboys to challenge this fellow to a race. Another cowboy, Dutch Hazelbush, said, "Lowry, just go ahead and race him."

At first he was reluctant, but finally decided to, and with their encouragement he stopped his horse, jumped down and pulled the saddle off. The cowboys drew a starting line in the sand and a finish line. They bet Lowry's horse against his horse. Whoever wins gets the other guy's horse to keep. Lowry jumped on bareback, and the race was on and away they went. Lowry really beat him, and it made that big cowboy angry, and he thought something wasn't right, something wasn't fair, and he wanted to run it again. So they ran it again and Lowry beat him again! With hooting and hollering and a lot of cheering those cowboys jerked the saddle off that cowboy's horse, built a fire and put Lowry's brand on that horse right then and there. That horse carried that brand until he died. Lowry won many races using him. He was a beautiful blue-gray.

It didn't take me a long time to adapt to life on a ranch. I liked the activity. There were lots of hard times, but like any marriage, you work through them. It has never been dull. There is always something going on with Lowry Seely. On the Fourth of July that first summer on the ranch, Lowry and Dave went to Craig, leaving Marjorie and me at the ranch alone. The young hired men and a neighbor's boy, Bill Urie, from an adjoining ranch came by. They were all bathed and sheiked up for a country dance at the Hamilton Schoolhouse and they invited us to go with the gang. We had a housekeeper named Mrs. Godlove at the

Crawford place. We cut one of her cakes to treat the boys with while we got ready for the dance. Then we took a second cake to the dance. Everyone took something to those old-timey dances. Well, the next day we were in trouble! Mrs. Godlove discovered the robbery and stuck a big butcher knife accusingly in the face of poor innocent Cookie, saying, "When I find who took my cake, I'll run this butcher knife through him and clinch it on the other side."

After the dance Lowry came in and exclaimed, " You went to the dance with all of those young bucks?"

I answered, sweetly, "I went with Marge."

He said, sternly, "You are a married woman!"

Marge and I still laugh over that episode. The next time the boys went to town, they came home to the ranch about daybreak singing. They called themselves "The Salty Seely Serenaders."

One June, about 1959, I had gone to Provo to bring Sunny home from the university. Lowry called and said, "See if you can find a boat and bring it home. I have a calf on an island in the river. The mother cow swam over, but it is too high and swift to get the baby back. I can't find a boat here I can use."

What an opportunity! And did we ever take advantage of it! We went shopping, all right, and bought a small boat and motor that could pull a water-skier. David and Sunny both chipped in all they had in savings. What fun we had water-skiing, the only real recreation and time off any of us had taken from the ranch.

It's a good thing I love to read and can and be happy with myself because there have been very few women friends, except when we moved to Craig. Although all of the ranch women are friendly, some are shy and reserved. I had Margaret, Hugh's wife, Mother Seely, and Lowry's sister Marjorie when she visited from Chicago, for gabbing partners. And when we had guests, there was always a lot of woman talk. I guess we were always too busy to ride horseback three or five miles to the Sullivans or Burgesses just to gab. Lowry worked long, long hours and usually came in so late. In Craig I joined clubs and participated in community and church activities.

The Yampa River here at this ranch in Craig has come out of its banks twice since we have been here. It hasn't been a threat to our lives, but it has been up to the top stair at our back door entrance. At that time the neighbors were here helping to start to move the furniture out. They had already moved the ranch machinery to higher ground. Everyone was here helping except Lowry. I finally was able to get him on the telephone out at the Williams Fork Ranch. I told him we were being flooded out and for him to come in.

He said, "Well, I can't come now because I've got a cow that's calving." So I told him to bring the cow in, calving or not, because we were going to be washed away if he didn't get in here now! The men from the church and our neighbors were down here shoveling. Everybody was helping but Lowry. Finally, he came in dragging the trailer with the cow. I watched the cow in the trailer and she had her calf without help. He could see that he had to get to work right away. Some of the livestock had gotten marooned on an island the flood had created and they had to be rescued. While the flood was taking place we kept calling Steamboat Springs and Hayden (both upstream) to ask about the crest, but luckily it crested about ten o'clock that night and it didn't come up above the top step of our rear entry.

We expected a flood this year, but we got cold weather and that slowed the runoff. Lowry had hired a machine to build a dike along the river, but we didn't need it. When we get to thinking about threats to our livelihood, I'm really concerned about the unreasonableness of the BLM and some environmentalists who put wildlife above human life and wilderness designations against a way of making a living. We have to be able to make a living and furnish food for our country. I've been concerned about trying to keep a balance between factions.

I have worked in campaigns for national and local politicians and have called our senators two or three times. I've written, too, but when I write it down, usually I am too frustrated and too angry, so I don't mail the letters. I'm always going to reconstruct the letter and then don't get it done. I have written on occasion to our state and national senators and representatives. I always get answers, which I appreciate.

Several exciting things have happened over the years. When I was young I won an essay contest sponsored by radio station KSL. My mother called up to me while I was still asleep that the station was going to announce the winners. I crawled out of bed, came downstairs and sat on one of the steps trying to hold my head up. My name was the second one announced! I was so excited I leapt over the last six steps into my daddy's arms. They took me to Salt Lake City where I got to read my essay over the radio. I had a choice for gifts and chose a beautiful, big doll buggy which I used later in my life for all of my babies.

Here in Craig we had a mooing man radio program. It had something to do with the milk program for the children. You were to write a jingle, and if your jingle won that day, you could guess who the mooing man was. His voice would come on with a big Moo. I guessed it right off, right at first, but I didn't try to write a jingle until the contest went on for a couple of weeks. I decided that nobody knew who it was, so I wrote a jingle and it was chosen and I won the contest.

It was disappointing and exciting once when Lowry and Hugh got me in a race. One time I said "I think it would be kind of exciting riding in one of those 'ride and tie' rodeos." That particular morning we were doing a float for our Ladies Recreation Club. Millie Bilsing and I had gotten up at four o'clock in the morning, after working very late on the float, to scrape the frost and the ice off the freezers because we needed frost and ice on the float to make snowballs to throw at the spectators. Then I drove the vehicle in the parade. Our place was always a gathering place, and when I got home everyone had come in from the ranch. We had this great big crowd to hurry and fix dinner for. In came Lowry and Hugh to tell me they had signed me up to run in the relay race.

I said, "Oh, no, I haven't ridden a horse for years. I need to get into shape."

They said, "Well, you're already signed up."

Then, instead of just a short race, they had stretched it out so we had to go around that whole race track three times. To start out with, it was not fair. We didn't have a starting gate, we just had a man who started the race by waving a flag, and you were to be off. The other contestant wouldn't come up to the start line, and my horse finally had just settled down, then here came the other contestant at a dead run. She went past me and my horse had to start from a dead stop. I started out behind and I caught up to her once, but that was the second round. I was so exhausted those guys just pulled me off and threw me on the different horses at the relay points. I couldn't even get off on my own. I came in close, but she still stayed ahead. When I got off, I was drained of strength and I just fainted. The ambulance came, but there was nothing really wrong with me. I was simply exhausted. In all the race was a mile and a half in length. Each horse was ridden a half mile on the relay. Lowry confessed later it was pretty dumb of him to enter me in a race when I hadn't ridden in a long time, and had been up late the night before working on the float, and also had been at it since four in the morning getting the float ready for the parade.

Another highlight in my activities was when I was chosen to serve on the anchor committee for Craig's Golden Jubilee Pageant. I was one of the narrators for the history section of the pageant.

When people talk about excitement in life, I found excitement in most everything I did. I loved school, I liked all my teachers. I liked the activities. I wasn't good at anything, but I did everything in sports: ball, rifle, swimming, dancing, and tennis. My father had a beautiful home with a tennis court. I loved playing tennis. I loved riding. I ran for rodeo queen; I was the first attendant, once as a teenager in Idaho and later in Craig. I danced, I sang, was in plays and lots of clubs. When I moved into Craig I belonged to the Ladies Recreation Club. I enjoyed that club because many of our activities would involve the family—Lowry, and sometimes the children. I frequently was asked to judge speech contests at the school, and for the queen contests for radio functions. I belonged to the Community Club. I helped to get people to start thinking about getting rid of the mosquitos here. There were no outside activities, no flowers, yards, no outside furniture sold in the stores. It was impossible to live outside because of the mosquitos. I have been active with the Wool Growers Association, the Cow Belles, I worked in the church, the Missing in Action Organization, the Republican Women, and the PTA. And I was a room mother. At the school each room has a room mother. Every year I invited the children's teachers to a dinner. I love to entertain and I did a lot of it. It seemed like everything I joined, I was eventually asked to be president. I think my talent was organizing and delegating. I could get people to work, to cooperate with each other.

Other exciting things were our trips to Europe and Mexico, and a stay in New York City where we saw *The Sound of Music* on stage. Those were exciting for me. Another time we were guests of Milburn Keith in Kentucky for the Kentucky Derby. We attended the Governor's Derby Breakfast at Spindeltop Mansion. That was fun. We also met and visited with President and Mrs. Nixon.

Lowry had racehorses. Winning was very exciting, and so was learning the personality and disposition of each of those beautiful animals. Riding one of them, Ute Chief, frightened me a little because I felt I did not have complete control of all of his power and strength and high spirit.

Then we started showing purebred Hereford bulls at the National Livestock Show in Denver. Later we took fancy club calves to many shows—Phoenix, the Cow Palace in San Francisco, Los Angeles, and Denver, as well as to private sales in California. These calves were for 4-H, Future Farmers of America, and college kids with fat steer projects. The fancy club calves were so beautiful and uniform when washed, scrubbed, dressed, clipped, and sprayed. Even their ears got cleaned and their tails combed and fluffed. They won many grand champion prizes.

We often attended the 26-Bar Bull Sale in Arizona. It was owned by Louis Johnson and John Wayne. I enjoyed the personality of the "Big Duke" and his patriotism. The sale was quite a social event with their parties for the bull buyers. We also traveled to Oklahoma City for the National Quarter Horse Show where Lowry also won championships.

Then there were, and still are, innumerable roping events. I remember telling him, "Our lives are in a rut and they are full of manure. Animals control our lives."

It has been satisfying for me to see David take his responsibilities in jobs in the community—scouting, church, president of the Cattlemen's Association and president of the Farm Bureau. Geddes was an active member of the Jaycees and worked enthusiastically.

I really enjoyed the life we lived in Grand Junction. Lowry had bought a stable and with it came a lovely, large house. It was an interesting, but challenging house; it had a swimming pool in the living room and beautiful flowers and fantastic views. We had many great friendships there. I was a licensed real estate agent and worked at that. That was a different kind of ranch life.

But all the way my priorities have been my husband, my children, and the ranch.

9

Chad Moore

Chad Moore's father, Andy Moore, has been described to me as the epitome of a western cowboy. With his two sons and an occasional ranch hand or two, Andy made a name for himself by developing a good-sized herd of cattle. In a tragic accident while on the range he lost one of his two sons. Chad was there at the time of the accident, but there was nothing he could do. Even today in this wild and dangerous country medical help is miles and miles away.

Chad lives in Green River and carries on running cattle at his ranch headquarters at the Texas Well. The well is about fifty miles south of town across some of the best grazing land imaginable. That is, when it rains! His dad cross-bred stock until he developed a breed that could withstand the desert life better than the pure Hereford. Chad has continued with that science, and I honestly think he will never retire from life on the range. Neither will he change his attitude about the BLM. He has very little good to say about that outfit. Just ask him!

July 21, 1994
Green River, Utah

My dad and his dad and the rest of the family left Texas and worked their way up to Wyoming. Dad and the family came to Green River after they left Wyoming. They ran horses out there on Dead Horse Point. They gathered a bunch of horses and shipped them to Boston to sell them. My uncle accompanied the horses to Boston, and when he came back he had on a new suit of clothes. They asked him how much money he got out of the horses, and he said, "That was it." So they sold

Chad Moore, 1994.

the horses. They had thoroughbred mares and Hambletonian studs. I don't know if they were selling the horses to the army or what, but when they didn't make any more money than that, they sold the mares for ten dollars a head. That is what they cleared after freight and feed costs were subtracted. The different family members all took their share of the money and went their own way. My dad went to work for Neal McMillan. He was down in Sevier County over near Richfield. That's where Mother was raised, and that is where he met her. They got married in 1920, and moved out here to Green River where we have been ever since.

Pa worked for McMillan until he went in the service, and when he came back out, McMillan had gone broke. Pa started buying a few cattle, and kept adding a little bit to them whenever he could. He ran his cattle just north of Green River where Wayne Smith runs today. From there he moved out onto the San Rafael River. He didn't like the river because of the mud in the spring. That's when he bought some springs off Neal McMillan and moved the head camp out further on the desert. Out there he bought Dugout Spring number one, number two and number three, and bought Twin Spring, too. It was there that he headquartered the camp. Back in those days if you owned the water, you had the land.

When some people in Green River wanted to sell a few head of cattle, then my dad would buy those and add to what he had. He didn't borrow from the bank. He didn't believe in borrowing money when he didn't know whether or not he could pay it back. We started from there, and after we got too big for that area, then we moved on up and bought the Tomlinsons' spring called the North Spring. We moved our headquarters up there. You couldn't get an automobile in there because it was too sandy. When we were little, Mother drove the wagon to get there. If it wasn't the wagon, it was pack mules. We stayed there at North Spring until 1939 when we bought the Texas Well from George Franz, and that is where we are headquartered today. We just kept adding to the place and we had it pretty good until the BLM came along. When they came along, things started going back downhill.

Every so often somebody would quit ranching and Pa would buy them out and we would get back up there a ways, then the BLM would give us another cut. Then someone else would quit, and we'd buy their grazing rights. We had to buy a ranch down on the San Rafael River to get our original grazing permit so we could have commensurates. We have to have deeded land that we own before we can get grazing rights or rights to use water on the public lands. So much deeded land allows one to have commensurate rights in the public domain. People can also get commensurate rights on springs or wells. We bought that land on the San Rafael River from the bank; it was 320 acres and Dad bought it for fifteen hundred dollars Noah Aubert had it and went broke. Then the bank had it and couldn't sell it because it was during the Great Depression of the 1930s, so Pa bought it. Then he picked up four hundred acres from the county in 1936 for a dollar an acre for taxes and added that to our place. We kept it until 1980 when we sold it to the Utah Power and Light Company.

When the BLM came along, we had a permit for six hundred head of cattle. This permit was on water and land both. You had to have feed in a four-mile radius around your water holes to take care of so many head of cattle, and on that land you had to raise feed to take care of so many for two months.

I don't remember the year that it was dry and the BLM cut everybody by one-third of their number. The rancher whose grazing rights were based on water was cut on water, and the one whose grazing rights were based on land, the number of cattle he could graze was cut. As we were based on both land and water, we took a double cut. We would have somebody from the BLM office come out and take a look, and it was just one man's opinion on how many cattle one could run. It didn't do any good to take them to court, which we did. We still lost, so we got cut back bad on that deal.

In 1980 we sold the ranch and the rest of the deeded land on the San Rafael, but we kept our permits for grazing. We had 718 acres of deeded land, and we ran six hundred head of cattle. We were up river about fourteen miles above the Chaffin Ranch. They kept cutting us down, so now we can't even run four hundred. The BLM haven't been our favorite people.

You have to have deeded land, or you have to have enough water to handle them. We had both. There were only two outfits that had both, ours and Pearl and Slim Baker at the Biddlecome place known as the Robbers Roost Ranch. Slim Baker was there when the BLM took effect. His grazing rights were all fixed on water. The Biddlecome Ranch sold to the Ekkers. The ranch house is at Crow Seep where a good spring flows.

We always had a dispute with the BLM over grazing. They say we can run four head to a section. We always said we could run eighteen, sixteen to eighteen. They wanted to know where we came up with that figure. I said, "I couldn't tell you. But," I says, "I know we can run more than four." My dad always said we could run about sixteen head. That was about all we wanted to run. They would eat off half the grass and leave half, so that's what we did. In 1939 we bought George Franz out. That was another permit, but we didn't get any deeded land with it. Then we had to lease a lot of school sections. At one time we had 104 state school sections leased. That is a lot of land, sixty-six thousand acres. We had some of them leased north of the town of Green River. It didn't make any difference where you had them leased just so it was on the books that you had that many acres leased. That was all the BLM cared about. Then finally they came and they were going to divide us up. That was when we took a big cut in our permit and they put us all under a fence. They wouldn't let us lease any sections that weren't under our fence. That really cut us back. They built boundary fences around each permit holder, and I couldn't have a lease over here in this other guy's allotment. We had those leases for twenty years, but we had to give them up, so we transferred them over to our deeded land.

We used to run six hundred head; we had a permit for six hundred when we first started. We never did own more than 718 deeded acres, but we had one hundred and some sections leased. We didn't run any sheep. To run the cattle we never did hire more than two men. I was going to school, so Dad hired one man to work the cattle and one man to farm at the ranch, just out there in the summertime. At melon picking time, the hired hand would leave the ranch and go pick melons. He could make more money doing that than farming on the ranch.

When the war came along we had three men working for us then. They kept drafting them as fast as we could get them. I was still going to school and my brother was going to college. Soon my dad and I were the only ones left. They had taken all the hired hands and Bill too. Bill, my brother, died in 1982. We were putting a well in out here on the desert, and he came down to help me. We had a winch truck out there. We broke a rod off, and when we went to pull it up a chain slipped. Everybody just stepped back when it slipped, and when Bill stepped back, he fell over backwards and hit his head on a bucket of cement and severed his spinal cord. He died right there.

We used to run up north into Antelope Valley all the way over to Horseshoe Canyon, but when the BLM divided it up, they took that away from us. They said we had too much country. We're the only outfit out there that ever drilled a well. The Chaffins were great hands to build ponds. They were underneath the ledge, so we never ran cattle with them. They had a few head of cattle down at their ranch that would get out here on the desert, but their main herd was Under the Ledge, so we never mixed with them.

The Chuchuru, a sheep outfit, bought the Tidwells out, and another sheep outfit, the Moyniers, bought the Chaffins grazing permits and ranch. The Chaffin Ranch was sold four times before it was sold to the Utah Power and Light Company. The old sheepherders, they got all over the area. The Moyniers had a herder named Pete Masset. Old Pete never had a big bunch of sheep, if I remember right. I just remember going out there with my dad in the wintertime on the weekends, and if they was going through the country, Pa always stopped and talked to them. I remember he liked kids, Pete did, and he was always friendly with me because I was just a kid. I never really knew him. I think the Moyniers were in bad financial trouble. I could be wrong about this, but I think he told his herders—Pete was one—if they would stick with him he would pay them in sheep. And he did. So they had a few sheep to call their own so they could sell the sheep and get a little bit of money. Then they got in the business that way. Pierre Moynier always paid them what he said he would.

The Tidwells grazed on the North Spur, north Horseshoe. They used the land, and now a cowman owns that land from Horseshoe Canyon over to the dirt road to Green River. But he has never had a cow or sheep out there for about six years now. There isn't any water in that area, that's why it looks good today. No one is going to run stock there if there isn't any water. Chuchuru bought Tidwells' ranch, and that is when they put that pipeline down in Horseshoe Canyon. They used to take sheep in there, into Horseshoe, to water them. In the spring when the ewes got heavy with lambs, they told me, the sheep can't take that. It's a long ways down there, and those sheep get full of water and they can't pull up out of there. There could be all the feed you want up on top, but there is no water up there, so they can't move back and forth. That is why they moved over to Keg Spring. There was a pipeline in the canyon down there, so they would move down there for maybe another three weeks. Depending on the weather, they might stay three weeks, but if it got cold the pipeline would freeze, and they couldn't even pump it. Then they would go back over to Colorado. But it got so it didn't snow any more around here, so they would go south and get over there where there was some feed and water. Got so it wasn't worth it to stay in the canyon.

Back there, anyone who looks at Antelope Valley says that's the most wonderful place on earth, but when they looked at it and there isn't a water hole on it, no wonder it's good-looking grass. You can't graze where there isn't any water.

I've never been Under the Ledge. When we bought George Franz's Texas Well out, he had a permit down there with the Chaffins, but the BLM wouldn't transfer that over to us. They told Pa he had too much anyhow, so outside of that we didn't have any reason to go down there.

They put sheep ahead of cows on these mountain pastures. The sheep go through and eat all of the larkspur out of the grass. The larkspur will kill a cow, but won't harm a sheep. So you know darn good and well that cows will follow sheep, eat in pastures the sheep have grazed in.

Larkspur isn't found on the desert. It belongs to the buttercup family. The western larkspur is a native to the Rocky Mountain country. It is highly toxic in higher elevations with larger leaves and taller than the species found at lower elevations. It is highly toxic to cattle, although the cattle can follow sheep on it, but it doesn't bother the sheep. If the sheep graze it first, then there is not enough left to bother the cattle. The only way you can kill it is to graze it with sheep or spray it.

Locoweed, sometimes called crazy weed, is a member of the pea family. Any livestock can be poisoned by eating locoweed. Horses never recover once they are poisoned. Cattle gain weight slowly and often will abort their calves after eating locoweed. Sheep abortions also are high after eating locoweed. Livestock generally avoid eating the crazy weed until feed is scarce, but once they have eaten it, they seek the plant out. In our area we have quite a lot of locoweed. In years past we have had to move off of certain areas until after the weed has come up and flowered out. It's worse when the weather is dry; in dry weather and after it has flowered out and dried out, the cattle will eat it. It seems to bother their nervous systems. They have no sense of balance or movement. Finally, they just die. They get to a water hole and just stand there and swallow, but never get their heads down and drink. It is a pitiful sight to see. One year Ekkers and we lost just about all of our replacement heifers because we had them in town and when they got out here the grass had just started up and the locoweed was thick. It got just about all of them.

One year out here on the desert we had a sheep outfit come in. They were south, between the Texas Well and the Dirty Devil River. There isn't any water down there and the sheep were eating the locoweed when it came up in the spring of the year. The sheepherder told the owner that he'd better do something, that the sheep were eating that water weed down there. The owner of the sheep said, "Just leave them down there. We don't have to haul water if they are eating that."

The sheepherder told the owner to ". . . find a replacement for me because I'm not staying. It makes the sheep go crazy." Within three weeks the sheep started dying. Their eyes rolled back in their heads and they died. They got some of them up to our corrals at the Texas Well and started skinning them. They were dying faster than they could skin them.

We tried to tell the owner that was what he was going to get into if they ate that weed, but he ignored us like he did his sheepherder. He tried to trail what was left of the herd over to Colorado, but he lost everything he had before he got to Colorado.

We do have coyotes in this country, but they aren't a great problem to us. We probably lose three or four calves a year, and we have calves with their tails bitten off. We don't have any lions or other predators, so we're pretty thankful we just have the coyotes to contend with.

I don't remember larkspur being a problem around Moab, but during the last ten years or so the Taylors had to buy some sheep to go ahead of the cows to eat the larkspur, especially in the timber. Over here at the M & O Ranch, the Mountain and Oak Springs Ranch, they went to sheep finally because so much larkspur has showed up.

I remember when the BLM first came into effect, the first thing they tried to do was take a well, our Texas Well out there, away from us. That was in '39. The BLM never did do nothing. I guess the sheepherders came from Colorado, we had eight or nine herds that came from there living out here. Well, when the BLM came in, that stopped that. Those boys didn't get to renew their permits. One guy owned I don't know how many permits, but he didn't even have any sheep. He just owned a lot of land there, and sheepmen leased the land from him. When the BLM came in effect, he was smart enough that he applied for permits down here attached to that land of his. So if you wanted to run out here, all you had to do was go talk to him. He'd let you run on his permits. He was making money off them. Finally those old boys got tired of paying him, and some of the permits got set aside. I don't know of any good the BLM did because everybody started going downhill after that. They never did anything to help you. They were always giving you a cut, or you can't do this, or trespass here. The BLM never did any good for anybody that stayed here. And they knew we had to stay here. We were here because there was no place else to go. So we just stayed there and made the best of it.

The sheepherders, though, they could pack up and trail the sheep. Back then they didn't haul them in semis. They'd trail them into Green River and go out across the ground and graze it. They had a cheaper rate at Thompson than what it was here in Green River, so they'd trail them from here to Thompson where they'd put them on the rail to send them to Montrose or even to Grand Junction. They got all over the country and ate it coming and going. That's what was wrong with the country.

There is no place in this country that has been hurt by overgrazing, because if you overgraze, you won't make any money off the land, so you won't hurt the land by overgrazing it. If we get enough moisture, you couldn't get enough stock together to eat it off. In good years we got plenty of feed; if it doesn't rain, then we haven't got it.

We had a little cabin over at North Springs. The roof half caved in and we didn't do anything about it. The BLM said you either fix it or get rid of it. I said, "That's a historic building. It's even on the map. It's a hundred years old, and you people have to take over." I was just kidding this old gal. She's the one I report to at the BLM.

She said, "That's right. We don't want to argue with you over that. We want it cleaned up." Well, it should be cleaned up and so we're going to do that. At the dugout we had a cabin where you could get in out of the weather. It didn't come up to their standards. Every Tom, Dick, and Harry that came by stole something from it. The table was gone, the stove was gone, the beds were gone. Everything had been taken out of it. We went down there the other day and set fire to it and buried the remains. And that was that.

We had another cabin up at what we call Little Flat Tops. We hauled it in from a mining outfit down at Hidden Splendor. When we got it up there, the BLM wouldn't let us set it down. They wouldn't give permission. We wanted to set it by our well, but they told us we didn't own the well and to move out. Without the BLM knowing it, I got the tag from the state, so the only thing the BLM could do to make it rough for us was not let us put the cabin down. The tag from the state is a copper tag that I attached to the well. That tag gives me the authority to put a stock watering tank there so the cattle can drink. It also allows me to build some troughs. Without the tag the BLM told me all I could do was let the cattle drink from the well hole. That wouldn't work! So the cabin just set there and rotted away and blowed down. We went down and burned the remains and cleaned up the ground.

At the Texas Well there was a lot of oil-drilling debris laying around. They told us we had to clean that up or they was going to cancel our permit. So we did that. I got a notice the other day that they had been out and inspected the site and it was okay, and they'd give us our permit.

The headquarters of the BLM is in Moab, but our district office is in Price. When we put that double-wide trailer and built a quonset hut at the Texas Well (the quonset is forty-two feet by fifty feet), the BLM said we didn't have any right to put that there. I said we did, that we had a Section 4. They said the Section 4 called for a line cabin and a granary. I said that's all it is. We do put our trucks and stuff in the granary, and the double-wide trailer is just enough rig for a cabin. They wanted me to tear them down. I talked to an attorney, and he told me don't worry about it. You have that Section 4 and there is not a court in the land that would hear the case. So now I lease the two acres the buildings are on. I pay the BLM fifty dollars a year for each acre. They told me they were going to cancel my Section 4, but the attorney says they can't cancel it. I'm the only one who can, and I'd have to give them notice that I'm not going to renew it.

I don't own any of that land, just have a government lease on the two acres, and have grazing permits on the rest of the land. Our permit covers the Sweetwater allotment. That allotment is a huge one; it covers the Dugout Springs, the North Springs, and the wells we have. Back when the BLM came into being they issued a Section 4 permit that gave us permission from the government to build a cabin, a granary, and corrals to operate our livestock business. That's why my attorney was so confident we were adhering to the regulations. No one else grazes down there in the summer. In the winter, over at the Jeffrey Well, an outfit runs cattle in there. Another outfit leases from the Utah Power and Light Company east of there.

I run Brangus, three-eighths Brahma and five-eighths Angus. That mix does well in this desert. Everyone tries to get bigger cattle all the time, and it doesn't make any difference how big a cow you get, in ten years she's going to be just the size the desert will take care of. We used to have polled Herefords, but they got pinkeye. The Brangus don't get it.

In 1980 when we sold out to Utah Power and Light, we went to New Mexico and bought a bunch of Brangus bulls, so we've been running strictly Brangus bulls since 1980. Our cattle weigh about four hundred pounds when we take them off the desert. Then we put them in a feed lot to winter them up. We feed them more now than we ever did. Our cows didn't used to know what a bale of hay was. We just run them on the desert grasses. Nowadays we feed them quite a lot of hay out there, and feed them protein block.

Our yearling heifers, when they are weaned, we take them over to the feed lot and in the spring we take them over to an irrigated pasture in Wayne County. In the fall we take them over here in Green River until February. Then we take them over and turn them loose in the desert, so they are never out of the corral from the time they are weaned. We never did believe in calving two-year-old heifers. I still don't, because if you get a good calf and you take good care of that calf and heifer, those heifers will weigh nine hundred pounds when we turn them out there when they are only two years old. They are as heavy as a regular cow, and if they calf when they are two, they won't when they are three. Our bigger percentage of drys come out of those three-year-olds. I'd rather have them calf when they are three, then I have someplace to put them. We sold them off last spring when the BLM cut us off.

The Utah Power and Light put in two power units, one at Castle Dale and one at Huntington, and they needed the water, so they bought up the water rights from the ranchers to cool the power units. At first, they were only interested in getting the water. They didn't care about the land, but Milt Oman had a lot to do with it, and he wanted them to take the land too. They were going to give us just as much for the water as for the land and we could keep the land, but old Milt Oman, a lawyer who had cattle on the San Rafael Desert a few years before, talked them into taking the land too. Then they leased the land back to him and he, in turn, leased it back to different people, and some of them leased it again. Some didn't even own any stock, but subleased it at a profit to cattlemen. We were all against that sublease arrangement. If Utah Power and Light had the permit, they were supposed to be the one to own and graze the stock. Every sublessor jacked the price up and made money on it. That is one good thing the BLM has done, they changed the rules so you can't do that any more. If I sublease my permit, all I can get out of it is what the BLM gets—$1.91 or $1.96 an animal unit. I can't jack the price up.

The Utah Power and Light was going to operate the ranches at one time, but decided against it. Nobody is going to go down there and live the way we had to, to farm those ranches. No electricity, no running water, and half the time the San Rafael River was dry. We always said we had an irrigated dry farm. We irrigated when we had water and dry farmed when we didn't. When they put that power plant in, we never got any high water to flush the channel out, so alkalies and sulphur and the weeds got so high with salts that when our hay would get to be four inches high, it would burn up. That's when we told the Utah Power and Light either return the water to us or buy it. So they bought it.

If the BLM would fix up a water hole, or do anything to help you, but they don't. Their attitude is, if you don't like the way we're running the land, then get off. The government is dumb. Why don't they sell all that land out there for a dollar an acre and get it on the tax rolls? But they want some two hundred dollars an acre, that was the cheapest. They will never make this land pay enough to break even on the salaries they pay all those BLM people. We have put in six wells on our own. The government never put a dime in any of them. When we hit water, we had to file on that water in the government's name. And they never put one penny in it. We even had to pay the filing fee.

We have wells wherever we run cattle. If the springs get low, our cattle can always get water. They won't choke. If one well breaks down, they can go to another. We use diesel generators with submersible pumps—no windmills. The wells are so deep it takes a pretty good wind to bring the water up, then the wind dies down and your water drops back down, and you wear out your leather rings. The diesels, with the submersibles, we run some of them for thirty-eight hours at a time to fill a tank. It takes about an hour a foot to fill a tank, those fifty-two-hundred-gallon tanks. We got a twelve-hundred-gallon tank on one. It takes two hours a foot to fill up.

There were a lot of young men that came along during the Great Depression. Like Bill Racy, they were riding the rails looking for work. Lot of them wanted to work as cowboys. They had nowhere to go, no food, no home. Ranchers used to hire them. At least on the ranch they could get shelter and food. The ranchers were not able to pay them much.

I don't think the cattle business in this area will be here for too many more years. The BLM is so rough we can't make it with them looking over our shoulders all the time. They want to raise the grazing fees to around six dollars a head, which is clear out of reach. We can lease private pastures where they take care of the cattle, furnish the feed, furnish the water, and still have our cattle. Whereas out here we have to take care of our cattle ourselves, supply our own water, and if we tell them the feed isn't there, they say, "Well then, get off the land."

We thought Babbitt would be a help to us because his family is cow people in Arizona. He said he was born to be Secretary of Interior and I don't think, in fact I know, he is not a help to us out here in the West raising cattle. I'd like to know what they are going to do in this country when we are gone.

If they would lay off and Mother Nature would give us some rain, I believe we could still make a good living out here. This is a hard place to make it; there is nothing that comes easy out here. We have been here since 1912; I've been here sixty-nine years myself. We have been making it, but it seems like these droughts have been getting a little worse all the time. The grass isn't like it was when I was a little kid. I don't think the livestock in this country has got much of a chance of surviving.

When you talk about the cowboys, this day and age there isn't such a thing as a young cowboy. None of them have an interest in it; it's too hard work for them. They only want to work eight hours a day. They want the weekend off, and they don't know one cow from another. All they think about is getting on a horse and running the cattle. It's not like we used to work cattle. They work cattle too fast.

I just don't think we have much going for us. The weather is against us, the BLM is against us, and there just aren't any good cowboys out there unless you had a family and raised your own to help out. You always want your kids to have better than what you had, so you send them off to school to get a higher education. They always write home for money from a cattle operation, so I guess we made just as good a showing as these highly educated kids do.

Index